The Essential
Slow Cooker
Cookbook For Beginners

1200+ Easy, Delicious & Healthy Slow Cooker
Recipes for Everyday Slow Cooking

Debbie Herrin

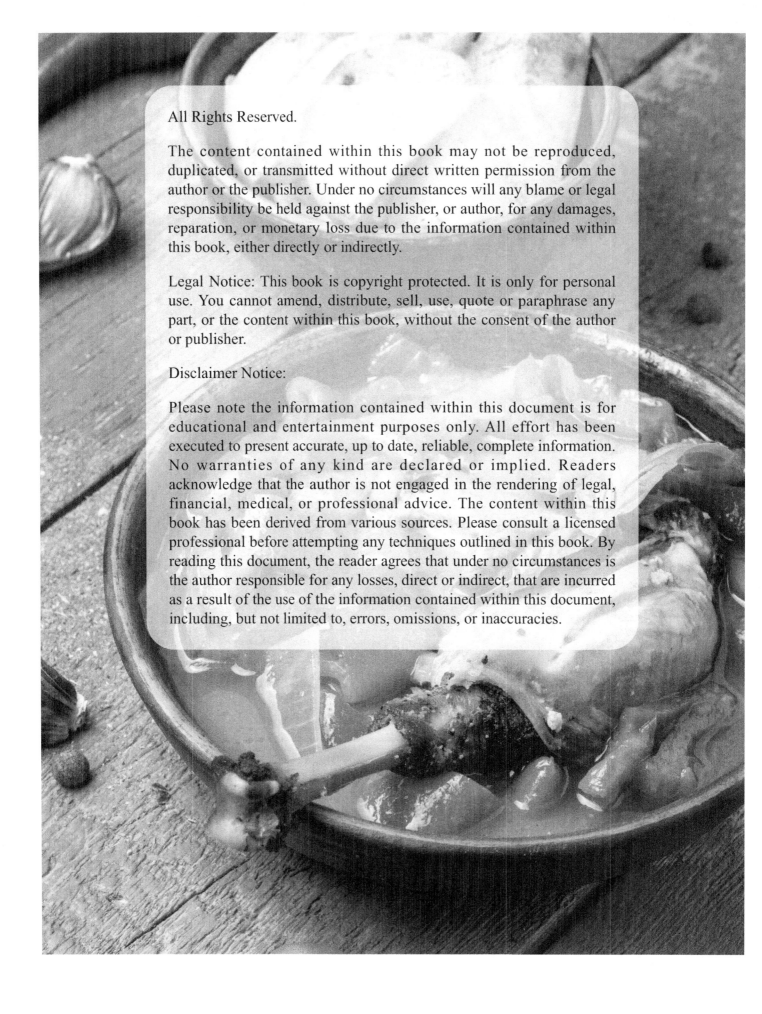

CONTENTS

Chapter 4 Beef, Pork & Lamb Recipes 32

Chapter 5 Fish & Seafood Recipes 43

Chapter 6 Poultry Recipes 54

Chapter 7 Vegetable & Vegetarian Recipes 65

Chapter 8 Side Dish Recipes 76

Chapter 12 Dessert Recipes 119

APPENDIX : Recipes Index... 129

INTRODUCTION

Hello, everyone! I'm glad that you bought this cookbook. Welcome to learn how to make healthy and delicious food with slow cooker with me! I'm Debbie Herrin. It seems that I grew up in the kitchen. My father is a chef in a starred hotel. I have admired his cooking skills since I was young. I hope I can become a cook as good as him when I grow up. So after graduating from high school, I went to learn cooking. It has been 15 years now. During the college, I worked in different restaurant for part-time job, which was an unforgettable time. I have carefully studied every process from cutting vegetables to cooking. With the development of cooking appliances, cooking becomes easier and easier. It seems that everyone can become a "chef" in their own kitchen. Therefore, I learned nutriology five years ago, thinking about how to mix daily food reasonably, so that they can give full play to their nutritional value. 15 years of cooking career has also enabled me to accumulate a lot of cooking tips, which are recorded in each of my cookbooks. I hope this book can help you discover the secrets of the kitchen and enjoy cooking!

The book begins with a brief introduction to slow cooker, which can help you know it better before you start cooking. There are 1200 easy to follow recipes in this book for your everyday meals. If you have no idea what to eat, just follow the cookbook!

Chapter 1 Before You Start Cooking

What Is a Slow Cooker?

When talking about Slow Cookers, we are actually talking about Slow Cookers.Over the decades Slow Cooker, the original slow cooker brand, has evolved from a single bean cooker into a diverse and extensive line of slow cookers and accessories that make meals and entertaining smarter, easier and more convenient for the many different styles of cooking today.

The composition of slow cooker is very simple. It includes a removable stoneware, a dishwasher safe stoneware& lid, the surface is stainless steel finish. And it has low, high and warm settings, which is easy to operate, friendly to beginners.

Benefits of Slow Cooker

1. Slow Cooker is more suitable for cooking meat cuts that are difficult to cook, such as pork shoulder, pork spine, beef brisket, etc.

2. Slow Cooker can help to make meat soften and tender, fall off the bone meat.

3. Vegetables cooked in a slow cooker can absorb spices and stock the fuller flavors.

4. The slow cooker is also used to cook dried beans. Add some water and you can do your own thing, because it needs more time.

5. In the process of slow stewing, the nutrition of food will be absorbed by the soup. Soup is more suitable for everyone.

6. Slow Cooker can directly cook frozen food taken from the refrigerator, but the cooking time is longer. Remember to add a spoonful of warm water to avoid rapid temperature change.

Cooking with Slow Cooker

Cooking with slow cooker is very simple. You need to pay attention to the following matters:

1. Always make sure to fill your slow cooker somewhere between one-half to three-fourths of the way to the top. If you fill up the pot to the top, it will affect cooking safety, cooking time and cooking quality.

2. When layering multiple ingredients, always try to follow the instructions. Vegetables are cook slower in slow cooker compare to meat and poultry. Place the vegetables first and second put the meat over it and last is top with broth, sauce or water in slow cooker.

3. Always put your slow cooker on high for the first hour then turn the setting high to low until finish cooking.

4. When cooking meat, always make sure to use cheaper cuts of meats, since they tend to work better with slow cooker. This is partly because they have less fat and are perfect for long cooking times, that results in tender delicious meats.

5. If you are cooking on Low Settings, try to avoid lifting up the lid from time to time. Each time you lift up the lid, heat will escape a little, adding another 20 minutes to your overall cooking time.

6. If you want to cook a large piece of meat, you'd better fry its skin to golden brown before putting it into the slow cooker, this will allow for more intense flavors to be developed.

Slow Cooker will certainly become a good helper in your kitchen, and will let you find the fun of cooking. Now, it's your time to find out more secrets of slow cooker. Let's start!

BASIC KITCHEN CONVERSIONS & EQUIVALENTS

DRY MEASUREMENTS CONVERSION CHART

3 TEASPOONS = 1 TABLESPOON = 1/16 CUP

6 TEASPOONS = 2 TABLESPOONS = 1/8 CUP

12 TEASPOONS = 4 TABLESPOONS = 1/4 CUP

24 TEASPOONS = 8 TABLESPOONS = 1/2 CUP

36 TEASPOONS = 12 TABLESPOONS = 3/4 CUP

48 TEASPOONS = 16 TABLESPOONS = 1 CUP

METRIC TO US COOKING CONVERSIONS

OVEN TEMPERATURES

120 °C = 250 °F

160 °C = 320 °F

180° C = 350 °F

205 °C = 400 °F

220 °C = 425 °F

LIQUID MEASUREMENTS CONVERSION CHART

8 FLUID OUNCES = 1 CUP = 1/2 PINT = 1/4 QUART

16 FLUID OUNCES = 2 CUPS = 1 PINT = 1/2 QUART

32 FLUID OUNCES = 4 CUPS = 2 PINTS = 1 QUART = 1/4 GALLON

128 FLUID OUNCES = 16 CUPS = 8 PINTS = 4 QUARTS = 1 GALLON

BAKING IN GRAMS

1 CUP FLOUR = 140 GRAMS

1 CUP SUGAR = 150 GRAMS

1 CUP POWDERED SUGAR = 160 GRAMS

1 CUP HEAVY CREAM = 235 GRAMS

VOLUME

1 MILLILITER = 1/5 TEASPOON

5 ML = 1 TEASPOON

15 ML = 1 TABLESPOON

240 ML = 1 CUP OR 8 FLUID OUNCES

1 LITER = 34 FL. OUNCES

WEIGHT

1 GRAM = .035 OUNCES

100 GRAMS = 3.5 OUNCES

500 GRAMS = 1.1 POUNDS

1 KILOGRAM = 35 OUNCES

US TO METRIC COOKING CONVERSIONS

1/5 TSP = 1 ML

1 TSP = 5 ML

1 TBSP = 15 ML

1 FL OUNCE = 30 ML

1 CUP = 237 ML

1 PINT (2 CUPS) = 473 ML

1 QUART (4 CUPS) = .95 LITER

1 GALLON (16 CUPS) = 3.8 LITERS

1 OZ = 28 GRAMS

1 POUND = 454 GRAMS

BUTTER

1 CUP BUTTER = 2 STICKS = 8 OUNCES = 230 GRAMS = 8 TABLESPOONS

WHAT DOES 1 CUP EQUAL

1 CUP = 8 FLUID OUNCES

1 CUP = 16 TABLESPOONS

1 CUP = 48 TEASPOONS

1 CUP = 1/2 PINT

1 CUP = 1/4 QUART

1 CUP = 1/16 GALLON

1 CUP = 240 ML

BAKING PAN CONVERSIONS

1 CUP ALL-PURPOSE FLOUR = 4.5 OZ

1 CUP ROLLED OATS = 3 OZ 1 LARGE EGG = 1.7 OZ

1 CUP BUTTER = 8 OZ 1 CUP MILK = 8 OZ

1 CUP HEAVY CREAM = 8.4 OZ

1 CUP GRANULATED SUGAR = 7.1 OZ

1 CUP PACKED BROWN SUGAR = 7.75 OZ

1 CUP VEGETABLE OIL = 7.7 OZ

1 CUP UNSIFTED POWDERED SUGAR = 4.4 OZ

BAKING PAN CONVERSIONS

9-INCH ROUND CAKE PAN = 12 CUPS

10-INCH TUBE PAN =16 CUPS

11-INCH BUNDT PAN = 12 CUPS

9-INCH SPRINGFORM PAN = 10 CUPS

9 X 5 INCH LOAF PAN = 8 CUPS

9-INCH SQUARE PAN = 8 CUPS

Chapter 2 Breakfast Recipes

Chapter 2 Breakfast Recipes

Chia Oatmeal

Servings: 2 | Cooking Time: 8 Hours

Ingredients:
- 2 cups almond milk
- 1 cup steel cut oats
- 2 tablespoons butter, soft
- ½ teaspoon almond extract
- 2 tablespoons chia seeds

Directions:
1. In your Slow Cooker, mix the oats with the chia seeds and the other ingredients, toss, put the lid on and cook on Low for 8 hours.
2. Stir the oatmeal one more time, divide into 2 bowls and serve.

Nutrition Info:
- calories 812, fat 71.4, fiber 9.4, carbs 41.1, protein 11

Lamb And Eggs Mix

Servings: 2 | Cooking Time: 6 Hours

Ingredients:
- 1 pound lamb meat, ground
- 4 eggs, whisked
- 1 tablespoon basil, chopped
- ½ teaspoon cumin powder
- 1 tablespoon chili powder
- 1 red onion, chopped
- 1 tablespoon olive oil
- A pinch of salt and black pepper

Directions:
1. Grease the Slow Cooker with the oil and mix the lamb with the eggs, basil and the other ingredients inside.
2. Toss, put the lid on, cook on Low for 6 hours, divide into bowls and serve for breakfast.

Nutrition Info:
- calories 220, fat 2, fiber 2, carbs 6, protein 2

Apple Crumble

Servings:2 | Cooking Time: 5 Hours

Ingredients:
- 1 tablespoon liquid honey
- 2 Granny Smith apples
- 4 oz granola
- 4 tablespoons water
- 1 tablespoon almond butter
- 1 teaspoon vanilla extract

Directions:
1. Cut the apple into small wedges.
2. Remove the seeds from the apples and chop them into small pieces.
3. Put them in the Slow Cooker.
4. Add water, almond butter, vanilla extract, and honey.
5. Cook the apples for 5 hours on Low.
6. Then stir them carefully.
7. Put the cooked apples and granola one-by-one in the serving glasses.

Nutrition Info:
- Per Serving: 268 calories, 10.8g protein, 71.4g carbohydrates, 18.5g fat, 11.3g fiber, 0mg cholesterol, 17mg sodium, 613mg potassium.

Hash Brown Mix

Servings: 6 | Cooking Time: 3 Hours

Ingredients:
- 3 tablespoons butter
- ½ cup sour cream
- ¼ cup mushrooms, sliced
- ¼ teaspoon garlic powder
- ¼ cup yellow onion, chopped
- 1 cup milk
- 3 tablespoons flour
- 20 ounces hash browns
- Salt and black pepper to the taste
- 1 cup cheddar cheese, shredded
- Cooking spray

Directions:
1. Heat up a pan with the butter over medium-high heat, add mushrooms, onion and garlic powder, stir and cook for a few minutes.
2. Add flour and whisk well.
3. Add milk, stir really well and transfer everything to your Slow Cooker greased with cooking spray.
4. Add hash browns, salt, pepper, sour cream and cheese, toss, cover and cook on High for 3 hours.
5. Divide between plates and serve for breakfast.

Nutrition Info:
- calories 262, fat 6, fiber 4, carbs 12, protein 6

Chicken Burrito Bowl

Servings: 6 | Cooking Time: 7 Hrs

Ingredients:
- 10 oz. chicken breast, sliced
- 1 tbsp chili flakes
- 1 tsp salt
- 1 tsp onion powder
- 1 tsp minced garlic
- ½ cup white beans, canned
- ¼ cup green peas
- 1 cup chicken stock
- ½ avocado, pitted and chopped
- 1 tsp ground black pepper

Directions:
1. Place the chicken breast in the Slow Cooker.
2. Drizzle salt, onion powder, chili flakes, black pepper, and minced garlic on top.
3. Pour the chicken stock on top of the chicken.
4. Put the cooker's lid on and set the cooking time to 2 hours on High settings.
5. Now add white beans and green peas to the chicken.
6. Close the lid again and cook for 5 hours on Low setting.
7. Shred the slow-cooked chicken and return to the bean's mix-

ture.
8. Mix well and add chopped avocado.
9. Serve the burrito with avocado on top.

Nutrition Info:
• Per Serving: Calories 192, Total Fat 7.7g, Fiber 5g, Total Carbs 15.66g, Protein 16g

Spinach Frittata
Servings:6 | Cooking Time: 2 Hours

Ingredients:
• 2 cups spinach, chopped
• 1 teaspoon smoked paprika
• 1 teaspoon sesame oil
• 7 eggs, beaten
• 2 tablespoons coconut oil
• ¼ cup heavy cream

Directions:
1. Mix eggs with heavy cream.
2. Then grease the Slow Cooker with coconut oil and pour the egg mixture inside.
3. Add smoked paprika, sesame oil, and spinach.
4. Carefully mix the ingredients and close the lid.
5. Cook the frittata on High for 2 hours.

Nutrition Info:
• Per Serving: 140 calories, 6.9g protein, 1.1g carbohydrates, 12.3g fat, 0.4g fiber, 198mg cholesterol, 82mg sodium, 137mg potassium.

Sweet Toasts
Servings:4 | Cooking Time: 5 Hours

Ingredients:
• 4 slices of white bread
• 3 eggs, beaten
• 1 tablespoon sugar
• 1 teaspoon olive oil
• 1 teaspoon vanilla extract

Directions:
1. Mix eggs with sugar and vanilla extract.
2. Then pour the mixture in the Slow Cooker.
3. Add olive oil and bread slices.
4. Close the lid and cook the meal on Low for 5 hours.

Nutrition Info:
• Per Serving: 95 calories, 4.8g protein, 7.9g carbohydrates, 4.8g fat, 0.2g fiber, 123mg cholesterol, 108mg sodium, 55mg potassium

Apricot Butter
Servings:4 | Cooking Time: 7 Hours

Ingredients:
• 1 cup apricots, pitted, chopped
• 3 tablespoons butter
• 1 teaspoon ground cinnamon
• 1 teaspoon brown sugar

Directions:
1. Put all ingredients in the Slow Cooker and stir well
2. Close the lid and cook them on Low for 7 hours.
3. Then blend the mixture with the help of the immersion blender and cool until cold.

Nutrition Info:

• Per Serving: 99 calories, 0.6g protein, 5.5g carbohydrates, 8.9g fat, 1.1g fiber, 23mg cholesterol, 62mg sodium, 106mg potassium.

Scallions And Bacon Omelet
Servings:4 | Cooking Time: 2 Hours

Ingredients:
• 5 eggs, beaten
• 2 oz bacon, chopped, cooked
• 1 oz scallions, chopped
• 1 teaspoon olive oil
• ½ teaspoon ground black pepper
• ¼ teaspoon cayenne pepper

Directions:
1. Brush the Slow Cooker bowl bottom with olive oil.
2. After this, in the bowl mix eggs with bacon, scallions, ground black pepper, and cayenne pepper.
3. Pour the liquid in the Slow Cooker and close the lid.
4. Cook the meal on high for 2 hours.

Nutrition Info:
• Per Serving: 169 calories, 12.3g protein, 1.4g carbohydrates, 12.6g fat, 0.3g fiber, 220mg cholesterol, 406mg sodium, 179mg potassium

Breakfast Sausage & Cauliflower
Servings: 6 (serving Size Is 6.2 Ounces)
Cooking Time: 7 Hours And 15 Minutes

Ingredients:
• 10 eggs
• 1 lb. breakfast sausage, chopped
• 1 head cauliflower, shredded
• ½ teaspoon mustard
• ¼ cup milk
• 1 ½ cups cheddar cheese, shredded
• Salt and pepper to taste
• Olive oil

Directions:
1. Whisk together milk, mustard, eggs, salt, and pepper in a mixing bowl. Grease Crock-Pot with olive oil. Place one layer of sausage on the bottom, then cheese, and season with salt and pepper. Repeat layer. Pour egg mixture over all ingredients. Cover and cook on LOW for 6-7 hours or until eggs are set. Serve hot.

Nutrition Info:
• Calories: 324.42, Total Fat: 18.01 g, Saturated Fat: 6.96 g, Cholesterol: 259.93 mg, Sodium: 988.86 mg, Potassium: 222.34 mg, Total Carbohydrates: 7.23 g, Fiber: 3.08 g, Sugar: 1.77 g, Protein: 32.48 g

Green Muffins
Servings: 8 | Cooking Time: 2 ½ hrs

Ingredients:
• 1 cup spinach, washed
• 5 tbsp butter
• 1 cup flour
• 1 tsp salt
• ½ tsp baking soda
• 1 tbsp lemon juice
• 1 tbsp sugar
• 3 eggs

Directions:

1. Add the spinach leaves to a blender jug and blend until smooth.
2. Whisk the eggs in a bowl and add the spinach mixture.
3. Stir in baking soda, salt, sugar, flour, and lemon juice.
4. Mix well to form a smooth spinach batter.
5. Divide the dough into a muffin tray lined with muffin cups.
6. Place this muffin tray in the Slow Cooker.
7. Put the cooker's lid on and set the cooking time to 2 hours 30 minutes on High settings.
8. Serve.

Nutrition Info:
• Per Serving: Calories 172, Total Fat 6.1g, Fiber 1g, Total Carbs 9.23g, Protein 20g

Breakfast Potatoes

Servings: 8 | Cooking Time: 4 Hours

Ingredients:
• 3 potatoes, peeled and cubed
• 1 green bell pepper, chopped
• 1 red bell pepper, chopped
• 1 yellow onion, chopped
• 12 ounces smoked chicken sausage, sliced
• 1 and ½ cups cheddar cheese, shredded
• ¼ teaspoon oregano, dried
• ½ cup sour cream
• ¼ teaspoon basil, dried
• 10 ounces cream of chicken soup
• 2 tablespoons parsley, chopped
• Salt and black pepper to the taste

Directions:
1. In your Slow Cooker, mix potatoes with red bell pepper, green bell pepper, sausage, onion, oregano, basil, cheese, salt, pepper and cream of chicken, cover and cook on Low for 4 hours.
2. Add parsley, divide between plates and serve for breakfast.

Nutrition Info:
• calories 320, fat 5, fiber 7, carbs 10, protein 5

Breakfast Zucchini Oatmeal

Servings: 4 | Cooking Time: 8 Hours

Ingredients:
• ½ cup steel cut oats
• 1 carrot, grated
• 1 and ½ cups coconut milk
• ¼ zucchini, grated
• A pinch of cloves, ground
• A pinch of nutmeg, ground
• ½ teaspoon cinnamon powder
• 2 tablespoons brown sugar
• ¼ cup pecans, chopped

Directions:
1. In your Slow Cooker, mix oats with carrot, milk, zucchini, cloves, nutmeg, cinnamon and sugar, stir, cover and cook on Low for 8 hours.
2. Add pecans, toss, divide into bowls and serve.

Nutrition Info:
• calories 251, fat 6, fiber 8, carbs 19, protein 6

Sage Chicken Strips

Servings:6 | Cooking Time: 4 Hours

Ingredients:
• ½ cup coconut cream
• 1-pound chicken fillet, cut into the strips
• 2 tablespoons cornflour
• 1 teaspoon ground black pepper
• 1 teaspoon dried sage
• 2 tablespoons sour cream

Directions:
1. Sprinkle the chicken strips with ground black pepper, dried sage, and sour cream.
2. Then coat every chicken strip in the cornflour and arrange it in the Slow Cooker.
3. Top the chicken with coconut cream and close the lid.
4. Cook the chicken strips on High for 4 hours.

Nutrition Info:
• Per Serving: 208 calories, 22.7g protein, 3.5g carbohydrates, 11.3g fat, 0.8g fiber, 69mg cholesterol, 70mg sodium, 255mg potassium.

Apple Spread

Servings: 2 | Cooking Time: 4 Hours

Ingredients:
• 2 apples, cored, peeled and pureed
• ½ cup coconut cream
• 2 tablespoons apple cider
• 2 tablespoons sugar
• ¼ teaspoon cinnamon powder
• ½ teaspoon lemon juice
• ¼ teaspoon ginger, grated

Directions:
1. In your Slow Cooker, mix the apple puree with the cream, sugar and the other ingredients, whisk, put the lid on and cook on High for 4 hours.
2. Blend using an immersion blender, cool down and serve for breakfast.

Nutrition Info:
• calories 172, fat 3, fiber 3, carbs 8, protein 3

Giant Pancake

Servings:4 | Cooking Time: 4 Hours

Ingredients:
• 1 cup pancake mix
• ½ cup milk
• 2 eggs, beaten
• 1 tablespoon coconut oil, melted

Directions:
1. Whisk pancake mix with milk, and eggs.
2. Then brush the Slow Cooker mold with coconut oil from inside.
3. Pour the pancake mixture in the Slow Cooker and close the lid.
4. Cook it on High for 4 hours.

Nutrition Info:
• Per Serving: 225 calories, 7.8g protein, 29.9g carbohydrates, 8.1g fat, 1g fiber, 94mg cholesterol, 529mg sodium, 7.8mg potassium.

Crock-pot Breakfast Casserole

Servings: 8 | Cooking Time: 10-12 Hours

Ingredients:
- 1 lb. ground sausage, cooked, drained
- 12-ounce package bacon slices, crumbled, cooked, drained
- 1 dozen eggs
- 1 cup heavy white cream
- ½ cup feta cheese, chopped
- 1 teaspoon sea salt
- 1 teaspoon black pepper
- 2 cups Monterrey Jack cheese, shredded
- 1 ½ cups spinach, fresh
- 1 ½ cups mushrooms, fresh, sliced
- 1 green bell pepper, diced
- 1 medium sweet yellow onion, diced
- 4 cups daikon radish hashed browns

Directions:
1. Place a layer of hashed browns on bottom of Crock-Pot. Follow with a layer of sausage and bacon, then add onions, spinach, green pepper, mushrooms and cheese. In a mixing bowl, beat the eggs, cream, salt, and pepper together. Pour over mixture in Crock-Pot. Cover and cook on LOW for 10-12 hours.

Nutrition Info:
- Calories: 443.6, Carbohydrates: 8 g, Fiber: 1.95 g, Net Carbohydrates: 6.05 g, Protein: 18.1 g, Fat: 38.25 g

Eggs And Sweet Potato Mix

Servings: 2 | Cooking Time: 6 Hours

Ingredients:
- ½ red onion, chopped
- ½ green bell pepper, chopped
- 2 sweet potatoes, peeled and grated
- ½ red bell pepper, chopped
- 1 garlic clove, minced
- ½ teaspoon olive oil
- 4 eggs, whisked
- 1 tablespoon chives, chopped
- A pinch of red pepper, crushed
- A pinch of salt and black pepper

Directions:
1. In a bowl, mix the eggs with the onion, bell peppers and the other ingredients except the oil and whisk well.
2. Grease your Slow Cooker with the oil, add the eggs and potato mix, spread, put the lid on and cook on Low for 6 hours.
3. Divide everything between plates and serve.

Nutrition Info:
- calories 261, fat 6, fiber 6, carbs 16, protein 4

Mixed Egg And Sausage Scramble

Servings: 6 | Cooking Time: 6 Hours

Ingredients:
- 12 eggs
- 14 ounces sausages, sliced
- 1 cup milk
- 16 ounces cheddar cheese, shredded
- A pinch of salt and black pepper
- 1 teaspoon basil, dried
- 1 teaspoon oregano, dried
- Cooking spray

Directions:

1. Grease your Slow Cooker with cooking spray, spread sausages on the bottom, crack eggs, add milk, basil, oregano, salt and pepper, whisk a bit, sprinkle cheddar all over, cover and cook on Low for 6 hours.
2. Divide egg and sausage scramble between plates and serve.

Nutrition Info:
- calories 267, fat 4, fiber 5, carbs 12, protein 9

Eggs And Sausage Casserole

Servings: 4 | Cooking Time: 8 Hours

Ingredients:
- 8 eggs, whisked
- 1 yellow onion, chopped
- 1 pound pork sausage, chopped
- 2 teaspoons basil, dried
- 1 tablespoon garlic powder
- Salt and black pepper to the taste
- 1 yellow bell pepper, chopped
- 1 teaspoon olive oil

Directions:
1. Grease your Slow Cooker with the olive oil, add eggs, onion, pork sausage, basil, garlic powder, salt, pepper and yellow bell pepper, toss, cover and cook on Low for 8 hours.
2. Slice, divide between plates and serve for breakfast.

Nutrition Info:
- calories 301, fat 4, fiber 4, carbs 14, protein 7

Boiled Bacon Eggs

Servings: 6 | Cooking Time: 2 Hrs

Ingredients:
- 7 oz. bacon, sliced
- 1 tsp salt
- 6 eggs, hard-boiled, peeled
- ½ cup cream
- 3 tbsp mayonnaise
- 1 tbsp minced garlic
- 1 tsp ground black pepper
- 4 oz. Parmesan cheese, shredded
- 1 tsp dried dill

Directions:
1. Place a non-skillet over medium heat and add bacon slices.
2. Drizzle salt and black pepper on top, then cook for 1 minute per side.
3. Transfer the bacon slices to a plate and keep them aside.
4. Whisk mayonnaise with minced garlic, dried dill, and cream in a bowl.
5. Spread this creamy mixture into the base of your Slow Cooker.
6. Take the peeled eggs and wrap then with cooked bacon slices.
7. Place the wrapped eggs in the creamy mixture.
8. Drizzle shredded cheese over the wrapped eggs.
9. Put the cooker's lid on and set the cooking time to 2 hours on High settings.
10. Serve and devour.

Nutrition Info:
- Per Serving: Calories 381, Total Fat 31g, Fiber 1g, Total Carbs 8.07g, Protein 19g

Cheddar Eggs

Servings:4 | Cooking Time: 2 Hours

Ingredients:
- 1 teaspoon butter, softened
- 4 eggs
- ½ teaspoon salt
- 1/3 cup Cheddar cheese, shredded

Directions:
1. Grease the Slow Cooker bowl with butter and crack the eggs inside.
2. Sprinkle the eggs with salt and shredded cheese.
3. Close the lid and cook on High for 2 hours.

Nutrition Info:
- Per Serving: 109 calories, 7.9g protein, 0.5g carbohydrates, 8.5g fat, 0g fiber, 176mg cholesterol, 418mg sodium, 69mg potassium.

Ham Pockets

Servings:4 | Cooking Time: 1 Hour

Ingredients:
- 4 pita bread
- ½ cup Cheddar cheese, shredded
- 4 ham slices
- 1 tablespoon mayonnaise
- 1 teaspoon dried dill

Directions:
1. Mix cheese with mayonnaise and dill.
2. Then fill the pita bread with sliced ham and cheese mixture.
3. Wrap the stuffed pitas in the foil and place it in the Slow Cooker.
4. Cook them on High for 1 hour.

Nutrition Info:
- Per Serving: 283 calories, 13.7g protein, 35.7g carbohydrates, 9.1g fat, 1.7g fiber, 32mg cholesterol, 801mg sodium, 175mg potassium.

Breakfast Meatballs

Servings:8 | Cooking Time: 7 Hours

Ingredients:
- 2 cups ground pork
- 1 egg, beaten
- 1 teaspoon garlic powder
- 1 tablespoon semolina
- ½ cup heavy cream
- 1 teaspoon cayenne pepper

Directions:
1. Mix ground pork with egg, garlic powder, and semolina,
2. Then make the meatballs and put them in the Slow Cooker.
3. Sprinkle them with cayenne pepper.
4. After this, add heavy cream and close the lid.
5. Cook the meatballs on low for 7 hours.

Nutrition Info:
- Per Serving: 98 calories, 6.1g protein, 1.6g carbohydrates, 7.4g fat, 0.1g fiber, 49mg cholesterol, 31mg sodium, 24mg potassium.

Smoked Salmon Omelet

Servings:4 | Cooking Time: 2 Hours

Ingredients:
- 4 oz smoked salmon, sliced
- 5 eggs, beaten
- 1 teaspoon ground coriander
- 1 teaspoon butter, melted

Directions:
1. Brush the Slow Cooker bottom with melted butter.
2. Then mix eggs with ground coriander and pour the liquid in the Slow Cooker.
3. Add smoked salmon and close the lid.
4. Cook the omelet on High for 2 hours.

Nutrition Info:
- Per Serving: 120 calories, 12.1g protein, 0.4g carbohydrates, 7.7g fat, 0g fiber, 214mg cholesterol, 651mg sodium, 124mg potassium

Shrimp Omelet

Servings:4 | Cooking Time: 3.5 Hours

Ingredients:
- 4 eggs, beaten
- 4 oz shrimps, peeled
- ½ teaspoon ground turmeric
- ½ teaspoon ground paprika
- ¼ teaspoon salt
- Cooking spray

Directions:
1. Mix eggs with shrimps, turmeric, salt, and paprika.
2. Then spray the Slow Cooker bowl with cooking spray.
3. After this, pour the egg mixture inside. Flatten the shrimps and close the lid.
4. Cook the omelet for 3.5 hours on High.

Nutrition Info:
- Per Serving: 98 calories, 12.1g protein, 1.1g carbohydrates, 4.9g fat, 0.2g fiber, 223mg cholesterol, 278mg sodium, 120mg potassium.

Tomato Eggs

Servings:4 | Cooking Time: 2.5 Hours

Ingredients:
- 2 cups tomatoes, chopped
- ¼ cup tomato juice
- 1 onion, diced
- 1 teaspoon olive oil
- ½ teaspoon ground black pepper
- 4 eggs

Directions:
1. Pour olive oil in the Slow Cooker.
2. Add onion, tomato juice, and tomatoes.
3. Close the lid and cook the mixture on High for 1 hour.
4. Then mix the tomato mixture and crack the eggs inside.
5. Close the lid and cook them on High for 1.5 hours more.

Nutrition Info:
- Per Serving: 103 calories, 6.8g protein, 7.2g carbohydrates, 5.8g fat, 1.8g fiber, 164mg cholesterol, 108mg sodium, 350mg potassium

Quinoa And Banana Mix

Servings: 8 | Cooking Time: 6 Hours

Ingredients:
- 2 cups quinoa
- 2 bananas, mashed
- 4 cups water
- 2 cups blueberries
- 2 teaspoons vanilla extract
- 2 tablespoons maple syrup
- 1 teaspoon cinnamon powder
- Cooking spray

Directions:
1. Grease your Slow Cooker with cooking spray, add quinoa, bananas, water, blueberries, vanilla, maple syrup and cinnamon, stir, cover and cook on Low for 6 hours.
2. Stir again, divide into bowls and serve for breakfast.

Nutrition Info:
- calories 200, fat 4, fiber 6, carbs 12, protein 4

Santa Fe's Frittata

Servings:12 | Cooking Time: 4 Hours

Ingredients:
- 10 organic eggs
- ½ cup milk
- Salt and pepper to taste
- 8 ounces ground pork
- 2 cups red and yellow sweet peppers, diced
- ½ cup pepper jack cheese

Directions:
1. Beat eggs and milk in a mixing bowl. Season with salt and pepper to taste. Set aside.
2. Heat a skillet over medium high flame and sauté the ground pork until lightly golden.
3. Pour into the CrockPot and add in the sweet peppers.
4. Pour in the egg mixture and sprinkle cheese on top.
5. Close the lid and cook on high for 3 hours or on low for 4 hours.

Nutrition Info:
- Calories per serving: 169; Carbohydrates: 2.8g; Protein: 11.2g; Fat:11.9 g; Sugar: 0g; Sodium: 269mg; Fiber: 0.5g

Vanilla Oats

Servings: 4 | Cooking Time: 8 Hours

Ingredients:
- 1 cup steel cut oats
- 2 teaspoons vanilla extract
- 2 cups vanilla almond milk
- 2 tablespoons maple syrup
- 2 teaspoons cinnamon powder
- 2 cups water
- 2 teaspoons flaxseed
- Cooking spray
- 2 tablespoons blackberries

Directions:
1. Grease your Slow Cooker with the cooking spray and add oats, vanilla extract, almond milk, maple syrup, cinnamon, water and flaxseed, cover and cook on Low for 8 hours.
2. Stir oats, divide into bowls, sprinkle blackberries on top and serve for breakfast.

Nutrition Info:
- calories 200, fat 3, fiber 6, carbs 9, protein 3

Arugula Frittata

Servings: 4 | Cooking Time: 4 Hours

Ingredients:
- 8 eggs
- Salt and black pepper to the taste
- ½ cup milk
- 1 teaspoon oregano, dried
- 4 cups baby arugula
- 1 and ¼ cup roasted red peppers, chopped
- ½ cup red onion, chopped
- ¾ cup goat cheese, crumbled
- Cooking spray

Directions:
1. In a bowl, mix the eggs with milk, oregano, salt and pepper and whisk well.
2. Grease your Slow Cooker with cooking spray and spread roasted peppers, onion and arugula.
3. Add eggs mix, sprinkle goat cheese all over, cover, cook on Low for 4 hours, divide frittata between plates and serve for breakfast.

Nutrition Info:
- calories 269, fat 3, fiber 6, carbs 15, protein 4

Potato Omelet

Servings:4 | Cooking Time: 6 Hours

Ingredients:
- 1 cup potatoes, sliced
- 1 onion, sliced
- 6 eggs, beaten
- 2 tablespoons olive oil
- 1 teaspoon salt
- ½ teaspoon ground black pepper

Directions:
1. Mix potatoes with ground black pepper and salt.
2. Transfer them in the Slow Cooker, add olive oil and cook on high for 30 minutes.
3. Then mix the potatoes and add onion and eggs.
4. Stir the mixture and cook the omelet on Low for 6 hours.

Nutrition Info:
- Per Serving: 192 calories, 9.3g protein, 9.1g carbohydrates, 13.6g fat, 1.6g fiber, 246mg cholesterol, 677mg sodium, 285mg potassium

Chicken Frittata

Servings: 2 | Cooking Time: 3 Hours

Ingredients:
- ½ cup chicken, cooked and shredded
- 1 teaspoon mustard
- 1 tablespoon mayonnaise
- 1 tomato, chopped
- 2 bacon slices, cooked and crumbled
- 4 eggs
- 1 small avocado, pitted, peeled and chopped
- Salt and black pepper to the taste

Directions:
1. In a bowl, mix the eggs with salt, pepper, chicken, avocado, tomato, bacon, mayo and mustard, toss, transfer to your Slow

Cooker, cover and cook on Low for 3 hours.
2. Divide between plates and serve for breakfast

Nutrition Info:
- calories 300, fat 32, fiber 6, carbs 15, protein 25

Romano Cheese Frittata
Servings:4 | Cooking Time: 3 Hours

Ingredients:
- 4 oz Romano cheese, grated
- 5 eggs, beaten
- ¼ cup of coconut milk
- ½ cup bell pepper, chopped
- ½ teaspoon ground white pepper
- 1 teaspoon olive oil
- ½ teaspoon ground coriander

Directions:
1. Mix eggs with coconut milk, ground white pepper, bell pepper, and ground coriander.
2. Then brush the Slow Cooker bowl with olive oil.
3. Pour the egg mixture in the Slow Cooker.
4. Cook the frittata on High for 2.5 hours.
5. Then top the frittata with Romano cheese and cook for 30 minutes on High.

Nutrition Info:
- Per Serving: 238 calories, 16.5g protein, 3.6g carbohydrates, 17.9g fat, 0.6g fiber, 234mg cholesterol, 420mg sodium, 169mg potassium.

Broccoli Egg Casserole
Servings:5 | Cooking Time: 3 Hours

Ingredients:
- 4 eggs, beaten
- ½ cup full-fat milk
- 3 tablespoons grass-fed butter, melted
- 1 ½ cup broccoli florets, chopped
- Salt and pepper to taste

Directions:
1. Beat the eggs and milk in a mixing bowl.
2. Grease the bottom of the CrockPot with melted butter.
3. Add in the broccoli florets in the CrockPot and pour the egg mixture.
4. Season with salt and pepper to taste.
5. Close the lid and cook on high for 2 hours or on low for 3 hours.

Nutrition Info:
- Calories per serving: 217; Carbohydrates:4.6 g; Protein: 11.6g; Fat: 16.5g; Sugar: 0.7g; Sodium: 674mg; Fiber: 2.3g

Kale & Feta Breakfast Frittata
Servings: 6 (4.8 Ounces Per Serving)
Cooking Time: 3 Hours And 5 Minutes

Ingredients:
- 2 cups kale, chopped
- ½ cup feta, crumbled
- 2 teaspoons olive oil
- Salt and pepper to taste
- 3 green onions, chopped
- 1 large green pepper, diced
- 8 eggs

Directions:

1. Heat the olive oil in Crock-Pot and sauté the kale, diced pepper, and chopped green onion for about 2-3 minutes. Beat the eggs in a mixing bowl, pour over other ingredients, and stir. Add salt and pepper and sprinkle crumbled feta cheese on top. Cover and cook on LOW for 2-3 hours, or until the cheese has melted. Serve hot.

Nutrition Info:
- Calories: 160.1, Total Fat: 10.71 g, Saturated Fat: 4.2 g, Cholesterol: 259.13 mg, Sodium: 245.78 mg, Potassium: 263.49 mg, Total Carbohydrates: 4.92 g, Fiber: 1.06 g, Sugar: 1.52 g, Protein: 11.24 g

Milk Oatmeal
Servings:4 | Cooking Time: 2 Hours

Ingredients:
- 2 cups oatmeal
- 1 cup of water
- 1 cup milk
- 1 tablespoon liquid honey
- 1 teaspoon vanilla extract
- 1 tablespoon coconut oil
- ¼ teaspoon ground cinnamon

Directions:
1. Put all ingredients except liquid honey in the Slow Cooker and mix.
2. Close the lid and cook the meal on High for 2 hours.
3. Then stir the cooked oatmeal and transfer in the serving bowls.
4. Top the meal with a small amount of liquid honey.

Nutrition Info:
- Per Serving: 234 calories, 7.4g protein, 35.3g carbohydrates, 7.3g fat, 4.2g fiber, 5mg cholesterol, 33mg sodium, 189mg potassium.

Fried Apple Slices
Servings: 6 | Cooking Time: 6 Hours 10 Minutes

Ingredients:
- 1 teaspoon ground cinnamon
- 3 tablespoons cornstarch
- 3 pounds Granny Smith apples
- ¼ teaspoon nutmeg, freshly grated
- 1 cup sugar, granulated
- 2 tablespoons butter

Directions:
1. Put the apple slices in the slow cooker and stir in nutmeg, cinnamon, sugar and cornstarch.
2. Top with butter and cover the lid.
3. Cook on LOW for about 6 hours, stirring about halfway.
4. Dish out to serve hot.

Nutrition Info:
- Calories: 234 Fat: 4.1g Carbohydrates: 52.7g

Swiss Ham Quiche
Servings: 6 | Cooking Time: 3 Hrs

Ingredients:
- 1 pie crust
- 1 cup ham, cooked and chopped
- 2 cups Swiss cheese, shredded
- 6 eggs
- 1 cup whipping cream
- 4 green onions, chopped

- Salt and black pepper to the taste
- A pinch of nutmeg, ground
- Cooking spray

Directions:
1. Grease the base of your Slow Cooker with cooking spray.
2. Spread the pie crust in the Slow Cooker.
3. Put the cooker's lid on and set the cooking time to 1 hour 30 minutes on High settings.
4. Meanwhile, beat eggs with cream, nutmeg, black pepper, and salt in a bowl.
5. Pour the egg mixture in the pie crust and top it with cheese, green onions, and ham.
6. Put the cooker's lid on and set the cooking time to 1 hour 30 minutes on High settings.
7. Slice and serve.

Nutrition Info:
- Per Serving: Calories 300, Total Fat 4g, Fiber 7g, Total Carbs 15g, Protein 5g

Raspberry Chia Porridge

Servings:4 | Cooking Time: 4 Hours

Ingredients:
- 1 cup raspberry
- 3 tablespoons maple syrup
- 1 cup chia seeds
- 4 cups of milk

Directions:
1. Put chia seeds and milk in the Slow Cooker and cook the mixture on low for 4 hours.
2. Meanwhile, mix raspberries and maple syrup in the blender and blend the mixture until smooth.
3. When the chia porridge is cooked, transfer it in the serving bowls and top with blended raspberry mixture.

Nutrition Info:
- Per Serving: 315 calories, 13.1g protein, 37.7g carbohydrates, 13.9g fat, 11.7g fiber, 20mg cholesterol, 121mg sodium, 332mg potassium

Dates Quinoa

Servings: 4 | Cooking Time: 3 Hours

Ingredients:
- 1 cup quinoa
- 4 medjol dates, chopped
- 3 cups milk
- 1 apple, cored and chopped
- ¼ cup pepitas
- 2 teaspoons cinnamon powder
- 1 teaspoon vanilla extract
- ¼ teaspoon nutmeg, ground

Directions:
1. In your Slow Cooker, mix quinoa with dates, milk, apple, pepitas, cinnamon, nutmeg and vanilla, stir, cover and cook on High for 3 hours.
2. Stir again, divide into bowls and serve.

Nutrition Info:
- calories 241, fat 4, fiber 4, carbs 10, protein 3

Chicken Cabbage Medley

Servings: 5 | Cooking Time: 4.5 Hrs

Ingredients:
- 6 oz. ground chicken
- 10 oz. cabbage, chopped
- 1 white onion, sliced
- ½ cup tomato juice
- 1 tsp sugar
- ½ tsp salt
- 1 tsp ground black pepper
- 4 tbsp chicken stock
- 2 garlic cloves

Directions:
1. Whisk tomato juice with black pepper, salt, sugar, and chicken stock in a bowl.
2. Spread the onion slices, chicken, and cabbage in the Slow Cooker.
3. Pour the tomato-stock mixture over the veggies and top with garlic cloves.
4. Put the cooker's lid on and set the cooking time to 4 hours 30 minutes on High settings.
5. Serve.

Nutrition Info:
- Per Serving: Calories 91, Total Fat 3.1g, Fiber 2g, Total Carbs 9.25g, Protein 8g

Breakfast Salad

Servings:4 | Cooking Time: 2.5 Hours

Ingredients:
- 1 cup ground beef
- 1 teaspoon chili powder
- 1 onion, diced
- 1 tablespoon olive oil
- 2 cups arugula, chopped
- 1 cup tomatoes, chopped

Directions:
1. Mix ground beef with chili powder, diced onion, and olive oil.
2. Put the mixture in the Slow Cooker and close the lid.
3. Cook it on High for 2.5 hours.
4. Then transfer the mixture in the salad bowl, cool gently.
5. Add tomatoes and arugula. Mix the salad.

Nutrition Info:
- Per Serving: 128 calories, 12.3g protein, 5.1g carbohydrates, 6.7g fat, 1.5g fiber, 34mg cholesterol, 45mg sodium, 373mg potassium

Sweet Vegetable Rice Pudding

Servings:4 | Cooking Time: 1 Hour

Ingredients:
- 2 cups cauliflower, shredded
- 3 cups of milk
- 1 tablespoon potato starch
- 2 tablespoons maple syrup

Directions:
1. Mix potato starch with milk and pour in the Slow Cooker.
2. Add maple syrup and cauliflower shred. Cook the mixture on High for 1 hour.

Nutrition Info:
- Per Serving: 140 calories, 7g protein, 20.9g carbohydrates, 3.8g fat, 1.3g fiber, 15mg cholesterol, 102mg sodium, 277mg potassium

Raisins And Rice Pudding

Servings:4 | Cooking Time: 6 Hours

Ingredients:
- 1 cup long-grain rice
- 2.5 cups organic almond milk
- 2 tablespoons cornstarch
- 1 teaspoon vanilla extract
- 2 tablespoons raisins, chopped

Directions:
1. Put all ingredients in the Slow Cooker and carefully mix.
2. Then close the lid and cook the pudding for 6 hours on Low.

Nutrition Info:
- Per Serving: 238 calories, 4.1g protein, 49.4g carbohydrates, 1.9g fat, 0.8g fiber, 0mg cholesterol, 91mg sodium, 89mg potassium

Cranberry Oatmeal

Servings: 4 | Cooking Time: 8 Hours 15 Minutes

Ingredients:
- 1 cup dried cranberries
- 1 cup steel cut oats
- 1 cup dates, chopped
- 4 cups water
- 2 tablespoons honey
- ½ cup half and half

Directions:
1. Grease a crockpot and add all the ingredients except the half and half and honey.
2. Cover and cook on LOW for about 8 hours.
3. Stir in honey and half and half and dish out to serve.

Nutrition Info:
- Calories: 289 Fat: 5g Carbohydrates: 59.7g

Artichoke Pepper Frittata

Servings: 4 | Cooking Time: 3 Hrs

Ingredients:
- 14 oz. canned artichokes hearts, drained and chopped
- 12 oz. roasted red peppers, chopped
- 8 eggs, whisked
- ¼ cup green onions, chopped
- 4 oz. feta cheese, crumbled
- Cooking spray

Directions:
1. Coat the base of your Slow Cooker with cooking spray.
2. Add green onions, roasted peppers, and artichokes to the Slow Cooker.
3. Pour whisked eggs over the veggies and drizzle cheese on top.
4. Put the cooker's lid on and set the cooking time to 3 hours on Low settings.
5. Slice and serve.

Nutrition Info:
- Per Serving: Calories 232, Total Fat 7g, Fiber 9g, Total Carbs 17g, Protein 6g

Baby Spinach Rice Mix

Servings: 4 | Cooking Time: 6 Hours

Ingredients:
- ¼ cup mozzarella, shredded
- ½ cup baby spinach
- ½ cup wild rice
- 1 and ½ cups chicken stock
- ½ teaspoon turmeric powder
- ½ teaspoon oregano, dried
- A pinch of salt and black pepper
- 3 scallions, minced
- ¾ cup goat cheese, crumbled

Directions:
1. In your Slow Cooker, mix the rice with the stock, turmeric and the other ingredients, toss, put the lid on and cook on Low for 6 hours.
2. Divide the mix into bowls and serve for breakfast.

Nutrition Info:
- calories 165, fat 1.2, fiber 3.5, carbs 32.6, protein 7.6

Squash Bowls

Servings: 2 | Cooking Time: 6 Hours

Ingredients:
- 2 tablespoons walnuts, chopped
- 2 cups squash, peeled and cubed
- ½ cup coconut cream
- ½ teaspoon cinnamon powder
- ½ tablespoon sugar

Directions:
1. In your Slow Cooker, mix the squash with the nuts and the other ingredients, toss, put the lid on and cook on Low for 6 hours.
2. Divide into bowls and serve.

Nutrition Info:
- calories 140, fat 1, fiber 2, carbs 2, protein 5

Peppers And Eggs Mix

Servings: 2 | Cooking Time: 4 Hours

Ingredients:
- 4 eggs, whisked
- ½ teaspoon coriander, ground
- ½ teaspoon rosemary, dried
- 2 spring onions, chopped
- 1 red bell pepper, cut into strips
- 1 green bell pepper, cut into strips
- 1 yellow bell pepper, cut into strips
- ¼ cup heavy cream
- ½ teaspoon garlic powder
- A pinch of salt and black pepper
- 1 teaspoon sweet paprika
- Cooking spray

Directions:
1. Grease your Slow Cooker with the cooking spray, and mix the eggs with the coriander, rosemary and the other ingredients into the pot.
2. Put the lid on, cook on Low for 4 hours, divide between plates and serve for breakfast.

Nutrition Info:
- calories 172, fat 6, fiber 3, carbs 6, protein 7

Chapter 3 Appetizers Recipes

Chapter 3 Appetizers Recipes

Sweet Corn Crab Dip

Servings: 20 | Cooking Time: 2 1/4 Hours

Ingredients:
- 2 tablespoons butter
- 1 cup canned sweet corn, drained
- 2 red bell peppers, cored and diced
- 2 garlic cloves, chopped
- 2 poblano peppers, chopped
- 1 cup sour cream
- 1 can crab meat, drained
- 1 teaspoon Worcestershire sauce
- 1 teaspoon hot sauce
- 1 cup grated Cheddar cheese

Directions:
1. Mix all the ingredients in your Slow Cooker.
2. Cover the pot with its lid and cook on low settings for 2 hours.
3. Serve the dip warm or chilled.

Artichoke Bread Pudding

Servings: 10 | Cooking Time: 6 1/2 Hours

Ingredients:
- 6 cups bread cubes
- 6 artichoke hearts, drained and chopped
- 1/2 cup grated Parmesan
- 4 eggs
- 1/2 cup sour cream
- 1 cup milk
- 4 oz. spinach, chopped
- 1 tablespoon chopped parsley
- 2 tablespoons olive oil
- Salt and pepper to taste
- 1/2 teaspoon dried oregano
- 1/2 teaspoon dried basil

Directions:
1. Combine the bread cubes, artichoke hearts and Parmesan in your Slow Cooker. Add the spinach and parsley as well.
2. In a bowl, mix the eggs, sour cream, milk, oregano and basil, as well as salt and pepper.
3. Pour this mixture over the bread and press the bread slightly to make sure it soaks up all the liquid.
4. Cover the pot with its lid and cook on low settings for 6 hours.
5. The bread can be served both warm and chilled.

Southwestern Nacho Dip

Servings: 10 | Cooking Time: 6 1/4 Hours

Ingredients:
- 1 pound ground pork
- 1 cup apple juice
- 4 garlic cloves, chopped
- 2 cups BBQ sauce
- 2 tablespoons brown sugar
- Salt and pepper to taste
- 1 1/2 cups sweet corn
- 1 can black beans, drained
- 1 cup diced tomatoes
- 2 jalapeno peppers, chopped
- 2 tablespoons chopped cilantro
- 2 cups grated Cheddar
- 1 lime, juiced
- Nachos for serving

Directions:
1. Heat a skillet over medium flame and add the pork. Cook for a few minutes, stirring often.
2. Transfer the pork in your Slow Cooker and add the apple juice, garlic, BBQ sauce, brown sugar, salt and pepper.
3. Cook on high settings for 2 hours.
4. After 2 hours, add the remaining ingredients and continue cooking for 4 hours on low settings.
5. Serve the dip warm with nachos.

Marinara Turkey Meatballs

Servings: 8 | Cooking Time: 6 1/2 Hours

Ingredients:
- 2 pounds ground turkey
- 1 carrot, grated
- 1 potato, grated
- 1 shallot, chopped
- 1 tablespoon chopped parsley
- 1 tablespoon chopped cilantro
- 4 basil leaves, chopped
- 1/2 teaspoon dried mint
- 1 egg
- 1/4 cup breadcrumbs
- Salt and pepper to taste
- 2 cups marinara sauce

Directions:
1. Mix the turkey, carrot, potato, shallot, parsley, cilantro, basil, mint, egg and breadcrumbs in a bowl.
2. Add salt and pepper to taste and mix well.
3. Pour the marinara sauce in your Slow Cooker then form meatballs and drop them in the sauce.
4. Cover the pot with its lid and cook on low settings for 6 hours.
5. Serve the meatballs warm or chilled.

Nacho Sauce

Servings: 12 | Cooking Time: 6 1/4 Hours

Ingredients:
- 2 pounds ground beef
- 2 tablespoons Mexican seasoning
- 1 teaspoon chili powder
- 1 can diced tomatoes
- 2 shallots, chopped
- 4 garlic cloves, minced
- 1 can sweet corn, drained
- 2 cups grated Cheddar cheese

Directions:
1. Combine all the ingredients in your Slow Cooker.
2. Cook on low settings for 6 hours.
3. This dip is best served warm.

Bean Queso

Servings: 10 | Cooking Time: 6 1/4 Hours

Ingredients:
- 1 can black beans, drained
- 1 cup chopped green chiles
- 1/2 cup red salsa
- 1 teaspoon dried oregano
- 1/2 teaspoon cumin powder
- 1 cup light beer
- 1 1/2 cups grated Cheddar
- Salt and pepper to taste

Directions:
1. Combine the beans, chiles, oregano, cumin, salsa, beer and cheese in your Slow Cooker.
2. Add salt and pepper as needed and cook on low settings for 6 hours.
3. Serve the bean queso warm.

Quick Parmesan Bread

Servings: 8 | Cooking Time: 1 1/4 Hours

Ingredients:
- 4 cups all-purpose flour
- 1/2 teaspoon salt
- 1/2 cup grated Parmesan cheese
- 1 teaspoon baking soda
- 2 cups buttermilk
- 2 tablespoons olive oil

Directions:
1. Mix the flour, salt, parmesan cheese and baking soda in a bowl.
2. Stir in the buttermilk and olive oil and mix well with a fork.
3. Shape the dough into a loaf and place it in your Slow Cooker.
4. Cover with its lid and cook on high heat for 1 hour.
5. Serve the bread warm or chilled.

Charred Tomato Salsa

Servings: 8 | Cooking Time: 3 Hours

Ingredients:
- 4 ripe tomatoes, sliced
- 2 tablespoons olive oil
- 1 teaspoon dried basil
- 1/2 teaspoon dried mint
- 2 shallots, chopped
- 1 jalapeno pepper, chopped
- 1 can black beans, drained
- 1/4 cup chicken stock
- 1 bay leaf
- Salt and pepper to taste

Directions:
1. Place the tomato slices in a baking tray and sprinkle with salt, pepper, basil and mint.
2. Drizzle with olive oil and cook in the preheated oven at 350F for 35-40 minutes until the slices begin to caramelize.
3. Transfer the tomatoes in a Slow Cooker and add the remaining ingredients.
4. Cook on high settings for 2 hours and serve the salsa warm or chilled.

Oriental Chicken Bites

Servings: 10 | Cooking Time: 7 1/4 Hours

Ingredients:
- 4 chicken breasts, cubed
- 2 sweet onions, sliced
- 1 teaspoon grated ginger
- 4 garlic cloves, minced
- 1/2 teaspoon cinnamon powder
- 1 teaspoon smoked paprika
- 1 teaspoon cumin powder
- 1 cup chicken stock
- 1/2 lemon, juiced
- 2 tablespoons olive oil
- Salt and pepper to taste

Directions:
1. Combine all the ingredients in your Slow Cooker.
2. Add salt and pepper to taste and mix well until the ingredients are evenly distributed.
3. Cover and cook on low settings for 7 hours.
4. Serve the chicken bites warm or chilled.

Green Vegetable Dip

Servings: 12 | Cooking Time: 2 1/4 Hours

Ingredients:
- 10 oz. frozen spinach, thawed and drained
- 1 jar artichoke hearts, drained
- 1 cup chopped parsley
- 1 cup cream cheese
- 1 cup sour cream
- 1/2 cup grated Parmesan cheese
- 1/2 cup feta cheese, crumbled
- 1/2 teaspoon onion powder
- 1/4 teaspoon garlic powder

Directions:
1. Combine all the ingredients in your Slow Cooker and mix gently.
2. Cover with its lid and cook on high settings for 2 hours.
3. Serve the dip warm or chilled with crusty bread, biscuits or other salty snacks or even vegetable sticks.

Bacon Wrapped Dates

Servings: 8 | Cooking Time: 1 3/4 Hours

Ingredients:
- 16 dates, pitted
- 16 almonds
- 16 slices bacon

Directions:
1. Stuff each date with an almond.
2. Wrap each date in bacon and place the wrapped dates in your Slow Cooker.
3. Cover with its lid and cook on high settings for 1 1/4 hours.
4. Serve warm or chilled.

Cheeseburger Meatballs

Servings 8

Cooking Time 6 14 Hours

Ingredients:
- 2 pounds ground pork
- 1 shallot, chopped
- 2 tablespoons beef stock
- 1 egg
- 14 cup breadcrumbs
- 1 teaspoon Cajun seasoning
- 12 teaspoon dried basil
- Salt and pepper to taste
- 2 cups shredded processed cheese

Directions:
1. Mix the pork, shallot, beef stock, egg, breadcrumbs, Cajun seasoning and basil in a bowl.
2. Add salt and pepper to taste and mix well.
3. Form small meatballs and place them in the Slow Cooker.
4. Top with shredded cheese and cook on low settings for 6 hours.
5. Serve the meatballs warm.

Sausage And Pepper Appetizer

Servings: 8 | Cooking Time: 6 1/4 Hours

Ingredients:
- 6 fresh pork sausages, skins removed
- 2 tablespoons olive oil
- 1 can fire roasted tomatoes
- 4 roasted bell peppers, chopped
- 1 poblano pepper, chopped
- 1 shallot, chopped
- 1 cup grated Provolone cheese
- Salt and pepper to taste

Directions:
1. Heat the oil in a skillet and stir in the sausage meat. Cook for 5 minutes, stirring often.
2. Transfer the meat in your Slow Cooker and add the remaining ingredients.
3. Season with salt and pepper and cook on low settings for 6 hours.
4. Serve the dish warm or chilled.

Creamy Spinach Dip

Servings: 30 | Cooking Time: 2 1/4 Hours

Ingredients:
- 1 can crab meat, drained
- 1 pound fresh spinach, chopped
- 2 shallots, chopped
- 2 jalapeno peppers, chopped
- 1 cup grated Parmesan
- 1/2 cup whole milk
- 1 cup sour cream
- 1 cup cream cheese
- 1 cup grated Cheddar cheese
- 1 tablespoon sherry vinegar
- 2 garlic cloves, chopped

Directions:
1. Combine all the ingredients in your Slow Cooker.
2. Cover with its lid and cook on high settings for 2 hours.
3. Serve the spinach dip warm or chilled with vegetable stick or your favorite salty snacks.

Bacon Black Bean Dip

Servings: 6 | Cooking Time: 6 1/4 Hours

Ingredients:
- 6 bacon slices
- 2 cans black beans, drained
- 2 shallots, sliced
- 1 garlic cloves, chopped
- 1 cup red salsa
- 1/2 cup beef stock
- 1 tablespoon brown sugar
- 1 tablespoon molasses
- 1/2 teaspoon chili powder
- 1 tablespoon apple cider vinegar
- 2 tablespoons Bourbon
- Salt and pepper to taste

Directions:
1. Heat a skillet over medium flame and add the bacon. Cook until crisp then transfer the bacon and its fat in your Slow Cooker.
2. Stir in the remaining ingredients and cook on low settings for 6 hours.
3. When done, partially mash the beans and serve the dip right away.

Chipotle Bbq Meatballs

Servings: 10 | Cooking Time: 7 1/2 Hours

Ingredients:
- 3 pounds ground pork
- 2 garlic cloves, minced
- 2 shallots, chopped
- 2 chipotle peppers, chopped
- Salt and pepper to taste
- 2 cups BBQ sauce
- 1/4 cup cranberry sauce
- 1 bay leaf

Directions:
1. Mix the ground pork, garlic, shallots, chipotle peppers, salt and pepper in a bowl.
2. Combine the BBQ sauce, cranberry sauce, bay leaf, salt and pepper in your Slow Cooker.
3. Form small meatballs and drop them in the sauce.
4. Cover the pot with its lid and cook on low settings for 7 hours.
5. Serve the meatballs warm or chilled with cocktail skewers or toothpicks.

Party Mix

Servings: 20 | Cooking Time: 1 3/4 Hours

Ingredients:
- 4 cups cereals
- 4 cups crunchy cereals
- 2 cups mixed nuts
- 1 cup mixed seeds
- 1/2 cup butter, melted
- 2 tablespoons Worcestershire sauce
- 1 teaspoon hot sauce
- 1 teaspoon salt
- 1/2 teaspoon cumin powder

Directions:
1. Combine all the ingredients in your Slow Cooker and toss around until evenly coated.
2. Cook on high settings for 1 1/2 hours.
3. Serve the mix chilled.

Beer Cheese Fondue

Servings: 8 | Cooking Time: 2 1/4 Hours

Ingredients:
- 1 shallot, chopped
- 1 garlic clove, minced
- 1 cup grated Gruyere cheese
- 2 cups grated Cheddar
- 1 tablespoon cornstarch
- 1 teaspoon Dijon mustard
- 1/2 teaspoon cumin seeds
- 1 cup beer
- Salt and pepper to taste

Directions:
1. Combine the shallot, garlic, cheeses, cornstarch, mustard, cumin seeds and beer in your Slow Cooker.
2. Add salt and pepper to taste and mix well.
3. Cover the pot with its lid and cook on high settings for 2 hours.
4. Serve the fondue warm.

Cheesy Chicken Bites

Servings: 10 | Cooking Time: 6 1/4 Hours

Ingredients:
- 4 chicken breasts, cut into bite-size cubes
- 1/4 cup all-purpose flour
- Salt and pepper to taste
- 1 cup cream cheese
- 2 roasted red bell peppers
- 1 cup shredded mozzarella
- 1/4 teaspoon chili powder

Directions:
1. Mix the cream cheese, bell peppers, chili powder, salt and pepper in a blender and pulse until smooth.
2. Pour the mixture in your Slow Cooker and add the remaining ingredients.
3. Cook on low settings for 6 hours.
4. Serve the chicken bites warm or chilled.

Artichoke Dip

Servings: 20 | Cooking Time: 6 1/4 Hours

Ingredients:
- 2 sweet onions, chopped
- 1 red chili, chopped
- 2 garlic cloves, chopped
- 1 jar artichoke hearts, drained and chopped
- 1 cup cream cheese
- 1 cup heavy cream
- 2 oz. blue cheese, crumbled
- 2 tablespoons chopped cilantro

Directions:
1. Mix the onions, chili, garlic, artichoke hearts, cream cheese, heavy cream and blue cheese in a Slow Cooker.
2. Cook on low settings for 6 hours.
3. When done, stir in the cilantro and serve the dip warm or chilled.

Tahini Chickpea Dip

Servings: 6 | Cooking Time: 6 1/4 Hours

Ingredients:
- 2 cups dried chickpeas, rinsed
- 5 cups water
- 1 bay leaf
- Salt and pepper to taste
- 1 lemon, juiced
- 1/4 cup tahini paste
- 2 tablespoons olive oil
- 1 pinch red pepper flakes

Directions:
1. Combine the chickpeas, water, bay leaf, salt and pepper in a Slow Cooker.
2. Cook on low settings for 6 hours then drain and transfer in a food processor.
3. Stir in the remaining ingredients and pulse until smooth.
4. Spoon into a bowl and serve fresh or store in an airtight container in the fridge.

Balsamico Pulled Pork

Servings: 6 | Cooking Time: 8 1/4 Hours

Ingredients:
- 2 pounds boneless pork shoulder
- 2 tablespoons honey
- 1/4 cup balsamic vinegar
- 1/4 cup hoisin sauce
- 1 tablespoon Dijon mustard
- 1/4 cup chicken stock
- 2 garlic cloves, minced
- 2 shallots, sliced
- 2 tablespoons soy sauce

Directions:
1. Combine the honey, vinegar, hoisin sauce, mustard, stock, garlic, shallots and soy sauce in your Slow Cooker.
2. Add the pork shoulder and roll it in the mixture until evenly coated.
3. Cover the Slow Cooker and cook on low settings for 8 hours.
4. When done, shred the meat into fine pieces and serve warm or chilled.

Spanish Chorizo Dip

Servings: 8 | Cooking Time: 6 1/4 Hours

Ingredients:
- 8 chorizo links, diced
- 1 can diced tomatoes
- 1 chili pepper, chopped
- 1 cup cream cheese
- 2 cups grated Cheddar cheese
- 1/4 cup white wine

Directions:
1. Combine all the ingredients in your Slow Cooker.
2. Cook the dip on low settings for 6 hours.
3. Serve the dip warm.

Chili Corn Cheese Dip

Servings: 8 | Cooking Time: 2 1/4 Hours

Ingredients:
- 1 pound ground beef
- 2 tablespoons olive oil
- 1 shallot, chopped
- 1 can sweet corn, drained
- 1 can kidney beans, drained
- 1/2 cup beef stock
- 1 cup diced tomatoes
- 1/2 cup black olives, pitted and chopped
- 1 teaspoon dried oregano
- 1/2 teaspoon chili powder
- 1/2 teaspoon cumin powder
- 1/4 teaspoon garlic powder
- 2 cups grated Cheddar cheese
- Tortilla chips for serving

Directions:
1. Heat the oil in a skillet and stir in the ground beef. Cook for 5-7 minutes, stirring often.
2. Transfer the meat in a Slow Cooker and add the remaining ingredients.
3. Add salt and pepper to taste and cover with its lid.
4. Cook on high settings for 2 hours.
5. Serve the dip warm with tortilla chips.

Spicy Chicken Taquitos

Servings: 8 | Cooking Time: 6 1/2 Hours

Ingredients:
- 4 chicken breasts, cooked and diced
- 1 cup cream cheese
- 2 jalapeno peppers, chopped
- 1/2 cup canned sweet corn, drained
- 1/2 teaspoon cumin powder
- 4 garlic cloves, minced
- 16 taco-sized flour tortillas
- 2 cups grated Cheddar cheese

Directions:
1. In a bowl, mix the chicken, cream cheese, garlic, cumin, poblano peppers and corn. Stir in the cheese as well.
2. Place your tortillas on your working surface and top each tortilla with the cheese mixture.
3. Roll the tortillas tightly to form an even roll.
4. Place the rolls in your Slow Cooker.
5. Cook on low settings for 6 hours.
6. Serve warm.

Five-spiced Chicken Wings

Servings: 8 | Cooking Time: 7 1/4 Hours

Ingredients:
- 1/2 cup plum sauce
- 1/2 cup BBQ sauce
- 2 tablespoons butter
- 1 tablespoon five-spice powder
- 1 teaspoon salt
- 1/2 teaspoon chili powder
- 4 pounds chicken wings

Directions:
1. Combine the plum sauce and BBQ sauce, as well as butter, five-spice, salt and chili powder in a slow cooker.

2. Add the chicken wings and mix well until well coated.
3. Cover and cook on low settings fir 7 hours.
4. Serve warm or chilled.

Boiled Peanuts With Skin On

Servings: 8 | Cooking Time: 7 1/4 Hours

Ingredients:
- 2 pounds uncooked, whole peanuts
- 1/2 cup salt
- 4 cups water

Directions:
1. Combine all the ingredients in your Slow Cooker.
2. Cover and cook on low settings for 7 hours.
3. Drain and allow to cool down before servings.

Mixed Olive Dip

Servings: 10 | Cooking Time: 1 3/4 Hours

Ingredients:
- 1 pound ground chicken
- 2 tablespoons olive oil
- 1 green bell pepper, cored and diced
- 1/2 cup Kalamata olives, pitted and chopped
- 1/2 cup green olives, chopped
- 1/2 cup black olives, pitted and chopped
- 1 cup green salsa
- 1/2 cup chicken stock
- 1 cup grated Cheddar cheese
- 1/2 cup shredded mozzarella

Directions:
1. Combine all the ingredients in your Slow Cooker.
2. Cover with its lid and cook on high settings for 1 1/2 hours.
3. The dip is best served warm.

Chili Chicken Wings

Servings: 8 | Cooking Time: 7 1/4 Hours

Ingredients:
- 4 pounds chicken wings
- 1/4 cup maple syrup
- 1 teaspoon garlic powder
- 1 teaspoon chili powder
- 2 tablespoons balsamic vinegar
- 1 tablespoon Dijon mustard
- 1 teaspoon Worcestershire sauce
- 1/2 cup tomato sauce
- 1 teaspoon salt

Directions:
1. Combine the chicken wings and the remaining ingredients in a Slow Cooker.
2. Toss around until evenly coated and cook on low settings for 7 hours.
3. Serve the chicken wings warm or chilled.

Stuffed Artichokes

Servings: 6 | Cooking Time: 6 1/2 Hours

Ingredients:
- 6 fresh artichokes
- 6 anchovy fillets, chopped
- 4 garlic cloves, minced
- 2 tablespoons olive oil
- 1 cup breadcrumbs
- 1 tablespoon chopped parsley
- Salt and pepper to taste
- 1/4 cup white wine

Directions:
1. Cut the stem of each artichoke so that it sits flat on your chopping board then cut the top off and trim the outer leaves, cleaning the center as well.
2. In a bowl, mix the anchovy fillets, garlic, olive oil, breadcrumbs and parsley. Add salt and pepper to taste.
3. Top each artichoke with breadcrumb mixture and rub it well into the leaves.
4. Place the artichokes in your Slow Cooker and pour in the white wine.
5. Cook on low settings for 6 hours.
6. Serve the artichokes warm or chilled.

Wild Mushroom Dip

Servings: 20 | Cooking Time: 4 1/4 Hours

Ingredients:
- 1 pound wild mushrooms, chopped
- 1 can condensed cream of mushroom soup
- 1 cup white wine
- 1 cup cream cheese
- 1 cup heavy cream
- 1/2 cup grated Parmesan
- 1 teaspoon dried tarragon
- 1/2 teaspoon dried oregano
- 1/2 teaspoon ground black pepper
- Salt and pepper to taste

Directions:
1. Combine all the ingredients in your Slow Cooker.
2. Adjust the taste with salt and pepper and cook on low settings for 4 hours.
3. Serve the dip warm or chilled.

Bacon Wrapped Chicken Livers

Servings: 6 | Cooking Time: 3 1/2 Hours

Ingredients:
- 2 pounds chicken livers
- Bacon slices as needed

Directions:
1. Wrap each chicken liver in one slice of bacon and place all the livers in your slow cooker.
2. Cook on high heat for 3 hours.
3. Serve warm or chilled.

Hoisin Chicken Wings

Servings: 8 | Cooking Time: 7 1/4 Hours

Ingredients:
- 4 pounds chicken wings
- 2/3 cup hoisin sauce
- 4 garlic cloves, minced
- 1 teaspoon grated ginger
- 1 teaspoon sesame oil
- 1 tablespoon molasses
- 1 teaspoon hot sauce
- 1/4 teaspoon ground black pepper
- 1/2 teaspoon salt

Directions:
1. Mix the hoisin sauce, garlic, ginger, sesame oil, molasses, hot sauce, black pepper and salt in your Slow Cooker.
2. Add the chicken wings and toss them around until evenly coated.
3. Cover with a lid and cook on low settings for 7 hours.
4. Serve the wings warm or chilled.

Marmalade Glazed Meatballs

Servings: 8 | Cooking Time: 7 1/2 Hours

Ingredients:
- 2 pounds ground pork
- 1 shallot, chopped
- 4 garlic cloves, minced
- 1 carrot, grated
- 1 egg
- Salt and pepper to taste
- 1 cup orange marmalade
- 2 cups BBQ sauce
- 1 bay leaf
- 1 teaspoon Worcestershire sauce
- Salt and pepper to taste

Directions:
1. Mix the ground pork, shallot, garlic, carrot, egg, salt and pepper in a bowl.
2. Form small meatballs and place them on your working surface.
3. For the sauce, mix the orange marmalade, sauce, bay leaf, Worcestershire sauce, salt and pepper in your Slow Cooker.
4. Place the meatballs in the sauce. Cover with its lid and cook on low settings for 7 hours.
5. Serve the meatballs warm.

Glazed Peanuts

Servings: 8 | Cooking Time: 2 1/4 Hours

Ingredients:
- 2 pounds raw, whole peanuts
- 1/4 cup brown sugar
- 1/2 teaspoon garlic powder
- 2 tablespoons salt
- 1 tablespoon Cajun seasoning
- 1/2 teaspoon red pepper flakes
- 1/4 cup coconut oil

Directions:
1. Combine all the ingredients in your Slow Cooker.
2. Cover and cook on high settings for 2 hours.
3. Serve chilled.

Baba Ganoush

Servings: 4 | Cooking Time: 4 1/4 Hours

Ingredients:
- 1 large eggplant, halved
- 2 garlic cloves, minced
- 2 tablespoons olive oil
- 1 tablespoon tahini paste
- 1 tablespoon lemon juice
- 1 tablespoon chopped parsley
- Salt and pepper to taste

Directions:
1. Spread the garlic over each half of eggplant. Season them with salt and pepper and drizzle with olive oil.
2. Place the eggplant halves in your Slow Cooker and cook on low settings for 4 hours.
3. When done, scoop out the eggplant flesh and place it in a bowl. Mash it with a fork.
4. Stir in the tahini paste, lemon juice and parsley and mix well.
5. Serve the dip fresh.

Mozzarella Stuffed Meatballs

Servings: 8 | Cooking Time: 6 1/2 Hours

Ingredients:
- 2 pounds ground chicken
- 1 teaspoon dried basil
- 1/2 teaspoon dried oregano
- 1 egg
- 1/2 cup breadcrumbs
- Salt and pepper to taste
- Mini-mozzarella balls as needed
- 1/2 cup chicken stock

Directions:
1. Mix the ground chicken, basil, oregano, egg, breadcrumbs, salt and pepper in a bowl.
2. Take small pieces of the meat mixture and flatten it in your palm. Place a mozzarella ball in the center and gather the meat around the mozzarella.
3. Shape the meatballs, making sure they are well sealed and place them in a Slow Cooker.
4. Add the chicken stock and cook on low settings for 6 hours.
5. Serve the meatballs warm or chilled.

Spicy Enchilada Dip

Servings: 8 | Cooking Time: 6 1/4 Hours

Ingredients:
- 1 pound ground chicken
- 1/2 teaspoon chili powder
- 1 shallot, chopped
- 2 garlic cloves, chopped
- 1 red bell pepper, cored and diced
- 2 tomatoes, diced
- 1 cup tomato sauce
- Salt and pepper to taste
- 1 1/2 cups grated Cheddar cheese

Directions:
1. Combine the ground chicken with chili powder, shallot and garlic in your Slow Cooker.
2. Add the remaining ingredients and cook on low settings for 6 hours.
3. Serve the dip warm with tortilla chips.

Cheese And Beer Fondue

Servings: 10 | Cooking Time: 2 1/4 Hours

Ingredients:
- 4 tablespoons butter
- 1 shallot, chopped
- 2 garlic cloves, minced
- 2 tablespoons all-purpose flour
- 2 poblano peppers, chopped
- 1 cup milk
- 1 cup light beer
- 2 cups grated Cheddar
- 1/2 teaspoon chili powder

Directions:
1. Melt the butter in a saucepan and stir in the shallot and garlic. Sauté for 2 minutes then add the flour and cook for 2 additional minutes.
2. Stir in the milk and cook until thickened, about 5 minutes.
3. Pour the mixture in your Slow Cooker and stir in the remaining ingredients.
4. Cook on high settings for 2 hours and serve the fondue warm with biscuits or other salty snacks.

Bacon New Potatoes

Servings: 6 | Cooking Time: 3 1/4 Hours

Ingredients:
- 3 pounds new potatoes, washed and halved
- 12 slices bacon, chopped
- 2 tablespoons white wine
- Salt and pepper to taste
- 1 rosemary sprig

Directions:
1. Place the potatoes, wine and rosemary in your Slow Cooker.
2. Add salt and pepper to taste and top with chopped bacon.
3. Cook on high settings for 3 hours.
4. Serve the potatoes warm.

Cheesy Beef Dip

Servings: 8 | Cooking Time: 3 1/4 Hours

Ingredients:
- 2 pounds ground beef
- 1 pound grated Cheddar
- 1/2 cup cream cheese
- 1/2 cup white wine
- 1 poblano pepper, chopped

Directions:
1. Combine all the ingredients in a slow cooker.
2. Cook on high settings for 3 hours.
3. Serve preferably warm.

Spicy Monterey Jack Fondue

Servings: 6 | Cooking Time: 4 1/4 Hours

Ingredients:
- 1 garlic clove
- 1 cup white wine
- 2 cups grated Monterey Jack cheese
- 1/2 cup grated Parmesan
- 1 red chili, seeded and chopped
- 1 tablespoon cornstarch
- 1/2 cup milk
- 1 pinch nutmeg
- 1 pinch salt
- 1 pinch ground black pepper

Directions:
1. Rub the inside of your Slow Cooker's pot with a garlic clove just to infuse it with aroma.
2. Add the white wine into the pot and stir in the cheeses, red chili, cornstarch and milk.
3. Season with nutmeg, salt and black pepper and cook on low heat for 4 hours.
4. The fondue is best served warm with bread sticks or vegetables.

Creamy Chicken Dip

Servings: 6 | Cooking Time: 3 1/4 Hours

Ingredients:
- 1 cup cream cheese
- 1 1/2 cups cooked and diced chicken
- 2 cups shredded Monterey Jack cheese
- 1/4 cup white wine
- 1 lime, juiced
- 1/4 teaspoon cumin powder
- 2 garlic cloves, chopped
- Salt and pepper to taste

Directions:
1. Combine all the ingredients in your Slow Cooker.
2. Add salt and pepper to taste and cook on low settings for 3 hours.
3. The dip is best served warm with tortilla chips or bread sticks.

Candied Kielbasa

Servings: 8 | Cooking Time: 6 1/4 Hours

Ingredients:
- 2 pounds kielbasa sausages
- 1/2 cup brown sugar
- 1 cup BBQ sauce
- 1 teaspoon prepared horseradish
- 1/2 teaspoon black pepper
- 1/4 teaspoon cumin powder

Directions:
1. Combine all the ingredients in a Slow Cooker, adding salt if needed.
2. Cook on low settings for 6 hours.
3. Serve the kielbasa warm or chilled.

Bacon Crab Dip

Servings: 20 | Cooking Time: 2 1/4 Hours

Ingredients:
- 1 pound bacon, diced
- 1 cup cream cheese
- 1/2 cup grated Parmesan cheese
- 1 teaspoon Worcestershire sauce
- 1 teaspoon Dijon mustard
- 1 can crab meat, drained and shredded
- 1 teaspoon hot sauce

Directions:
1. Heat a skillet over medium flame and add the bacon. Sauté for 5 minutes until fat begins to drain out.
2. Transfer the bacon in a Slow Cooker.
3. Stir in the remaining ingredients and cook on high settings for 2 hours.
4. Serve the dip warm or chilled.

Sausage Dip

Servings: 8 | Cooking Time: 6 1/4 Hours

Ingredients:
- 1 pound fresh pork sausages
- 1 pound spicy pork sausages
- 1 cup cream cheese
- 1 can diced tomatoes
- 2 poblano peppers, chopped

Directions:
1. Combine all the ingredients in a slow cooker.
2. Cook on low settings for 6 hours.
3. Serve warm or chilled.

Rosemary Potatoes

Servings: 8 | Cooking Time: 2 1/4 Hours

Ingredients:
- 4 pounds small new potatoes
- 1 rosemary sprig, chopped
- 1 shallot, sliced
- 2 garlic cloves, chopped
- 1 teaspoon smoked paprika
- 1 teaspoon salt
- 1/4 teaspoon ground black pepper
- 1/4 cup chicken stock

Directions:
1. Combine all the ingredients in your Slow Cooker.
2. Cover with its lid and cook on high settings for 2 hours.
3. Serve the potatoes warm or chilled.

Creamy Potatoes

Servings: 6 | Cooking Time: 6 1/4 Hours

Ingredients:
- 3 pounds small new potatoes, washed
- 4 bacon slices, chopped
- 1 teaspoon dried oregano
- 1 shallot, chopped
- 2 tablespoons olive oil
- 2 garlic cloves, chopped
- Salt and pepper to taste
- 1 cup sour cream
- 2 green onions, chopped
- 2 tablespoons chopped parsley

Directions:
1. Combine the potatoes, bacon, oregano, shallot, olive oil and garlic in a Slow Cooker.
2. Add salt and pepper and mix until the ingredients are well distributed.
3. Cover the pot with its lid and cook on low settings for 6 hours.
4. When done, mix the cooked potatoes with sour cream, onions and parsley and serve right away.

Pork Ham Dip

Servings: 20 | Cooking Time: 6 1/4 Hours

Ingredients:
- 2 cups diced ham
- 1 pound ground pork
- 1 shallot, chopped
- 2 garlic cloves, chopped
- 1 teaspoon Dijon mustard
- 1 cup tomato sauce
- 1/2 cup chili sauce
- 1/2 cup cranberry sauce
- Salt and pepper to taste

Directions:
1. Heat a skillet over medium flame and add the ground pork. Cook for 5 minutes, stirring often.
2. Transfer the ground pork in a Slow Cooker and add the remaining ingredients.
3. Adjust the taste with salt and pepper and cook on low settings for 6 hours.
4. Serve the dip warm or chilled.

Cheeseburger Dip

Servings: 20 | Cooking Time: 6 1/4 Hours

Ingredients:
- 2 pounds ground beef
- 1 tablespoon canola oil
- 2 sweet onions, chopped
- 4 garlic cloves, chopped
- 1/2 cup tomato sauce
- 1 tablespoon Dijon mustard
- 2 tablespoons pickle relish
- 1 cup shredded processed cheese
- 1 cup grated Cheddar

Directions:
1. Heat the canola oil in a skillet and stir in the ground beef. Sauté for 5 minutes then add the meat in your Slow Cooker.
2. Stir in the remaining ingredients and cover with the pot's lid.
3. Cook on low settings for 6 hours.
4. The dip is best served warm.

Chapter 4 Beef, Pork & Lamb Recipes

Chapter 4 Beef, Pork & Lamb Recipes

Crockpot Moroccan Beef

Servings:8 | Cooking Time: 10 Hours

Ingredients:
- 2 pounds beef roast, cut into strips
- ½ cup onions, sliced
- 4 tablespoons garam masala
- 1 teaspoon salt
- ½ cup bone broth

Directions:
1. Place all ingredients in the CrockPot.
2. Give a good stir.
3. Close the lid and cook on high for 8 hours or on low for 10 hours.

Nutrition Info:
- Calories per serving: 310; Carbohydrates: 0.7g; Protein: 30.3g; Fat: 25.5g; Sugar: 0g; Sodium: 682mg; Fiber: 0.5g

Sweet Pork Strips

Servings:2 | Cooking Time: 5 Hours

Ingredients:
- 6 oz pork loin, cut into strips
- 1 tablespoon maple syrup
- 1 teaspoon ground paprika
- ½ teaspoon salt
- 1 teaspoon butter
- 1 cup of water

Directions:
1. Pour water in the Slow Cooker.
2. Add salt and pork strips.
3. Cook the meat on High for 4 hours.
4. Then drain water and transfer the meat in the skillet.
5. Add butter, ground paprika, and roast the meat for 2 minutes per side.
6. Then sprinkle the meat with maple syrup and carefully mix.

Nutrition Info:
- Per Serving: 252 calories, 23.4g protein, 7.3g carbohydrates, 13.9g fat, 0.4g fiber, 73mg cholesterol, 652mg sodium, 407mg potassium

Bavarian Style Sausages

Servings:4 | Cooking Time: 4 Hours

Ingredients:
- 12 oz beef sausages
- ½ cup beer
- ¼ cup tomato sauce
- 1 tablespoon garlic, crushed
- 1 tablespoon olive oil
- 1 teaspoon cumin seeds

Directions:
1. In the mixing bowl, mix olive oil with cumin seeds, crushed garlic, and tomato sauce.
2. Then sprinkle the beef sausages with olive oil mixture and put in the Slow Cooker.
3. Add tomato sauce and beer.

4. Close the lid and cook the meal on high for 4 hours.

Nutrition Info:
- Per Serving: 361 calories, 12.3g protein, 5.2g carbohydrates, 31.2g fat, 0.4g fiber, 60mg cholesterol, 786mg sodium, 238mg potassium.

Ham Terrine

Servings:4 | Cooking Time: 8 Hours

Ingredients:
- 2 smoked ham hock, cooked
- 1 onion, chopped
- 1 carrot, grated
- 1 tablespoon fresh parsley, chopped
- 1 tablespoon mustard
- 3 oz prosciutto, sliced
- 1 teaspoon sunflower oil
- 1 cup of water

Directions:
1. Chop the ham hock into small pieces and mix with onion, carrot, parsley, and mustard.
2. Then brush the loaf mold with sunflower oil from inside.
3. Make the pie crust from prosciutto in the loaf mold.
4. Add ham hock mixture over the prosciutto and wrap it.
5. Pour water in the Slow Cooker.
6. Then insert the loaf mild with terrine inside and close the lid.
7. Cook the meal on Low for 8 hours.

Nutrition Info:
- Per Serving: 179 calories, 17.9g protein, 5.4g carbohydrates, 9.3g fat, 1.4g fiber, 52mg cholesterol, 296mg sodium, 334mg potassium

Worcestershire Pork Chops

Servings: 4 | Cooking Time: 7 Hours And 12 Minutes

Ingredients:
- 4 medium pork chops
- 1 teaspoon Dijon mustard
- 1 tablespoon Worcestershire sauce
- 1 teaspoon lemon juice
- 1 tablespoon water
- Salt and black pepper to the taste
- 1 teaspoon lemon pepper
- 1 tablespoon olive
- 1 tablespoon chives, chopped

Directions:
1. In a bowl, mix water with Worcestershire sauce, mustard and lemon juice and whisk well.
2. Heat up a pan with the oil over medium heat, add pork chops, season with salt, pepper and lemon pepper, cook them for 6 minutes, flip and cook for 6 more minutes and transfer to your Slow Cooker.
3. Add Worcestershire sauce mix, toss, cover and cook on Low for 7 hours.
4. Divide pork chops on plates, sprinkle chives on top and serve.

Nutrition Info:
- calories 132, fat 5, fiber 1, carbs 12, protein 18

Beef With Greens

Servings:3 | Cooking Time: 8 Hours

Ingredients:
- 1 cup fresh spinach, chopped
- 9 oz beef stew meat, cubed
- 1 cup swiss chard, chopped
- 2 cups of water
- 1 teaspoon olive oil
- 1 teaspoon dried rosemary

Directions:
1. Heat olive oil in the skillet.
2. Add beef and roast it for 1 minute per side.
3. Then transfer the meat in the Slow Cooker.
4. Add swiss chard, spinach, water, and rosemary.
5. Close the lid and cook the meal on Low for 8 hours.

Nutrition Info:
- Per Serving: 177 calories, 26.3g protein, 1.1g carbohydrates, 7g fat, 0.6g fiber, 76mg cholesterol, 95mg sodium, 449mg potassium.

Mole Pork Chops

Servings:3 | Cooking Time: 10 Hours

Ingredients:
- 1 tablespoon butter, melted
- 3 pork chops, bone in
- 2 teaspoons paprika
- ½ teaspoon cocoa powder, unsweetened
- Salt and pepper to taste

Directions:
1. Place the butter into the crockpot.
2. Season the pork chops with paprika, cocoa powder, salt and pepper.
3. Arrange in the crockpot.
4. Close the lid and cook on low for 10 hours or on high for 8 hours.
5. Halfway through the cooking time, be sure to flip the pork chops.

Nutrition Info:
- Calories per serving: 579; Carbohydrates: 1.2g; Protein: 41.7g; Fat: 34.7g; Sugar: 0g; Sodium: 753mg; Fiber: 0g

Tarragon Pork Chops

Servings: 2 | Cooking Time: 6 Hours

Ingredients:
- ½ pound pork chops
- ¼ tablespoons olive oil
- 2 garlic clove, minced
- ¼ teaspoon chili powder
- ½ cup beef stock
- ½ teaspoon coriander, ground
- Salt and black pepper to the taste
- ¼ teaspoon mustard powder
- 1 tablespoon tarragon, chopped

Directions:
1. Grease your Slow Cooker with the oil and mix the pork chops with the garlic, stock and the other ingredients inside.
2. Toss, put the lid on, cook on Low for 6 hours, divide between plates and serve with a side salad.

Nutrition Info:
- calories 453, fat 16, fiber 8, carbs 7, protein 27

Sandwich Pork Chops

Servings:2 | Cooking Time: 4.5 Hours

Ingredients:
- 2 pork chops
- 1 teaspoon mayonnaise
- 1 teaspoon ground black pepper
- ¼ teaspoon garlic powder
- ½ cup of water

Directions:
1. Pour water in the Slow Cooker.
2. Add garlic powder and ground black pepper.
3. Then add pork chops and cook them on High for 4.5 hours.
4. Remove the cooked pork chops from the water and brush with mayonnaise.

Nutrition Info:
- Per Serving: 269 calories, 18.2g protein, 1.5g carbohydrates, 20.7g fat, 0.3g fiber, 69mg cholesterol, 76mg sodium, 293mg potassium.

Habanero Pork Chops

Servings:4 | Cooking Time: 7 Hours

Ingredients:
- 1 habanero pepper, chopped
- 1 teaspoon tabasco
- 2 tablespoons maple syrup
- 1 teaspoon lemon zest
- 4 pork chops
- 1 tablespoon butter
- ½ cup of water

Directions:
1. Put all ingredients in the Slow Cooker and close the lid.
2. Cook the meat on low for 7 hours.

Nutrition Info:
- Per Serving: 313 calories, 18.3g protein, 7.8g carbohydrates, 22.8g fat, 0.2g fiber, 76mg cholesterol, 87mg sodium, 336mg potassium

Shredded Meat Dip With Pickles

Servings:4 | Cooking Time: 4 Hours

Ingredients:
- 1 tablespoon ketchup
- 2 oz dill pickles, shredded
- 1 cup of water
- 9 oz pork tenderloin
- 1 teaspoon ground cinnamon
- 1 teaspoon brown sugar

Directions:
1. Pour water in the Slow Cooker.
2. Add pork tenderloin and ground cinnamon.
3. Cook the meat on High for 4 hours.
4. Then remove the meat from the Slow Cooker and put it in the big bowl.
5. Shred the meat with the help of the fork.
6. Add ketchup, brown sugar, and dill pickles.
7. Carefully mix the meal.

Nutrition Info:
- Per Serving: 101 calories, 16.8g protein, 2.5g carbohydrates, 2.3g fat, 0.5g fiber, 47mg cholesterol, 251mg sodium, 290mg potassium

Pork And Chilies Mix

Servings: 2 | Cooking Time: 7 Hours

Ingredients:
- 1 pound pork stew meat, cubed
- 1 tablespoon olive oil
- ½ green bell pepper, chopped
- 1 red onion, sliced
- ½ red bell pepper, chopped
- 1 garlic clove, minced
- 2 ounces canned green chilies, chopped
- ½ cup tomato passata
- Salt and black pepper to the taste
- 1 tablespoon chili powder
- 1 tablespoon cilantro, chopped

Directions:
1. In your Slow Cooker, mix the pork with the oil, bell pepper and the other ingredients, toss, put the lid on and cook on Low for 7 hours.
2. Divide into bowls and serve right away.

Nutrition Info:
- calories 400, fat 14, fiber 5, carbs 29, protein 22

Flavored And Spicy Beef Mix

Servings: 6 | Cooking Time: 8 Hours

Ingredients:
- 1 and ½ pounds beef, ground
- 1 sweet onion, chopped
- Salt and black pepper to the taste
- 16 ounces mixed beans, soaked overnight and drained
- 28 ounces canned tomatoes, chopped
- 17 ounces beef stock
- 12 ounces pale ale
- 6 garlic cloves, chopped
- 7 jalapeno peppers, diced
- 2 tablespoons vegetable oil
- 4 carrots, chopped
- 3 tablespoons chili powder
- 1 bay leaf
- 1 teaspoon chipotle powder

Directions:
1. In your Slow Cooker, mix oil with beef, onion, salt, pepper, beans, tomatoes, stock, garlic, jalapenos, carrots, chili powder, bay leaf, chipotle powder and pale ale, toss, cover and cook on Low for 8 hours.
2. Divide into bowls and serve.

Nutrition Info:
- calories 300, fat 4, fiber 5, carbs 20, protein 16

Pork Meatloaf

Servings:4 | Cooking Time: 4 Hours

Ingredients:
- 8 oz pork mince
- ¼ cup onion, diced
- 1 teaspoon ground black pepper
- 1 teaspoon chili powder
- 1 egg, beaten
- 1 teaspoon olive oil
- ½ teaspoon salt
- 1 teaspoon tomato paste
- Cooking spray

Directions:
1. Spray the bottom of the Slow Cooker with cooking spray.
2. After this, mix the pork mince, onion, ground black pepper, chili powder, egg, olive oil, and salt.
3. Transfer the mixture in the Slow Cooker and flatten it.
4. Then brush the surface of the meatloaf with tomato paste and cook it on High for 4 hours.

Nutrition Info:
- Per Serving: 188 calories, 1.7g protein, 36.9g carbohydrates, 4.7g fat, 1.1g fiber, 41mg cholesterol, 314mg sodium, 58mg potassium

Beef Heart Saute

Servings:4 | Cooking Time: 6 Hours

Ingredients:
- 1-pound beef heart, chopped
- 1 teaspoon fresh ginger, minced
- 2 tablespoons apple cider vinegar
- 1 sweet pepper, chopped
- 1 red onion, chopped
- 2 cups tomatoes
- 2 tablespoons sunflower oil
- 1 cup of water

Directions:
1. Heat the sunflower oil until hot in the skillet.
2. Add chopped beef heart and roast it for 10 minutes on medium heat.
3. Then transfer it in the Slow Cooker.
4. Add all remaining ingredients and close the lid.
5. Cook the saute on low for 6 hours.

Nutrition Info:
- Per Serving: 289 calories, 33.7g protein, 8.9g carbohydrates, 12.7g fat, 2.1g fiber, 240mg cholesterol, 75mg sodium, 570mg potassium.

Aromatic Meatloaf

Servings:6 | Cooking Time: 6 Hours

Ingredients:
- 1 potato, grated
- 1 teaspoon garlic powder
- 1 onion, minced
- 10 oz minced beef
- 1 egg, beaten
- 1 teaspoon avocado oil
- 1 cup of water

Directions:
1. In the mixing bowl, mix grated potato, garlic powder, minced onion, minced beef, and egg.
2. Then brush the meatloaf mold with avocado oil.
3. Place the minced beef mixture inside and flatten it.
4. Then pour the water in the Slow Cooker.
5. Place the mold with meatloaf in water.
6. Close the lid and cook the meal on High for 6 hours.

Nutrition Info:
- Per Serving: 130 calories, 16.1g protein, 7.1g carbohydrates, 3.8g fat, 1.1g fiber, 69mg cholesterol, 45mg sodium, 354mg potassium.

Beef Roast With Cauliflower

Servings: 6 | Cooking Time: 8 Hrs. 30 Minutes

Ingredients:
- 4 lbs. beef chuck roast
- 1 cup veggie stock
- 1 tbsp coconut oil
- 1 bay leaf
- 10 thyme sprigs
- 4 garlic cloves, minced
- 1 carrot, roughly chopped
- 1 yellow onion, roughly chopped
- 2 celery ribs, roughly chopped
- 1 cauliflower head, florets separated
- Salt and black pepper to the taste

Directions:
1. Place a suitable pan over medium-high heat and add oil to it.
2. Toss in the beef and drizzle salt and black pepper over it.
3. Sear the seasoned beef for 5 minutes per side then transfer to the insert of the Slow Cooker.
4. Toss in the garlic, thyme springs, stock, bay leaf, celery, carrot, and onion.
5. Put the cooker's lid on and set the cooking time to 8 hours on Low settings.
6. Stir in cauliflower then cover again to cook for 20 minutes on High settings.
7. Serve warm.

Nutrition Info:
- Per Serving: Calories: 340, Total Fat: 5g, Fiber: 3g, Total Carbs: 14g, Protein: 22g

Garlic Lamb Chilli

Servings: 7 | Cooking Time: 10 Hrs.

Ingredients:
- 2 oz fresh rosemary, chopped
- ½ cup fresh cilantro, chopped
- ¼ cup coriander leaves, chopped
- 2 lbs. lamb fillet
- 1 tsp salt
- 1 tsp black peas
- 1 tsp chili flakes
- 1 cup garlic
- 1 tsp garlic powder
- 6 cups of water

Directions:
1. Spread all the greens and lamb fillet in the insert of the Slow Cooker.
2. Stir in garlic, garlic powder, black peas, chili flakes, salt, and water.
3. Put the cooker's lid on and set the cooking time to 10 hours on Low settings.
4. Strain the excess liquid from the lamb and serve warm.

Nutrition Info:
- Per Serving: Calories: 375, Total Fat: 22.4g, Fiber: 2g, Total Carbs: 8.71g, Protein: 33g

Winter Pork With Green Peas

Servings:4 | Cooking Time: 7 Hours

Ingredients:
- 1-pound pork shoulder, boneless, chopped
- 1 cup green peas
- 3 cups of water
- 1 cup carrot, chopped
- 1 teaspoon chili powder
- 1 teaspoon dried thyme

Directions:
1. Sprinkle the pork shoulder with chili powder and dried thyme. Transfer the meat in the Slow Cooker.
2. Add carrot, water, and green peas.
3. Close the lid and cook the meal on low for 7 hours.

Nutrition Info:
- Per Serving: 374 calories, 28.7g protein, 8.5g carbohydrates, 24.5g fat, 2.8g fiber, 102mg cholesterol, 110mg sodium, 566mg potassium

Cider Pork Roast

Servings:4 | Cooking Time: 8 Hours

Ingredients:
- 1-pound pork roast
- 1 cup cider
- 1 apple, chopped
- 1 teaspoon peppercorns
- ½ cup of water
- 1 teaspoon chili flakes

Directions:
1. Put all ingredients in the Slow Cooker.
2. Close the lid and cook the meat on low for 8 hours.

Nutrition Info:
- Per Serving: 294 calories, 32.6g protein, 15.3g carbohydrates, 10.9g fat, 1.6g fiber, 98mg cholesterol, 67mg sodium, 597mg potassium

Chili Crockpot Brisket

Servings:4 | Cooking Time: 12 Hours

Ingredients:
- 4 pounds beef brisket
- 1 bottle chili sauce
- Salt and pepper to taste
- 1 cup onion, chopped
- 1/8 cup water

Directions:
1. Place all ingredients in the crockpot.
2. Give a good stir.
3. Close the lid and cook on low for 12 hours or on high for 10 hours.

Nutrition Info:
- Calories per serving: 634; Carbohydrates: 2.1g; Protein: 30.2g; Fat: 45.4g; Sugar:0 g; Sodium: 835mg; Fiber: 1.4g

Crockpot Lamb Roast

Servings: 8 | Cooking Time: 8 Hours

Ingredients:
- 2 pounds leg of lamb
- ¼ cup olive oil
- 2 tablespoons mustard
- 4 sprigs thyme
- 7 leaves of mint
- ¾ teaspoon dried rosemary
- 4 cloves of garlic
- Salt and pepper to taste

Directions:
1. Mix all ingredients in the mixing bowl. Allow to rest in the fridge to marinate.
2. Line the bottom of the CrockPot with aluminum foil.
3. Grease the foil with butter or ghee.
4. Place the lamb leg in the CrockPot.
5. Close the lid and cook on high for 8 hours or on low for 10 hours.

Nutrition Info:
- Calories per serving: 414; Carbohydrates: 0.3g; Protein: 26.7g; Fat: 35.2g; Sugar: 0g; Sodium: 827mg; Fiber: 0g

Crockpot Beef Rendang

Servings:8 | Cooking Time: 10 Hours

Ingredients:
- ½ cup desiccated coconut, toasted
- 6 dried birds eye chilies, chopped
- 1 teaspoon ground cumin
- 2 teaspoon ground coriander
- 1 teaspoon turmeric powder
- 1 teaspoon salt
- 6 cloves of garlic, minced
- ½ cup water
- 1 tablespoon coconut oil
- 6 kafir lime leaves
- 2 stalks lemon grass
- 1 cup coconut cream
- 1 beef shoulder, cut into chunks
- ½ cup cilantro leaves, chopped

Directions:
1. Place all ingredients except the cilantro leaves in the CrockPot.
2. Give a good stir.
3. Close the lid and cook on high for 8 hours or on low for 10 hours.
4. Garnish with cilantro once cooked.

Nutrition Info:
- Calories per serving:305; Carbohydrates: 6.5g; Protein: 32.3g; Fat: 18.7g; Sugar: 0g; Sodium: 830mg; Fiber: 3.7g

Lamb Shoulder With Artichokes

Servings: 6 | Cooking Time: 8 Hrs. 10 Minutes

Ingredients:
- 3 lbs. lamb shoulder, boneless
- 3 onions, roughly chopped
- 1 tbsp olive oil
- 1 tbsp oregano, chopped
- 6 garlic cloves, minced
- 1 tbsp lemon zest, grated
- Salt and black pepper to the taste
- ½ tsp allspice
- 1 and ½ cups veggie stock
- 14 oz. canned artichoke hearts, chopped
- ¼ cup tomato paste
- 2 tbsp parsley, chopped

Directions:
1. Place a suitable pan over medium-high heat and add oil.
2. Add lamb to the hot oil and cook for 5 minutes per side.
3. Transfer the lamb to the insert of the Slow Cooker then stir in remaining ingredients except for the artichokes.
4. Put the cooker's lid on and set the cooking time to 8 hours on Low settings.
5. Stir in artichokes and cook for 15 minutes on low heat.
6. Serve warm.

Nutrition Info:
- Per Serving: Calories: 370, Total Fat: 4g, Fiber: 5g, Total Carbs: 12g, Protein: 16g

Lamb Chops

Servings:4 | Cooking Time: 5 Hours

Ingredients:
- 1 teaspoon ground black pepper
- ½ teaspoon salt
- 1 teaspoon sesame oil
- 4 lamb chops
- 1/3 cup water

Directions:
1. Sprinkle the lamb chops with sesame oil, salt, and ground black pepper.
2. Place the lamb chops in the Slow Cooker and add water.
3. Close the lid and cook the meal on High for 5 hours.

Nutrition Info:
- Per Serving: 169 calories, 23.9g protein, 0.3g carbohydrates, 7.4g fat, 0.1g fiber, 77mg cholesterol, 356mg sodium, 292mg potassium.

Simple Pork Chop Casserole

Servings:4 | Cooking Time: 10 Hours

Ingredients:
- 4 pork chops, bones removed and cut into bite-sized pieces
- 3 tablespoons minced onion
- ½ cup water
- Salt and pepper to taste
- 1 cup heavy cream

Directions:
1. Place the pork chop slices, onions, and water in the crockpot.
2. Season with salt and pepper to taste.
3. Close the lid and cook on low for 10 hours or on high for 8 hours.
4. Halfway through the cooking time, pour in the heavy cream.

Nutrition Info:
- Calories per serving: 515; Carbohydrates: 2.5g; Protein: 39.2g; Fat: 34.3g; Sugar: 0g; Sodium: 613mg; Fiber:0.9 g

Cumin Pork

Servings:6 | Cooking Time: 5 Hours

Ingredients:
- 1-pound pork shoulder, chopped
- 1 teaspoon cumin seeds
- 1 teaspoon garlic powder
- 1 teaspoon ground nutmeg
- 1 carrot, diced
- 2 cup of water
- 1 teaspoon salt

Directions:
1. Roast the cumin seeds in the skillet for 2-3 minutes or until the seeds start to smell.
2. Then place them in the Slow Cooker.
3. Add all remaining ingredients and close the lid.
4. Cook the pork on high for 5 hours.

Nutrition Info:
- Per Serving: 230 calories, 17.8g protein, 1.7g carbohydrates, 16.4g fat, 0.4g fiber, 68mg cholesterol, 449mg sodium, 295mg potassium

Lamb Leg With Sweet Potatoes

Servings: 4 | Cooking Time: 8 Hrs.

Ingredients:
- 2 tbsp olive oil
- 1 lamb leg, bone-in
- 1 garlic head, peeled and cloves separated
- 5 sweet potatoes, cubed
- 5 rosemary springs
- 2 cups chicken stock
- Salt and black pepper to the taste

Directions:
1. Liberally rub the lamb leg with salt, black pepper, and oil.
2. Place the lamb leg along with other ingredients in the Slow Cooker.
3. Put the cooker's lid on and set the cooking time to 8 hours on Low settings.
4. Serve warm.

Nutrition Info:
- Per Serving: Calories: 350, Total Fat: 6g, Fiber: 5g, Total Carbs: 12g, Protein: 22g

Lamb Shoulder

Servings: 6 | Cooking Time: 8 Hours And 10 Minutes

Ingredients:
- 3 pounds lamb shoulder, boneless
- 3 onions, roughly chopped
- 1 tablespoon olive oil
- 1 tablespoon oregano, chopped
- 6 garlic cloves, minced
- 1 tablespoon lemon zest, grated
- Salt and black pepper to the taste
- ½ teaspoon allspice
- 1 and ½ cups veggie stock
- 14 ounces canned artichoke hearts, chopped
- ¼ cup tomato paste

- 2 tablespoons parsley, chopped

Directions:
1. Heat up a pan with the oil over medium-high heat, add lamb, brown for 5 minutes on each side, transfer to your Slow Cooker, add onion, lemon zest, garlic, a pinch of salt, pepper, oregano, allspice, stock and tomato paste, cover and cook on Low for 7 hours and 45 minutes.
2. Add artichokes and parsley, stir gently, cover, cook on Low for 15 more minutes, divide into bowls and serve hot.

Nutrition Info:
- calories 370, fat 4, fiber 5, carbs 12, protein 16

Beef And Artichokes Bowls

Servings:2 | Cooking Time: 7 Hours

Ingredients:
- 6 oz beef sirloin, chopped
- ½ teaspoon cayenne pepper
- ½ teaspoon white pepper
- 4 artichoke hearts, chopped
- 1 cup of water
- 1 teaspoon salt

Directions:
1. Mix meat with white pepper and cayenne pepper. Transfer it in the Slow Cooker bowl.
2. Add salt, artichoke hearts, and water.
3. Close the lid and cook the meal on Low for 7 hours.

Nutrition Info:
- Per Serving: 313 calories, 36.5g protein, 34.6g carbohydrates, 5.9g fat, 17.8g fiber, 76mg cholesterol, 1527mg sodium, 1559mg potassium.

Green Curry Lamb

Servings: 2 | Cooking Time: 6 Hours

Ingredients:
- 1 pound lamb stew meat, cubed
- 2 garlic cloves, minced
- 1 tablespoon green curry paste
- A pinch of salt and black pepper
- 1 cup beef stock
- ½ teaspoon rosemary, dried
- 1 tablespoon cilantro, chopped

Directions:
1. In your Slow Cooker, mix the lamb with the garlic, curry paste and the other ingredients, toss, put the lid on and cook on Low for 6 hours.
2. Divide the mix between plates and serve.

Nutrition Info:
- calories 264, fat 14, fiber 2, carbs 8, protein 12

Mustard Beef

Servings:4 | Cooking Time: 8 Hours

Ingredients:
- 1-pound beef sirloin, chopped
- 1 tablespoon capers, drained
- 1 cup of water
- 2 tablespoons mustard
- 1 tablespoon coconut oil

Directions:
1. Mix meat with mustard and leave for 10 minutes to marinate.
2. Then melt the coconut oil in the skillet.
3. Add meat and roast it for 1 minute per side on high heat.
4. After this, transfer the meat in the Slow Cooker.
5. Add water and capers.
6. Cook the meal on Low for 8 hours.

Nutrition Info:
- Per Serving: 267 calories, 35.9g protein, 2.1g carbohydrates, 12.1g fat, 0.9g fiber, 101mg cholesterol, 140mg sodium, 496mg potassium.

Lamb And Spinach Salad

Servings: 4 | Cooking Time: 7 Hours

Ingredients:
- 1 tablespoon olive oil
- 2 garlic cloves, minced
- 2 cups veggie stock
- 3 pounds leg of lamb, bone discarded
- Salt and black pepper to the taste
- 1 teaspoon cumin, ground
- ¼ teaspoon thyme, dried
- For the salad:
- 4 ounces feta cheese, crumbled
- ½ cup pecans, toasted
- 2 cups spinach
- 1 and ½ tablespoons lemon juice
- ¼ cup olive oil
- 1 cup mint, chopped

Directions:
1. In your Slow Cooker, mix 1 tablespoon oil with garlic, stock, lamb, salt, pepper, cumin and thyme, cover and cook on Low for 7 hours.
2. Leave leg of lamb aside to cool down, slice and divide between plates.
3. In a bowl, mix spinach with mint, feta cheese, ¼ cup olive oil, lemon juice, pecans, salt and pepper, toss and divide next to lamb slices.
4. Serve right away.

Nutrition Info:
- calories 234, fat 20, fiber 3, carbs 12, protein 32

Crockpot Cheeseburgers Casserole

Servings:4 | Cooking Time: 8 Hours

Ingredients:
- 1 white onion, chopped
- 1 ½ pounds lean ground beef
- 2 tablespoons mustard
- 1 teaspoon dried basil leaves
- 2 cups cheddar cheese

Directions:
1. Heat skillet over medium flame and sauté both white onions

and ground beef for 3 minutes. Continue stirring until lightly brown.
2. Transfer to the crockpot and stir in mustard and basil leaves. Season with salt and pepper.
3. Add cheese on top.
4. Close the lid and cook on low for 8 hours and on high for 6 hours.

Nutrition Info:
- Calories per serving: 472; Carbohydrates: 3g; Protein: 32.7g; Fat: 26.2g; Sugar: 0g; Sodium: 429mg; Fiber: 2.4g

Saucy French Lamb

Servings: 4 | Cooking Time: 8 Hrs.

Ingredients:
- 4 lamb chops
- 1 cup onion, chopped
- 2 cups canned tomatoes, chopped
- 1 cup leek, chopped
- 2 tbsp garlic, minced
- 1 tsp herbs de Provence
- Salt and black pepper to the taste
- 3 cups of water

Directions:
1. Add lamb chops, onion, and all other ingredients to the insert of the Slow Cooker.
2. Put the cooker's lid on and set the cooking time to 8 hours on Low settings.
3. Serve warm.

Nutrition Info:
- Per Serving: Calories: 430, Total Fat: 12g, Fiber: 8g, Total Carbs: 20g, Protein: 18g

Mexican Lamb Fillet

Servings: 4 | Cooking Time: 8 Hrs.

Ingredients:
- 1 chili pepper, deseeded and chopped
- 1 jalapeno pepper, deseeded and chopped
- 1 cup sweet corn
- 1 cup chicken stock
- 14 oz lamb fillet
- 1 tsp salt
- 1 tsp ground black pepper
- 1 tbsp ground paprika
- 1 tsp grated ginger
- 1 cup tomato juice
- 1 tbsp white sugar

Directions:
1. Add the peppers, ginger, and ground paprika to the blender jug.
2. Blend this peppers mixture for 30 seconds until smooth.
3. Place the lamb fillet to the insert of the Slow Cooker.
4. Add pepper mixture, tomato juice, white sugar, black pepper, and salt to the lamb.
5. Lastly, add sweet corn and chicken stock.
6. Put the cooker's lid on and set the cooking time to 8 hours on Low settings.
7. Shred the cooked lamb and return the cooker.
8. Mix well and serve warm.

Nutrition Info:
- Per Serving: Calories: 348, Total Fat: 18.3g, Fiber: 3g, Total Carbs: 19.26g, Protein: 28g

Chili Beef Strips

Servings:4 | Cooking Time: 6 Hours

Ingredients:
- 1-pound beef loin, cut into strips
- 1 chili pepper, chopped
- 2 tablespoons coconut oil
- 1 teaspoon salt
- 1 teaspoon chili powder

Directions:
1. Sprinkle the beef strips with salt and chili powder.
2. Then put the chili pepper in the Slow Cooker.
3. Add coconut oil and beef strips.
4. Close the lid and cook the meal on Low for 6 hours.

Nutrition Info:
- Per Serving: 267 calories, 30.4g protein, 0.5g carbohydrates, 16.4g fat, 0.3g fiber, 81mg cholesterol, 650mg sodium, 401mg potassium.

Italian Sausage Soup

Servings: 12 | Cooking Time: 6 Hours

Ingredients:
- 64 ounces chicken stock
- 1 teaspoon olive oil
- 1 cup heavy cream
- 10 ounces spinach
- 6 bacon slices, chopped
- 1 pound radishes, chopped
- 2 garlic cloves, minced
- Salt and black pepper to the taste
- A pinch of red pepper flakes, crushed
- 1 yellow onion, chopped
- 1 and ½ pounds hot pork sausage, chopped

Directions:
1. Heat up a pan with the oil over medium-high heat, add sausage, onion and garlic, stir, brown for a few minutes and transfer to your Slow Cooker.
2. Add stock, spinach, radishes, bacon, cream, salt, pepper and red pepper flakes, stir, cover and cook on Low for 6 hours.
3. Ladle soup into bowls and serve.

Nutrition Info:
- calories 291, fat 22, fiber 2, carbs 14, protein 17

Beef Bolognese

Servings:4 | Cooking Time: 5 Hours

Ingredients:
- ½ cup onion, diced
- 1 teaspoon dried basil
- 1 teaspoon dried cilantro
- ½ cup tomato juice
- 1 tablespoon sesame oil
- 1-pound ground beef
- 2 oz parmesan, grated

Directions:
1. In the mixing bowl mix ground beef with cilantro, basil, and onion.
2. Pour the sesame oil in the Slow Cooker.
3. Add tomato juice and ground beef mixture.
4. Cook it on high for 3 hours.
5. Then add parmesan and carefully mix.
6. Cook the meal on low for 2 hours more.

Nutrition Info:
- Per Serving: 297 calories, 39.4g protein, 3.2g carbohydrates, 13.5g fat, 0.4g fiber, 111mg cholesterol, 289mg sodium, 548mg potassium.

Beef Burger

Servings:4 | Cooking Time: 6 Hours

Ingredients:
- 1 teaspoon ground black pepper
- 12 oz ground beef
- ¼ cup Cheddar cheese, shredded
- 1 teaspoon salt
- 1 tablespoon sunflower oil
- ¼ cup cream

Directions:
1. Mix ground beef with salt, and ground black pepper.
2. Then add shredded cheese and carefully mix the meat mixture.
3. Pour sunflower oil in the Slow Cooker.
4. Then make the burgers and place them in the Slow Cooker.
5. Add cream and close the lid.
6. Cook the meal on Low for 6 hours.

Nutrition Info:
- Per Serving: 228 calories, 27.7g protein, 0.9g carbohydrates, 12g fat, 0.1g fiber, 86mg cholesterol, 686mg sodium, 362mg potassium.

Crockpot Beef Stew

Servings:8 | Cooking Time: 10 Hours

Ingredients:
- 1-pound grass-fed beef stew meat, cubed
- 1 onion, chopped
- 1 cup tomatoes, crushed
- 2 cloves of garlic, minced
- 4 sprigs of thyme
- 3 stalks of celery, chopped
- 2 bay leaves
- 2 tablespoons parsley, chopped
- 2 tablespoons apple cider vinegar
- Salt and pepper to taste

Directions:
1. Place all ingredients in the CrockPot.
2. Close the lid and cook on high for 8 hours or on low for 10 hours.

Nutrition Info:
- Calories per serving:124; Carbohydrates: 2.1g; Protein: 11.5g; Fat: 8.9g; Sugar: 0g; Sodium: 420mg; Fiber: 0.8g

Beef Dip

Servings:6 | Cooking Time: 10 Hours

Ingredients:
- ½ cup heavy cream
- 1 onion, diced
- 1 teaspoon cream cheese
- ½ cup Cheddar cheese, shredded
- 1 teaspoon garlic powder
- 4 oz dried beef, chopped
- ½ cup of water

Directions:
1. Put all ingredients in the Slow Cooker.
2. Gently stir the ingredients and close the lid.
3. Cook the dip on Low for 10 hours.

Nutrition Info:
- Per Serving: 118 calories, 8.6g protein, 2.5g carbohydrates, 8.2g fat, 0.4g fiber, 41mg cholesterol, 78mg sodium, 126mg potassium.

Beef In Onion Dip

Servings:4 | Cooking Time: 6 Hours

Ingredients:
- 1-pound beef sirloin
- 1 cup onion, sliced
- 1 cup of water
- 3 tablespoons butter
- 1 teaspoon salt
- 1 teaspoon white pepper
- ½ teaspoon ground clove

Directions:
1. Toss the butter in the pan and melt it.
2. Add beef sirloin and roast it for 4 minutes per side on high heat.
3. After this, transfer the beef sirloin and liquid butter in the Slow Cooker.
4. Add onion, water, salt, white pepper, and ground clove.
5. Close the lid and cook the meal on High for 4 hours.
6. Then shred the beef and cook the dip for 2 hours on high more.

Nutrition Info:
- Per Serving: 301 calories, 34.9g protein, 3.2g carbohydrates, 15.8g fat, 0.9g fiber, 124mg cholesterol, 721mg sodium, 512mg potassium.

Smoke Infused Lamb

Servings: 4 | Cooking Time: 7 Hrs.

Ingredients:
- 4 lamb chops
- 1 tsp liquid smoke
- 1 cup green onions, chopped
- 2 cups canned tomatoes, chopped
- 1 tsp smoked paprika
- 2 tbsp garlic, minced
- Salt and black pepper to the taste
- 3 cups beef stock

Directions:
1. Add lamb, liquid smoke, and all other ingredients to the insert of Slow Cooker.
2. Put the cooker's lid on and set the cooking time to 7 hours on Low settings.
3. Serve warm.

Nutrition Info:
- Per Serving: Calories: 364, Total Fat: 12g, Fiber: 7g, Total Carbs: 29g, Protein: 28g

Beef With Green Beans And Cilantro

Servings: 2 | Cooking Time: 7 Hours

Ingredients:
- 1 pound beef stew meat, cubed
- 1 cup green beans, trimmed and halved
- 1 red onion, sliced
- ½ teaspoon chili powder
- ½ teaspoon rosemary, chopped
- 2 teaspoons olive oil
- 1 cup beef stock
- 1 tablespoon cilantro, chopped

Directions:
1. In your Slow Cooker, mix the beef with the green beans, onion and the other ingredients, toss, put the lid on and cook on Low for 7 hours.
2. Divide the mix between plates and serve right away.

Nutrition Info:
- calories 273, fat 14, fiber 2, carbs 6, protein 15

Beef Pot Roast

Servings:6 | Cooking Time: 12 Hours

Ingredients:
- 2 pounds shoulder pot roast, bones removed
- Salt and pepper to taste
- ¼ cup water
- 1 package mushrooms, sliced
- 1 tablespoon Worcestershire sauce

Directions:
1. Place all ingredients in the crockpot.
2. Give a good stir.
3. Close the lid and cook on low for 12 hours or on high for 10 hours.

Nutrition Info:
- Calories per serving: 419; Carbohydrates:3 g; Protein: 32.6g; Fat: 29.6g; Sugar: 0.7g; Sodium: 513mg; Fiber: 1.4g

Pork Belly And Applesauce

Servings: 6 | Cooking Time: 8 Hours

Ingredients:
- 2 tablespoons sugar
- 1 tablespoon lemon juice
- 1 quart water
- 17 ounces apples, cored and cut into wedges
- 2 pounds pork belly, scored
- Salt and black pepper to the taste
- A drizzle of olive oil

Directions:
1. In your blender, mix water with apples, lemon juice and sugar and pulse well
2. Put the pork belly in your Slow Cooker, add oil, salt, pepper and applesauce, toss, cover and cook on Low for 8 hours.
3. Slice pork roast, divide between plates and serve with the applesauce on top.

Nutrition Info:
- calories 456, fat 34, fiber 4, carbs 10, protein 25

Caribbean Pork Chop

Servings:4 | Cooking Time: 10 Hours

Ingredients:
- 1 tablespoon curry powder
- 1 teaspoon cumin
- Salt and pepper to taste
- 1-pound pork loin roast, bones removed
- ½ cup chicken broth

Directions:
1. Place all ingredients in the crockpot. Give a good stir.
2. Close the lid and cook on low for 8 to 10 hours or on high for 7 hours.

Nutrition Info:
- Calories per serving: 471; Carbohydrates: 0.9g; Protein: 43.8g; Fat: 35g; Sugar: 0g; Sodium:528mg; Fiber: 0g

Naked Beef Enchilada In A Crockpot

Servings:4 | Cooking Time: 6 Hours

Ingredients:
- 1-pound ground beef
- 2 tablespoons enchilada spice mix
- 1 cup cauliflower florets
- 2 cups Mexican cheese blend, grated
- ¼ cup cilantro, chopped

Directions:
1. In a skillet, sauté the ground beef over medium flame for 3 minutes.
2. Transfer to the crockpot and add the enchilada spice mix and cauliflower.
3. Stir to combine.
4. Add the Mexican cheese blend on top.
5. Cook on low for 6 hours or on high for 4 hours.
6. Sprinkle with cilantro on top.

Nutrition Info:
- Calories per serving: 481; Carbohydrates: 1g; Protein: 35.1g; Fat: 29.4g; Sugar: 0g; Sodium: 536mg; Fiber:0 g

Cajun Beef

Servings:4 | Cooking Time: 5 Hours

Ingredients:
- 1-pound beef ribs
- 1 tablespoon Cajun seasonings
- 3 tablespoons lemon juice
- 1 tablespoon coconut oil, melted
- ½ cup of water

Directions:
1. Rub the beef ribs with Cajun seasonings and sprinkle with lemon juice.
2. Then pour the coconut oil in the Slow Cooker.
3. Add beef ribs and water.
4. Close the lid and cook the beef on high for 5 hours.

Nutrition Info:
- Per Serving: 243 calories, 34.5g protein, 0.2g carbohydrates, 10.6g fat, 0.1g fiber, 101mg cholesterol, 115mg sodium, 471mg potassium.

Chapter 5 Fish & Seafood Recipes

Chapter 5 Fish & Seafood Recipes

Salmon With Green Sauce

Servings: 4 | Cooking Time: 2 Hrs And 30 Minutes

Ingredients:
- 2 garlic cloves, minced
- 4 salmon fillets, boneless
- ¾ cup cilantro, chopped
- 3 tbsp lime juice
- 1 tbsp olive oil
- Salt and black pepper to the taste

Directions:
1. Coat the base of your Slow Cooker with oil.
2. Place salmon along with all other ingredients in the cooker.
3. Put the cooker's lid on and set the cooking time to 2 hours 30minutes on Low settings.
4. Serve warm.

Nutrition Info:
- Per Serving: Calories 200, Total Fat 3g, Fiber 2g, Total Carbs 14g, Protein 8g

Garlic Sea Bass

Servings: 2 | Cooking Time: 4 Hours

Ingredients:
- 1 pound sea bass fillets, boneless
- 2 teaspoons avocado oil
- 3 garlic cloves, minced
- 1 green chili pepper, minced
- ½ teaspoon rosemary, dried
- ½ cup chicken stock
- A pinch of salt and black pepper
- 1 tablespoon cilantro, chopped

Directions:
1. In your Slow Cooker, mix the sea bass with the oil, garlic and the other ingredients, toss gently, put the lid on and cook on Low for 4 hours.
2. Divide the mix between plates and serve.

Nutrition Info:
- calories 232, fat 7, fiber 3, carbs 7, protein 9

Chicken Stuffed Squid

Servings: 4 | Cooking Time: 7 Hrs.

Ingredients:
- 1 lb. squid tubes
- 2 oz capers
- 1 cup tomatoes, chopped
- 1 tsp salt
- 1 tsp cayenne pepper
- 1 tsp ground black pepper
- 1 tsp butter
- 1 tbsp tomato paste
- 1 garlic clove, chopped
- 1 cup chicken stock
- 6 oz ground chicken
- 1 tsp cilantro

Directions:

1. Toss tomatoes with cayenne pepper, salt, black pepper, capers, butter, chicken, cilantro, and garlic in a bowl.
2. Stuff the squid tubes with chicken mixture.
3. Place these stuffed tubes in the insert of Slow Cooker and top then with tomato paste and stock.
4. Put the cooker's lid on and set the cooking time to 7 hours on Low settings.
5. Serve warm.

Nutrition Info:
- Per Serving: Calories: 216, Total Fat: 7g, Fiber: 1g, Total Carbs: 10.1g, Protein: 28g

Almond Shrimp And Cabbage

Servings: 2 | Cooking Time: 1 Hour

Ingredients:
- 1 pound shrimp, peeled and deveined
- 1 cup red cabbage, shredded
- 1 tablespoon almonds, chopped
- 1 cup cherry tomatoes, halved
- 1 tablespoon balsamic vinegar
- 2 tablespoons olive oil
- ½ cup tomato passata
- A pinch of salt and black pepper

Directions:
1. In your Slow Cooker, mix the shrimp with the cabbage, almonds and the other ingredients, toss, put the lid on and cook on High for 1 hour.
2. Divide everything into bowls and serve.

Nutrition Info:
- calories 200, fat 13, fiber 3, carbs 6, protein 11

Fish Pie

Servings:6 | Cooking Time: 7 Hours

Ingredients:
- 7 oz yeast dough
- 1 tablespoon cream cheese
- 8 oz salmon fillet, chopped
- 1 onion, diced
- 1 teaspoon salt
- 1 tablespoon fresh dill
- 1 teaspoon olive oil

Directions:
1. Brush the Slow Cooker bottom with olive oil.
2. Then roll up the dough and place it in the Slow Cooker.
3. Flatten it in the shape of the pie crust.
4. After this, in the mixing bowl mix cream cheese, salmon, onion, salt, and dill.
5. Put the fish mixture over the pie crust and cover with foil.
6. Close the lid and cook the pie on Low for 7 hours.

Nutrition Info:
- Per Serving: 158 calories, 9.5g protein, 18.6g carbohydrates, 5g fat, 1.3g fiber, 19mg cholesterol, 524mg sodium, 191mg potassium.

Shrimp Chicken Jambalaya

Servings: 8 | Cooking Time: 4 Hrs. 30 Minutes

Ingredients:
- 1 lb. chicken breast, chopped
- 1 lb. shrimp, peeled and deveined
- 2 tbsp extra virgin olive oil
- 1 lb. sausage, chopped
- 2 cups onions, chopped
- 1 and ½ cups of rice
- 2 tbsp garlic, chopped
- 2 cups green, yellow and red bell peppers, chopped
- 3 and ½ cups chicken stock
- 1 tbsp Creole seasoning
- 1 tbsp Worcestershire sauce
- 1 cup tomatoes, crushed

Directions:
1. Brush the insert of your Slow Cooker with oil.
2. Toss in sausage, chicken, bell peppers, garlic, onion, rice, tomatoes, stock, Worcestershire sauce, and seasoning.
3. Put the cooker's lid on and set the cooking time to 4 hours on High settings.
4. Stir in shrimp and cook for another 30 minutes on High settings.
5. Serve warm.

Nutrition Info:
- Per Serving: Calories: 251, Total Fat: 10g, Fiber: 3g, Total Carbs: 20g, Protein: 25g

Crockpot Fish Chowder

Servings:9 | Cooking Time: 3 Hours

Ingredients:
- 2 pounds catfish fillet, sliced
- 2 tablespoons butter
- ½ cup fresh oysters
- 1 onion, chopped
- 2 cups water
- 1 red bell pepper, chopped
- 1 yellow bell pepper, chopped
- Salt and pepper to taste
- 1 cup full-fat milk

Directions:
1. Place all ingredients in the CrockPot.
2. Give a good stir.
3. Close the lid and cook on high for 2 hours or on low for 3 hours.

Nutrition Info:
- Calories per serving: 172; Carbohydrates:6.1 g; Protein: 20.5g; Fat: 9.4g; Sugar: 1.3g; Sodium: 592mg; Fiber: 3.5g

Sea Bass And Squash

Servings: 2 | Cooking Time: 3 Hours

Ingredients:
- 1 pound sea bass, boneless and cubed
- 1 cup butternut squash, peeled and cubed
- 1 teaspoon olive oil
- ½ teaspoon turmeric powder
- ½ teaspoon Italian seasoning
- 1 cup chicken stock
- 1 tablespoon cilantro, chopped

Directions:

1. In your Slow Cooker, mix the sea bass with the squash, oil, turmeric and the other ingredients, toss, the lid on and cook on Low for 3 hours.
2. Divide everything between plates and serve.

Nutrition Info:
- calories 200, fat 12, fiber 3, carbs 7, protein 9

Mediterranean Octopus

Servings: 6 | Cooking Time: 3 Hours

Ingredients:
- 1 octopus, cleaned and prepared
- 2 rosemary springs
- 2 teaspoons oregano, dried
- ½ yellow onion, roughly chopped
- 4 thyme springs
- ½ lemon
- 1 teaspoon black peppercorns
- 3 tablespoons extra virgin olive oil
- For the marinade:
- ¼ cup extra virgin olive oil
- Juice of ½ lemon
- 4 garlic cloves, minced
- 2 thyme springs
- 1 rosemary spring
- Salt and black pepper to the taste

Directions:
1. Put the octopus in your Slow Cooker, add oregano, 2 rosemary springs, 4 thyme springs, onion, lemon, 3 tablespoons olive oil, peppercorns and salt, stir, cover and cook on High for 2 hours.
2. Transfer octopus on a cutting board, cut tentacles, put them in a bowl, mix with ¼ cup olive oil, lemon juice, garlic, 1 rosemary springs, 2 thyme springs, salt and pepper, toss to coat and leave aside for 1 hour.
3. Transfer octopus and the marinade to your Slow Cooker again, cover and cook on High for 1 more hour.
4. Divide octopus on plates, drizzle the marinade all over and serve.

Nutrition Info:
- calories 200, fat 4, fiber 3, carbs 10, protein 11

Octopus And Veggies Mix

Servings: 4 | Cooking Time: 3 Hours

Ingredients:
- 1 octopus, already prepared
- 1 cup red wine
- 1 cup white wine
- 1 cup water
- 1 cup olive oil
- 2 teaspoons pepper sauce
- 1 tablespoon hot sauce
- 1 tablespoon paprika
- 1 tablespoon tomato sauce
- Salt and black pepper to the taste
- ½ bunch parsley, chopped
- 2 garlic cloves, minced
- 1 yellow onion, chopped
- 4 potatoes, cut into quarters.

Directions:
1. Put octopus in a bowl, add white wine, red one, water, half of the oil, pepper sauce, hot sauce, paprika, tomato paste, salt, pepper and parsley, toss to coat, cover and keep in a cold place for 1

day.
2. Add the rest of the oil to your Slow Cooker and arrange onions and potatoes on the bottom.
3. Add the octopus and the marinade, stir, cover, cook on High for 3 hours, divide everything between plates and serve.

Nutrition Info:
- calories 230, fat 4, fiber 1, carbs 7, protein 23

Fish Soufflé

Servings:4 | Cooking Time: 7 Hours

Ingredients:
- 4 eggs, beaten
- 8 oz salmon fillet, chopped
- ¼ cup of coconut milk
- 2 oz Provolone cheese, grated

Directions:
1. Mix coconut milk with eggs and pour the liquid in the Slow Cooker.
2. Add salmon and cheese.
3. Close the lid and cook soufflé for 7 hours on low.

Nutrition Info:
- Per Serving: 222 calories, 20.5g protein, 1.5g carbohydrates, 15.2g fat, 0.3g fiber, 198mg cholesterol, 212mg sodium, 336mg potassium

Cod And Broccoli

Servings: 2 | Cooking Time: 3 Hours

Ingredients:
- 1 pound cod fillets, boneless
- 1 cup broccoli florets
- ½ cup veggie stock
- 2 tablespoons tomato paste
- 2 garlic cloves, minced
- 1 red onion, minced
- ½ teaspoon rosemary, dried
- A pinch of salt and black pepper
- 1 tablespoon chives, chopped

Directions:
1. In your Slow Cooker, mix the cod with the broccoli, stock, tomato paste and the other ingredients, toss, put the lid on and cook on Low for 3 hours.
2. Divide the mix between plates and serve.

Nutrition Info:
- calories 200, fat 13, fiber 3, carbs 6, protein 11

Bbq Shrimps

Servings:6 | Cooking Time: 40 Minutes

Ingredients:
- 1/3 cup BBQ sauce
- ¼ cup plain yogurt
- 1-pound shrimps, peeled
- 1 tablespoon butter

Directions:
1. Melt butter and mix it with shrimps.
2. Put the mixture in the Slow Cooker.
3. Add plain yogurt and BBQ sauce.
4. Close the lid and cook the meal on High for 40 minutes.

Nutrition Info:
- Per Serving: 135 calories, 17.8g protein, 6.9g carbohydrates,

3.4g fat, 0.1g fiber, 165mg cholesterol, 361mg sodium, 181mg potassium

Poached Cod And Pineapple Mix

Servings: 2 | Cooking Time: 4 Hours

Ingredients:
- 1 pound cod, boneless
- 6 garlic cloves, minced
- 1 small ginger pieces, chopped
- ½ tablespoon black peppercorns
- 1 cup pineapple juice
- 1 cup pineapple, chopped
- ¼ cup white vinegar
- 4 jalapeno peppers, chopped
- Salt and black pepper to the taste

Directions:
1. Put the fish in your crock, season with salt and pepper.
2. Add garlic, ginger, peppercorns, pineapple juice, pineapple chunks, vinegar and jalapenos.
3. Stir gently, cover and cook on Low for 4 hours.
4. Divide fish between plates, top with the pineapple mix and serve.

Nutrition Info:
- calories 240, fat 4, fiber 4, carbs 14, protein 10

Pineapple Milkfish

Servings:4 | Cooking Time: 3 Hours

Ingredients:
- 16 oz milkfish fillet, chopped
- ½ cup pineapple, chopped
- 1 cup of coconut milk
- 1 teaspoon white pepper
- ½ teaspoon curry powder

Directions:
1. Sprinkle the milkfish fillet with curry powder and white pepper.
2. Then put it in the Slow Cooker.
3. Top the fish with pineapple and coconut milk.
4. Close the lid and cook the fish on High for 3 hours.

Nutrition Info:
- Per Serving: 304 calories, 19.2g protein, 6.2g carbohydrates, 23g fat, 1.8g fiber, 53mg cholesterol, 70mg sodium, 555mg potassium

Calamari And Shrimp

Servings: 2 | Cooking Time: 2 Hours And 30 Minutes

Ingredients:
- 8 ounces calamari, cut into medium rings
- 7 ounces shrimp, peeled and deveined
- 3 tablespoons flour
- 1 tablespoon olive oil
- 2 tablespoons avocado, chopped
- 1 teaspoon tomato paste
- 1 tablespoon mayonnaise
- 1 teaspoon Worcestershire sauce
- 1 teaspoon lemon juice
- 2 lemon slices
- Salt and black pepper to the taste
- ½ teaspoon turmeric powder

Directions:

1. In your Slow Cooker, mix calamari with flour, oil, tomato paste, mayo, Worcestershire sauce, lemon juice, lemon slices, salt, pepper and turmeric, cover and cook on High for 2 hours.
2. Add shrimp, cover and cook on High for 30 minutes more.
3. Divide between plates and serve.

Nutrition Info:
- calories 368, fat 23, fiber 3, carbs 10, protein 34

Shrimps And Carrot Saute

Servings:4 | Cooking Time: 6 Hours

Ingredients:
- 1 cup carrot, diced
- 1-pound shrimps, peeled
- 1 cup tomatoes, chopped
- ½ cup of water
- 1 teaspoon fennel seeds

Directions:
1. Put all ingredients in the Slow Cooker.
2. Gently mix the mixture and close the lid.
3. Cook the saute on Low for 6 hours.

Nutrition Info:
- Per Serving: 156 calories, 26.5g protein, 6.4g carbohydrates, 2.1g fat, 1.4g fiber, 239mg cholesterol, 299mg sodium, 395mg potassium

Red Thai Salmon Curry

Servings:4 | Cooking Time: 4 Hours

Ingredients:
- 2 onions, chopped
- 4 salmon fillets
- 1 can coconut milk
- 1 teaspoon coconut oil
- 1 tablespoon curry powder
- 3 curry leaves
- 1 teaspoon coriander powder
- 1 teaspoon cayenne pepper
- ½ teaspoon cumin
- 1 teaspoon cinnamon
- 2 red bell peppers, julienned

Directions:
1. Place all ingredients in the CrockPot.
2. Give a good stir.
3. Close the lid and cook on high for 3 hours or on low for 4 hours.

Nutrition Info:
- Calories per serving: 499; Carbohydrates: 5.7g; Protein: 27.6g; Fat: 38.3g; Sugar: 0.8g; Sodium: 891mg; Fiber: 3.2g

Coconut Curry Cod

Servings:2 | Cooking Time: 2.5 Hours

Ingredients:
- 2 cod fillets
- ½ teaspoon curry paste
- 1/3 cup coconut milk
- 1 teaspoon sunflower oil

Directions:
1. Mix coconut milk with curry paste, add sunflower oil, and transfer the liquid in the Slow Cooker.
2. Add cod fillets.
3. Cook the meal on High for 2.5 hours.

Nutrition Info:
- Per Serving: 211 calories, 21g protein, 2.6g carbohydrates, 13.6g fat, 0.9g fiber, 55mg cholesterol, 76mg sodium, 105mg potassium

Balsamic-glazed Salmon

Servings: 7 | Cooking Time: 1.5 Hrs.

Ingredients:
- 5 tbsp brown sugar
- 2 tbsp sesame seeds
- 1 tbsp balsamic vinegar
- 1 tbsp butter
- 3 tbsp water
- 1 tsp salt
- ½ tsp ground black pepper
- 1 tsp ground paprika
- 1 tsp turmeric
- ¼ tsp fresh rosemary
- 1 tsp olive oil
- 21 oz salmon fillet

Directions:
1. Whisk rosemary, black pepper, salt, turmeric, and paprika in a small bowl.
2. Rub the salmon fillet with this spice's mixture.
3. Grease a suitable pan with olive oil and place it over medium-high heat.
4. Place the spiced salmon fillet in the hot pan and sear it for 3 minutes per side.
5. Add butter, sesame seeds, brown sugar, balsamic vinegar, and water to the insert of the Slow Cooker.
6. Put the cooker's lid on and set the cooking time to 30 minutes on High settings.
7. Stir this sugar mixture occasionally.
8. Place the salmon fillet in the Slow Cooker.
9. Put the cooker's lid on and set the cooking time to 1 hour on Low settings.
10. Serve warm.

Nutrition Info:
- Per Serving: Calories: 170, Total Fat: 9.9g, Fiber: 1g, Total Carbs: 1.43g, Protein: 18g

Hot Calamari

Servings:4 | Cooking Time: 1 Hour

Ingredients:
- 12 oz calamari, sliced
- ¼ cup of soy sauce
- 1 teaspoon cayenne pepper
- 1 garlic clove, crushed
- 1 teaspoon mustard
- ½ cup of water
- 1 teaspoon sesame oil

Directions:
1. In the bowl mix slices calamari, soy sauce, cayenne pepper, garlic, mustard, and sesame oil. Leave the ingredients for 10 minutes to marinate.
2. Then transfer the mixture in the Slow Cooker, add water, and close the lid.
3. Cook the meal on high for 1 hour.

Nutrition Info:
- Per Serving: 103 calories, 14.6g protein, 4.6g carbohydrates, 2.6g fat, 0.4g fiber, 198mg cholesterol, 937mg sodium, 262mg potassium.

Tacos Stuffing

Servings:4 | Cooking Time: 3 Hours

Ingredients:
- 1-pound trout fillet, sliced
- ¼ cup fresh cilantro, chopped
- 1 teaspoon taco seasoning
- 1 teaspoon olive oil
- 1 tablespoon tomato paste
- ½ cup of water
- 2 tablespoons lemon juice

Directions:
1. Pour water in the Slow Cooker.
2. Add tomato paste and stir the liquid until the tomato paste is dissolved.
3. Add sliced trout and taco seasonings.
4. Cook the fish on high for 3 hours.
5. Then drain water and mix the fish with olive oil, fresh cilantro, and lemon juice.
6. Shake the stuffing well.

Nutrition Info:
- Per Serving: 233 calories, 30.5g protein, 1.5g carbohydrates, 10.9g fat, 0.2g fiber, 84mg cholesterol, 136mg sodium, 581mg potassium.

Tuna With Potatoes

Servings: 8 | Cooking Time: 4 Hrs

Ingredients:
- 4 large potatoes, cut in half
- 8 oz. tuna, canned
- ½ cup cream cheese
- 4 oz. Cheddar cheese, shredded
- 1 garlic clove, minced
- 1 tsp onion powder
- ½ tsp salt
- 1 tsp ground black pepper
- 1 tsp dried dill

Directions:
1. Wrap the potatoes with an aluminum foil and put them in the Slow Cooker.
2. Put the cooker's lid on and set the cooking time to 2 hours on High settings.
3. Mix cream cheese with tuna, cheese, black pepper, salt, garlic, dill, and onion powder in a separate bowl.
4. Remove the potatoes from the foil and scoop out the flesh from each half.
5. Divide the tuna mixture in the potato shells then return then to the Slow Cooker.
6. Put the cooker's lid on and set the cooking time to 2 hours on High settings.
7. Serve warm.

Nutrition Info:
- Per Serving: Calories 247, Total Fat 5.9g, Fiber 4g, Total Carbs 35.31g, Protein 14g

Walnut Tuna Mix

Servings: 2 | Cooking Time: 3 Hours

Ingredients:
- 1 pound tuna fillets, boneless
- ½ tablespoon walnuts, chopped
- ½ cup chicken stock
- ½ teaspoon chili powder
- ½ teaspoon sweet paprika
- 1 red onion, sliced
- 2 tablespoons parsley, chopped
- A pinch of salt and black pepper

Directions:
1. In your Slow Cooker, mix the tuna with the walnuts, stock and the other ingredients, toss, put the lid on and cook on High for 3 hours.
2. Divide everything between plates and serve.

Nutrition Info:
- calories 200, fat 10, fiber 2, carbs 5, protein 9

White Fish With Olives Sauce

Servings: 4 | Cooking Time: 2 Hrs.

Ingredients:
- 4 white fish fillets, boneless
- 1 cup olives, pitted and chopped
- 1 lb. cherry tomatoes halved
- A pinch of thyme, dried
- 1 garlic clove, minced
- A drizzle of olive oil
- Salt and black pepper to the taste
- ¼ cup chicken stock

Directions:
1. Pour the stock into the insert of the Slow Cooker.
2. Add fish, tomatoes, olives, oil, black pepper, salt, garlic, and thyme to the stock.
3. Put the cooker's lid on and set the cooking time to 2 hours on High settings.
4. Serve warm.

Nutrition Info:
- Per Serving: Calories: 200, Total Fat: 3g, Fiber: 3g, Total Carbs: 12g, Protein: 20g

Lobster Colorado

Servings: 4 | Cooking Time: 6 Hours 30 Minutes

Ingredients:
- ½ teaspoon garlic powder
- Salt and black pepper, to taste
- 4 (8 ounce) beef tenderloin
- ½ cup butter, divided
- 4 slices bacon
- 8 ounces lobster tail, cleaned and chopped
- 1 teaspoon Old Bay Seasoning

Directions:
1. Season the beef tenderloins with garlic powder, salt and black pepper.
2. Transfer the beef tenderloins in the slow cooker and add butter.
3. Cover and cook on LOW for about 3 hours.
4. Add lobster and bacon and cover the lid.
5. Cook on LOW for another 3 hours and dish out to serve hot.

Nutrition Info:
- Calories: 825 Fat: 52.2g Carbohydrates: 0.6g

Herbed Octopus Mix

Servings: 6 | Cooking Time: 3 Hrs.

Ingredients:
- 1 octopus, cleaned and prepared
- 2 rosemary springs
- 2 tsp oregano, dried
- ½ yellow onion, roughly chopped
- 4 thyme sprigs
- ½ lemon
- 1 tsp black peppercorns
- 3 tbsp extra virgin olive oil
- For the marinade:
- ¼ cup extra virgin olive oil
- Juice of ½ lemon
- 4 garlic cloves, minced
- 2 thyme sprigs
- 1 rosemary spring
- Salt and black pepper to the taste

Directions:
1. Place the octopus in the insert of the Slow Cooker.
2. Add 2 rosemary springs, salt, peppercorns, lemon, onion, oregano, 3 tbsp olive oil, and 4 thyme springs.
3. Put the cooker's lid on and set the cooking time to 2 hours on High settings.
4. Transfer the cooked octopus to a cutting board and dice it.
5. Put the diced octopus in a suitable bowl then add ¼ cup olive oil, and remaining ingredients.
6. Mix well then transfer the octopus along with marinade to the Slow Cooker.
7. Put the cooker's lid on and set the cooking time to 1 hour on High settings.
8. Serve warm.

Nutrition Info:
- Per Serving: Calories: 200, Total Fat: 4g, Fiber: 3g, Total Carbs: 10g, Protein: 11g

Tuna Noodles Casserole

Servings: 12 | Cooking Time: 8 Hrs.

Ingredients:
- 8 oz wild mushrooms, chopped
- 8 oz noodles, cooked
- 1 lb. tuna, canned
- 3 potatoes, peeled and sliced
- 1 cup cream
- 7 oz Parmesan shredded
- 1 carrot, peeled, grated
- ½ cup green peas, frozen
- 1 tbsp salt
- 1 tsp ground ginger
- ½ tsp ground coriander
- ½ tsp cilantro
- 1 tbsp oregano
- 1 tsp olive oil
- 1 cup fresh dill, chopped
- 1 cup of water

Directions:
1. Place a suitable pan over medium-high heat and add olive oil.
2. Toss in mushrooms and stir cook for 6 minutes then transfer to the Slow Cooker.
3. Add sliced potatoes, carrot, tuna, cheese, and noodles.
4. Top these layers with green peas, salt, ground ginger, coriander

ground, cilantro, dill, water, cream, and oregano.
5. Put the cooker's lid on and set the cooking time to 8 hours on Low settings.
6. Serve warm.

Nutrition Info:
- Per Serving: Calories: 296, Total Fat: 5.8g, Fiber: 5g, Total Carbs: 44.39g, Protein: 19g

Mashed Potato Fish Casserole

Servings:4 | Cooking Time: 5 Hours

Ingredients:
- 1 cup potatoes, cooked, mashed
- 1 egg, beaten
- ½ cup Monterey Jack cheese, shredded
- 1 cup of coconut milk
- 1 tablespoon avocado oil
- ½ teaspoon ground black pepper
- 7 oz cod fillet, chopped

Directions:
1. Brush the Slow Cooker bottom with avocado oil.
2. Then mix chopped fish with ground black pepper and put in the Slow Cooker in one layer.
3. Top it with mashed potato and cheese.
4. Add egg and coconut milk.
5. Close the lid and cook the casserole on Low for 5 hours.

Nutrition Info:
- Per Serving: 283 calories, 16.9g protein, 9.8g carbohydrates, 20.7g fat, 2.4g fiber, 81mg cholesterol, 138mg sodium, 351mg potassium

Dill Trout

Servings: 4 | Cooking Time: 2 Hours

Ingredients:
- 2 lemons, sliced
- ¼ cup chicken stock
- Salt and black pepper to the taste
- 2 tablespoons dill, chopped
- 12 ounces spinach
- 4 medium trout

Directions:
1. Put the stock in your Slow Cooker, add the fish inside, season with salt and pepper, top with lemon slices, dill and spinach, cover and cook on High for 2 hours.
2. Divide fish, lemon and spinach between plates and drizzle some of the juice from the Slow Cooker all over.

Nutrition Info:
- calories 240, fat 5, fiber 4, carbs 9, protein 14

Braised Salmon

Servings:4 | Cooking Time: 1 Hour

Ingredients:
- 1 cup of water
- 2-pound salmon fillet
- 1 teaspoon salt
- 1 teaspoon ground black pepper

Directions:
1. Put all ingredients in the Slow Cooker and close the lid.
2. Cook the salmon on High for 1 hour.

Nutrition Info:
- Per Serving: 301 calories, 44.1g protein, 0.3g carbohydrates, 14g fat, 0.1g fiber, 100mg cholesterol, 683mg sodium, 878mg potassium.

Rosemary Shrimp

Servings: 2 | Cooking Time: 1 Hour

Ingredients:
- 1 pound shrimp, peeled and deveined
- 1 tablespoon avocado oil
- 1 tablespoon rosemary, chopped
- ½ teaspoon sweet paprika
- ½ teaspoon cumin, ground
- 3 garlic cloves, crushed
- 1 cup chicken stock
- A pinch of salt and black pepper

Directions:
1. In your Slow Cooker, mix the shrimp with the oil, rosemary and the other ingredients, toss, put the lid on and cook on High for 1 hour.
2. Divide the mix into bowls and serve.

Nutrition Info:
- calories 235, fat 8, fiber 4, carbs 7, protein 9

Mussels And Sausage Mix

Servings: 4 | Cooking Time: 2 Hours

Ingredients:
- 2 pounds mussels, scrubbed and debearded
- 12 ounces amber beer
- 1 tablespoon olive oil
- 1 yellow onion, chopped
- 8 ounces spicy sausage
- 1 tablespoon paprika

Directions:
1. Grease your Slow Cooker with the oil, add onion, paprika, sausage, mussels and beer, cover and cook on High for 2 hours.
2. Discard unopened mussels, divide the rest between bowls and serve.

Nutrition Info:
- calories 124, fat 3, fiber 1, carbs 7, protein 12

Butter Dipped Crab Legs

Servings: 4 | Cooking Time: 1 Hr. 30 Minutes

Ingredients:
- 4 lbs. king crab legs, broken in half
- 3 lemon wedges
- ¼ cup butter, melted
- ½ cup chicken stock

Directions:
1. Add crab legs, butter, and chicken stock to the insert of the Slow Cooker.
2. Put the cooker's lid on and set the cooking time to 1.5 hours on High settings.
3. Serve warm with lemon wedges.

Nutrition Info:
- Per Serving: Calories: 100, Total Fat: 1g, Fiber: 5g, Total Carbs: 12g, Protein: 3g

Spiced Mackerel

Servings:4 | Cooking Time: 4 Hours

Ingredients:
- 1-pound mackerel, peeled, cleaned
- 1 teaspoon salt
- 1 teaspoon ground black pepper
- ½ teaspoon ground clove
- 1 cup of water
- 1 tablespoon olive oil

Directions:
1. Sprinkle the fish with salt, ground black pepper, ground clove, and olive oil.
2. Then put the fish in the Slow Cooker. Add water.
3. Close the lid and cook the mackerel on high for 4 hours.

Nutrition Info:
- Per Serving: 329 calories, 27.1g protein, 0.5g carbohydrates, 23.8g fat, 0.2g fiber, 85mg cholesterol, 678mg sodium, 465mg potassium.

Hot Salmon And Carrots

Servings: 2 | Cooking Time: 3 Hours

Ingredients:
- 1 pound salmon fillets, boneless
- 1 cup baby carrots, peeled
- ½ teaspoon hot paprika
- ½ teaspoon chili powder
- ¼ cup chicken stock
- 2 scallions, chopped
- 1 tablespoon smoked paprika
- A pinch of salt and black pepper
- 2 tablespoons chives, chopped

Directions:
1. In your Slow Cooker, mix the salmon with the carrots, paprika and the other ingredients, toss, put the lid on and cook on Low for 3 hours.
2. Divide the mix between plates and serve.

Nutrition Info:
- calories 193, fat 7, fiber 3, carbs 6, protein 6

Ginger Cod

Servings:6 | Cooking Time: 5 Hours

Ingredients:
- 6 cod fillets
- 1 teaspoon minced ginger
- 1 tablespoon olive oil
- ¼ teaspoon minced garlic
- ¼ cup chicken stock

Directions:
1. In the mixing bowl mix minced ginger with olive oil and minced garlic.
2. Gently rub the fish fillets with the ginger mixture and put in the Slow Cooker.
3. Add chicken stock.
4. Cook the cod on Low for 5 hours.

Nutrition Info:
- Per Serving: 112 calories, 20.1g protein, 0.3g carbohydrates, 3.4g fat, 0g fiber, 55mg cholesterol, 102mg sodium, 5mg potassium

Crockpot Shrimp Gambas

Servings:4 | Cooking Time: 3 Hours

Ingredients:
- 1/3 cup extra virgin olive oil
- 5 cloves of garlic, chopped
- 1 teaspoon red pepper flakes
- 1 ¼ pounds shrimps, peeled and deveined
- 1 ¼ teaspoon Spanish paprika
- Salt and pepper to taste
- 2 tablespoons parsley, chopped

Directions:
1. Place all ingredients in the CrockPot.
2. Give a good stir.
3. Close the lid and cook on high for 2 hours or on low for 3 hours.

Nutrition Info:
- Calories per serving: 228; Carbohydrates: 3.8g; Protein: 29.8g; Fat: 12.6g; Sugar: 0g; Sodium: 633mg; Fiber: 2.1g

Bacon-wrapped Salmon

Servings:2 | Cooking Time: 6 Hours

Ingredients:
- 2 salmon fillets
- 1 teaspoon liquid honey
- ¼ teaspoon dried thyme
- 2 bacon slices
- 1 teaspoon sunflower oil
- ¼ cup of water

Directions:
1. Sprinkle the salmon fillets with dried thyme and wrap in the bacon.
2. Then pour water in the Slow Cooker.
3. Add sunflower oil and honey.
4. Then add wrapped salmon and close the lid.
5. Cook the meal on low for 6 hours.

Nutrition Info:
- Per Serving: 370 calories, 41.6g protein, 3.2g carbohydrates, 21.3g fat, 0.1g fiber, 99mg cholesterol, 518mg sodium, 794mg potassium

Harissa Dipped Cod

Servings: 6 | Cooking Time: 7 Hrs.

Ingredients:
- 2 tbsp harissa, dried
- 17 oz cod
- 1 tsp salt
- 1 tbsp minced garlic
- 1 tbsp sour cream
- ¼ cup of soy sauce
- 1 tbsp oyster sauce
- 1 tsp chili paste
- 1 tsp cilantro
- 1 red onion, peeled and sliced
- 1 cup fish stock
- ½ cup canned tomatoes
- 1 tbsp harissa sauce
- 4 tbsp orange juice

Directions:
1. Whisk dried harissa, sour cream, garlic, salt, harissa sauce, orange juice, fish stock, cilantro, chili paste, oyster sauce, and soy sauce in a bowl.
2. Spread the tomatoes in the insert of the Slow Cooker.
3. Place the cod over the tomatoes then add sliced onion on top.
4. Pour in the harissa mixture over the onion layer.
5. Put the cooker's lid on and set the cooking time to 7 hours on Low settings.
6. Give a gentle stir then serve warm.

Nutrition Info:
- Per Serving: Calories: 116, Total Fat: 2.9g, Fiber: 1g, Total Carbs: 7.4g, Protein: 15g

Calamari And Sauce

Servings: 2 | Cooking Time: 2 Hours And 20 Minutes

Ingredients:
- 1 squid, cut into medium rings
- A pinch of cayenne pepper
- 2 tablespoons flour
- Salt and black pepper to the taste
- ¼ cup fish stock
- 1 tablespoons lemon juice
- 4 tablespoons mayo
- 1 teaspoon sriracha sauce

Directions:
1. Season squid rings with salt, pepper and cayenne and put them in your Slow Cooker.
2. Add flour, stock, lemon juice and sriracha sauce, toss, cover and cook on High for 2 hour and 20 minutes.
3. Add mayo, toss, divide between plates and serve.

Nutrition Info:
- calories 345, fat 32, fiber 3, carbs 12, protein 13

Rosemary Sole

Servings:2 | Cooking Time: 2 Hours

Ingredients:
- 8 oz sole fillet
- 1 tablespoon dried rosemary
- 1 tablespoon avocado oil
- 1 tablespoon apple cider vinegar
- 5 tablespoons water

Directions:
1. Pour water in the Slow Cooker.
2. Then rub the sole fillet with dried rosemary and sprinkle with avocado oil and apple cider vinegar.
3. Put the fish fillet in the Slow Cooker and cook it on High for 2 hours.

Nutrition Info:
- Per Serving: 149 calories, 27.6g protein, 1.5g carbohydrates, 2.9g fat, 1g fiber, 77mg cholesterol, 122mg sodium, 434mg potassium.

Scallops In Lemon Butter Sauce

Servings:4 | Cooking Time: 3 Hours

Ingredients:
- 1-pound scallops, cleaned and patted dry
- Salt and pepper to taste
- 2 tablespoons olive oil
- 4 tablespoons butter
- 3 tablespoons lemon juice, freshly squeezed
- ¼ cup parsley, chopped

Directions:
1. Place all ingredients in the CrockPot.
2. Give a good stir.
3. Close the lid and cook on high for 2 hours or on low for 3 hours.
4. Garnish with parsley.

Nutrition Info:
- Calories per serving: 248; Carbohydrates: 2.1g; Protein: 14.7g; Fat: 18.9g; Sugar: 0g; Sodium: 791mg; Fiber: 0.6g

Butter Smelt

Servings:4 | Cooking Time: 6 Hours

Ingredients:
- 16 oz smelt fillet
- 1/3 cup butter
- 1 teaspoon dried thyme
- 1 teaspoon salt

Directions:
1. Sprinkle the fish with dried thyme and salt and put in the Slow Cooker.
2. Add butter and close the lid.
3. Cook the smelt on Low for 6 hours.

Nutrition Info:
- Per Serving: 226 calories, 17.2g protein, 0.2g carbohydrates, 17.4g fat, 0.1g fiber, 191mg cholesterol, 750mg sodium, 7mg potassium

Tomato Squid

Servings:4 | Cooking Time: 2 Hours

Ingredients:
- 1-pound squid tubes, cleaned
- 1 cup tomatoes, chopped
- ½ cup bell pepper, chopped
- 1 teaspoon cayenne pepper
- 1 cup of water
- 1 teaspoon avocado oil

Directions:
1. Chop the squid tube roughly and mix with avocado oil and cayenne pepper.
2. Put the squid in the Slow Cooker.
3. Add water, bell pepper, and tomatoes.
4. Close the lid and cook the squid on High for 2 hours.

Nutrition Info:
- Per Serving: 76 calories, 12.6g protein, 3.2g carbohydrates, 1.8g fat, 0.9g fiber, 351mg cholesterol, 546mg sodium, 148mg potassium.

Cod With Asparagus

Servings: 4 | Cooking Time: 2 Hrs

Ingredients:
- 4 cod fillets, boneless
- 1 bunch asparagus
- 12 tbsp lemon juice
- Salt and black pepper to the taste
- 2 tbsp olive oil

Directions:
1. Place the cod fillets in separate foil sheets.
2. Top the fish with asparagus spears, lemon pepper, oil, and lemon juice.
3. Wrap the fish with its foil sheet then place them in Slow Cooker.
4. Put the cooker's lid on and set the cooking time to 2 hours on High settings.
5. Unwrap the fish and serve warm.

Nutrition Info:
- Per Serving: Calories 202, Total Fat 3g, Fiber 6g, Total Carbs 7g, Protein 3g

Hot Salmon

Servings:4 | Cooking Time: 3 Hours

Ingredients:
- 1-pound salmon fillet, sliced
- 2 chili peppers, chopped
- 1 tablespoon olive oil
- 1 onion, diced
- ½ cup cream
- ½ teaspoon salt

Directions:
1. Mix salmon with salt, onion, and olive oil.
2. Transfer the ingredients in the Slow Cooker.
3. Add cream and onion.
4. Cook the salmon on high for 3 hours.

Nutrition Info:
- Per Serving: 211 calories, 22.6g protein, 3.7g carbohydrates, 12.2g fat, 0.7g fiber, 56mg cholesterol, 352mg sodium, 491mg potassium.

Coriander Cod Balls

Servings:3 | Cooking Time: 2 Hours

Ingredients:
- ½ teaspoon minced garlic
- 8 oz cod fillet, grinded
- 1 teaspoon dried cilantro
- 2 tablespoons cornflour
- 1 teaspoon avocado oil
- ¼ cup of water

Directions:
1. Mix minced garlic with grinded cod, dried cilantro, and cornflour.
2. Make the small balls.
3. After this, heat the avocado oil in the skillet well.
4. Add the fish balls and roast them on high heat for 2 minutes per side.
5. Transfer the fish balls in the Slow Cooker.
6. Add water and cook them on High for 2 hours.

Nutrition Info:
- Per Serving: 83 calories, 14.4g protein, 4g carbohydrates, 1.1g fat, 0.4g fiber, 39mg cholesterol, 50mg sodium, 23mg potassium

Tuna And Green Beans

Servings: 2 | Cooking Time: 3 Hours

Ingredients:
- 1 pound tuna fillets, boneless
- 1 cup green beans, trimmed and halved
- ½ cup chicken stock
- ½ teaspoon sweet paprika
- ½ teaspoon garam masala
- 3 scallions, minced
- ½ teaspoon ginger, ground
- 1 tablespoon olive oil
- 1 tablespoon chives, chopped
- Salt and black pepper to the taste

Directions:
1. In your Slow Cooker, mix the tuna with the green beans, stock and the other ingredients, toss gently, put the lid on and cook on High for 3 hours.
2. Divide the mix between plates and serve.

Nutrition Info:
- calories 182, fat 7, fiber 3, carbs 6, protein 9

Thyme Mussels

Servings:4 | Cooking Time: 2.5 Hours

Ingredients:
- 1-pound mussels
- 1 teaspoon dried thyme
- 1 teaspoon ground black pepper
- ½ teaspoon salt
- 1 cup of water
- ½ cup sour cream

Directions:
1. In the mixing bowl mix mussels, dried thyme, ground black pepper, and salt.
2. Then pour water in the Slow Cooker.
3. Add sour cream and cook the liquid on High for 1.5 hours.
4. After this, add mussels and cook them for 1 hour on High or until the mussels are opened.

Nutrition Info:
- Per Serving: 161 calories, 14.5g protein, 5.9g carbohydrates, 8.6g fat, 0.2g fiber, 44mg cholesterol, 632mg sodium, 414mg potassium.

Chapter 6 Poultry Recipes

Chapter 6 Poultry Recipes

Lime Dipped Chicken Drumsticks

Servings: 7 | Cooking Time: 3.5 Hours

Ingredients:
- 3 oz. garlic, peeled and minced
- 17 oz. chicken drumsticks
- 1 lime, finely chopped
- 1 tsp lemon zest
- 1 tsp kosher salt
- 1 tsp coriander
- 1 tsp butter

Directions:
1. Add butter, chicken and all other ingredients to the Slow Cooker.
2. Put the cooker's lid on and set the cooking time to 3.5 hours on High settings.
3. Serve warm.

Nutrition Info:
- Per Serving: Calories: 136, Total Fat: 7g, Fiber: 0g, Total Carbs: 4.68g, Protein: 13g

Chicken Liver Stew

Servings: 8 | Cooking Time: 2 Hours

Ingredients:
- 1 teaspoon olive oil
- ¾ pound chicken livers
- 1 yellow onion, chopped
- ¼ cup tomato sauce
- 1 bay leaf
- 1 tablespoons capers
- 1 tablespoon butter
- A pinch of salt and black pepper

Directions:
1. In your Slow Cooker, mix oil with chicken livers, onion, tomato sauce, bay leaf, capers, butter, salt and pepper, stir, cover and cook on High for 1 hour and 30 minutes.
2. Divide between plates and serve

Nutrition Info:
- calories 152, fat 4, fiber 2, carbs 5, protein 7

Cream Chicken With Spices

Servings:4 | Cooking Time: 7 Hours

Ingredients:
- 1 cup cream
- 1-pound chicken fillet, chopped
- 1 teaspoon dried sage
- 1 teaspoon dried lemongrass
- 1 teaspoon coriander seeds
- 1 teaspoon salt
- 1 tablespoon dried cilantro

Directions:
1. Pour cream in the Slow Cooker.
2. Add dried sage, dried lemongrass, coriander, seeds, salt, and dried cilantro.
3. Then add chicken and close the lid.
4. Cook the meal on Low for 7 hours.
5. Serve the chicken with fragrant cream gravy.

Nutrition Info:
- Per Serving: 255 calories, 33.3g protein, 2.1g carbohydrates, 11.8g fat, 0.1g fiber, 112mg cholesterol, 698mg sodium, 303mg potassium.

Creamy Spinach And Artichoke Chicken

Servings: 4 | Cooking Time: 4 Hours

Ingredients:
- 4 ounces cream cheese
- 4 chicken breasts, boneless and skinless
- 10 ounces canned artichoke hearts, chopped
- 10 ounces spinach
- ½ cup parmesan, grated
- 1 tablespoon dried onion
- 1 tablespoon garlic, dried
- Salt and black pepper to the taste
- 4 ounces mozzarella, shredded

Directions:
1. Place chicken breasts in your Slow Cooker season with salt and pepper, add artichokes, cream cheese, spinach, onion, garlic, spinach and top with mozzarella.
2. Cover Slow Cooker, cook on High for 4 hours, toss, divide everything between plates and serve.

Nutrition Info:
- calories 450, fat 23, fiber 1, carbs 14, protein 39

Mexican Black Beans Salad

Servings: 10 | Cooking Time: 10 Hrs

Ingredients:
- 1 cup black beans
- 1 cup sweet corn, frozen
- 3 tomatoes, chopped
- ½ cup fresh dill, chopped
- 1 chili pepper, chopped
- 7 oz. chicken fillet
- 5 oz. Cheddar cheese
- 4 tbsp mayonnaise
- 1 tsp minced garlic
- 1 cup lettuce, chopped
- 5 cups chicken stock
- 1 cucumber, chopped

Directions:
1. Add stock, chicken fillet, black beans, and corn to the Slow Cooker.
2. Put the cooker's lid on and set the cooking time to 10 hours on Low settings.
3. Now shred the cooked chicken with the help of two forks.
4. Add chicken shred, beans and all other ingredients in a salad bowl.
5. Toss them well and serve.

Nutrition Info:
- Per Serving: Calories 182, Total Fat 7.8g, Fiber 2g, Total Carbs 19.6g, Protein 9g

Chicken And Mustard Sauce

Servings: 3 | Cooking Time: 4 Hours

Ingredients:
- 8 bacon strips, cooked and chopped
- 1/3 cup Dijon mustard
- Salt and black pepper to the taste
- 1 cup yellow onion, chopped
- 1 tablespoon olive oil
- 1 and ½ cups chicken stock
- 3 chicken breasts, skinless and boneless
- ¼ teaspoon sweet paprika

Directions:
1. In a bowl, mix paprika with mustard, salt and pepper and stir well.
2. Spread this on chicken breasts and massage.
3. Heat up a pan with the oil over medium-high heat, add chicken breasts, cook for 2 minutes on each side and transfer to your Slow Cooker.
4. Add stock, bacon and onion, stir, cover and cook on High for 4 hours.
5. Divide chicken between plates, drizzle mustard sauce all over and serve.

Nutrition Info:
- calories 223, fat 8, fiber 1, carbs 13, protein 26

Honey Turkey Breast

Servings:4 | Cooking Time: 3.5 Hours

Ingredients:
- 1-pound turkey breast, skinless, boneless
- 3 tablespoons of liquid honey
- 1 teaspoon chili powder
- 1 teaspoon smoked paprika
- ½ teaspoon salt
- 1 cup of water
- 3 tablespoons butter

Directions:
1. Sprinkle the turkey breast with salt, smoked paprika, and chili powder.
2. Put the turkey in the Slow Cooker, add water, and close the lid.
3. Cook the meal on High for 3 hours.
4. Then drain water and sprinkle the turkey breast with butter and liquid honey. Carefully mix the turkey breast and cook it on High for 30 minutes.

Nutrition Info:
- Per Serving: 246 calories, 19.7g protein, 18.4g carbohydrates, 10.7g fat, 1g fiber, 72mg cholesterol, 1512mg sodium, 379mg potassium.

Chicken Wings In Vodka Sauce

Servings:4 | Cooking Time: 6 Hours

Ingredients:
- 1-pound chicken wings
- ½ cup vodka sauce
- 1 tablespoon olive oil

Directions:
1. Put all ingredients in the Slow Cooker and mix well.
2. Close the lid and cook the meal on Low for 6 hours.

Nutrition Info:
- Per Serving: 273 calories, 34.1g protein, 2.8g carbohydrates, 13.2g fat, 0g fiber, 102mg cholesterol, 208mg sodium, 276mg potassium.

Party Chicken Wings

Servings:4 | Cooking Time: 4 Hours

Ingredients:
- 1-pound chicken wings
- 3 tablespoons hot sauce
- 2 tablespoons butter
- ¼ cup of soy sauce

Directions:
1. Put all ingredients in the Slow Cooker and close the lid.
2. Cook the chicken wings on High for 4 hours.
3. Then transfer the chicken wings in the big bowl and sprinkle with hot sauce gravy from the Slow Cooker.

Nutrition Info:
- Per Serving: 276 calories, 33.9g protein, 1.4g carbohydrates, 14.2g fat, 0.2g fiber, 116mg cholesterol, 1322mg sodium, 327mg potassium.

Slow Cooked Turkey Delight

Servings: 8 | Cooking Time: 4 Hours

Ingredients:
- 4 cups zucchinis, cut with a spiralizer
- 1 egg, whisked
- 3 cups cabbage, shredded
- 3 cups turkey meat, cooked and shredded
- ½ cup turkey stock
- ½ cup cream cheese
- 1 teaspoon poultry seasoning
- 2 cup cheddar cheese, grated
- ½ cup parmesan cheese, grated
- Salt and black pepper to the taste
- ¼ teaspoon garlic powder

Directions:
1. In your Slow Cooker, mix the egg, stock, cream, parmesan, cheddar cheese, salt, pepper, poultry seasoning and garlic powder and stir.
2. Add turkey meat, cabbage and zucchini noodles, cover and cook on High for 4 hours.
3. Divide between plates and serve.

Nutrition Info:
- calories 240, fat 15, fiber 1, carbs 13, protein 25

Coca Cola Dipped Chicken

Servings: 4 | Cooking Time: 4 Hrs

Ingredients:
- 1 yellow onion, minced
- 4 chicken drumsticks
- 1 tbsp balsamic vinegar
- 1 chili pepper, chopped
- 15 oz. coca cola
- Salt and black pepper to the taste
- 2 tbsp olive oil

Directions:
1. Add chicken to a pan greased with oil and sear it until golden brown from both the sides.
2. Transfer the chicken to the Slow Cooker.
3. Stir in coca-cola, chili, onion, vinegar, black pepper, and salt to the cooker.
4. Put the cooker's lid on and set the cooking time to 4 hours on High settings.
5. Serve warm.

Nutrition Info:
- Per Serving: Calories: 372, Total Fat: 14g, Fiber: 3g, Total Carbs: 20g, Protein: 15g

Chopped Balls

Servings:4 | Cooking Time: 2.5 Hours

Ingredients:
- 1-pound chicken fillet, diced
- 2 tablespoon corn starch
- 1 tablespoon flour
- 1 teaspoon cayenne pepper
- ½ teaspoon salt
- 2 eggs, beaten
- 1 tablespoon coconut oil
- ½ cup of water

Directions:
1. Mix diced chicken fillet with corn starch, flour, cayenne pepper, salt, and eggs.
2. Then preheat the coconut oil in the skillet well.
3. With the help of the spoon make the chicken balls and put them in the hot skillet.
4. Roast them on high heat for 30 seconds per side.
5. Transfer the chicken balls in the Slow Cooker, add water, and close the lid.
6. Cook the meal on High for 2.5 hours.

Nutrition Info:
- Per Serving: 302 calories, 35.8g protein, 6.4g carbohydrates, 14.1g fat, 0.2g fiber, 183mg cholesterol, 420mg sodium, 317mg potassium.

Chicken And Dumplings

Servings: 4 | Cooking Time: 4 Hours

Ingredients:
- 1 yellow onion, chopped
- 1 and ½ pounds chicken breast, skinless and boneless
- Salt and black pepper to the taste
- 1 teaspoon oregano, dried
- 2 cups cream of chicken soup
- 2 cups chicken stock
- 4 thyme springs, chopped
- 1 bay leaf
- 2 celery stalks, chopped
- 2 carrots, chopped
- 1 cup peas
- 3 garlic cloves, minced
- ½ cup parmesan, grated
- 1 biscuit dough tube, cut into small pieces
- 1 tablespoon parsley, chopped

Directions:
1. In your Slow Cooker, mix onion with chicken, oregano, salt, pepper, cream of chicken soup, chicken stock, bay leaf and thyme, stir, cover and cook on High for 3 hours.
2. Discard bay leaf, add celery, carrots, peas, garlic and biscuit pieces, stir, cover and cook on High for 1 hour.
3. Add parmesan and parsley, divide into bowls and serve.

Nutrition Info:
- calories 311, fat 4, fiber 7, carbs 12, protein 5

Paella

Servings:6 | Cooking Time: 4 Hours

Ingredients:
- 12 oz chicken fillet, chopped
- 4 oz chorizo, chopped
- ½ cup white rice
- 1 teaspoon garlic, diced
- 2 cups chicken stock
- 1 teaspoon dried cilantro
- 1 teaspoon chili flakes
- Cooking spray

Directions:
1. Spray the skillet with cooking spray and put the chorizo inside.
2. Roast the chorizo for 2 minutes per side and transfer in the Slow Cooker.
3. Then put rice in the Slow Cooker.
4. Then add all remaining ingredients and carefully stir the paella mixture.
5. Cook it on High for 4 hours.

Nutrition Info:
- Per Serving: 254 calories, 22.3g protein, 13.1g carbohydrates, 11.7g fat, 0.2g fiber, 67mg cholesterol, 538mg sodium, 238mg potassium.

Turkey Chili

Servings: 2 | Cooking Time: 5 Hours

Ingredients:
- 1 pound turkey breast, skinless, boneless and cubed
- 1 red chili, minced
- 1 teaspoon chili powder
- 1 red onion, chopped
- 1 tablespoon avocado oil
- ½ cup tomato passata
- ½ cup chicken stock
- A pinch of salt and black pepper
- 1 tablespoon cilantro, chopped

Directions:
1. In your Slow Cooker, mix the turkey with the chili, chili powder and the other ingredients, toss, put the lid on and cook on High for 5 hours.
2. Divide the mix into bowls and serve.

Nutrition Info:
- calories 263, fat 12, fiber 2, carbs 7, protein 18

Chicken And Apples Mix

Servings: 2 | Cooking Time: 7 Hours

Ingredients:
- 1 pound chicken breast, skinless, boneless and sliced
- 1 cup apples, cored and cubed
- 1 teaspoon olive oil
- 1 red onion, sliced
- 1 tablespoon oregano, chopped
- ½ teaspoon turmeric powder
- ½ teaspoon chili powder
- 1 cup chicken stock
- A pinch of salt and black pepper
- 1 tablespoon chives, chopped

Directions:
1. Grease the Slow Cooker with the oil, and mix the chicken with the apples, onion and the other ingredients inside.
2. Toss, put the lid on, cook on Low for 7 hours, divide the mix between plates and serve.

Nutrition Info:
- calories 263, fat 13, fiber 2, carbs 7, protein 15

Crockpot Cheesy Buttermilk Drumsticks

Servings:8 | Cooking Time: 8 Hours

Ingredients:
- 2 tablespoons butter, melted
- 8 chicken drumsticks
- Salt and pepper to taste
- ¾ cup buttermilk
- 1/3 cup grated parmesan cheese

Directions:
1. Pour melted butter in the crockpot.
2. Season the chicken drumsticks with salt and pepper to taste.
3. Place in the crockpot and pour the buttermilk.
4. Top with parmesan cheese.
5. Close the lid and cook on low for 8 hours and on high for 6 hours.

Nutrition Info:
- Calories per serving: 264; Carbohydrates:2.3 g; Protein: 25.6g; Fat: 16.8g; Sugar: 0.4g; Sodium: 783mg; Fiber:0 g

Chicken Teriyaki

Servings:4 | Cooking Time: 4 Hours

Ingredients:
- 1-pound chicken wings
- ½ cup teriyaki sauce
- ½ cup of water
- 1 carrot, chopped
- 1 onion, chopped
- 1 teaspoon butter

Directions:
1. Toss butter in the pan and melt it.
2. Add onion and carrot and roast the vegetables for 5 minutes on medium heat.
3. Then transfer them in the Slow Cooker.
4. Add chicken wings, teriyaki sauce, and water.
5. Close the lid and cook the meal for 4 hours on High.

Nutrition Info:
- Per Serving: 273 calories, 35.4g protein, 9.7g carbohydrates, 9.4g fat, 1g fiber, 103mg cholesterol, 1497mg sodium, 446mg potassium.

Lemon Turkey And Spinach

Servings: 4 | Cooking Time: 7 Hours

Ingredients:
- 1 pound turkey breasts, skinless, boneless and roughly cubed
- 1 cup baby spinach
- Juice of ½ lemon
- 2 spring onions, chopped
- ½ teaspoon chili powder
- 1 cup chicken stock
- 1 tablespoon oregano, chopped
- A pinch of salt and black pepper
- 1 teaspoon garam masala

Directions:
1. In your Slow Cooker, mix the turkey with the lemon juice, spring onions and the other ingredients except the baby spinach, toss, put the lid on and cook on Low for 6 hours and 30 minutes.
2. Add the spinach, cook everything on Low for 30 minutes more, divide between plates and serve.

Nutrition Info:
- calories 258, fat 4.5, fiber 3, carbs 13.4, protein 40.1

Sesame Chicken Wings

Servings: 4 | Cooking Time: 4 Hrs

Ingredients:
- 1 lb. chicken wings
- ½ cup fresh parsley, chopped
- 1 tsp salt
- 1 tsp ground black pepper
- ¼ cup milk
- 1 tbsp sugar
- 5 tbsp honey
- 2 tbsp sesame seeds
- ¼ cup chicken stock
- 1 tsp soy sauce

Directions:
1. Rub the chicken wings with salt and black pepper.
2. Add this chicken to the Slow Cooker along with chicken stock and parsley.
3. Put the cooker's lid on and set the cooking time to 4 hours on High settings.
4. Mix milk with honey, sugar, and sesame seeds in a bowl.
5. Transfer the chicken to a baking tray.
6. Pour the sesame mixture over the chicken wings.
7. Bake them for 10 minutes at 350 degrees F in a preheated oven.
8. Enjoy.

Nutrition Info:
- Per Serving: Calories: 282, Total Fat: 7.5g, Fiber: 1g, Total Carbs: 27.22g, Protein: 27g

French-style Chicken

Servings:4 | Cooking Time: 7 Hours

Ingredients:
- 1 can onion soup
- 4 chicken drumsticks
- ½ cup celery stalk, chopped
- 1 teaspoon dried tarragon
- ¼ cup white wine

Directions:
1. Put ingredients in the Slow Cooker and carefully mix them.
2. Then close the lid and cook the chicken on low for 7 hours.

Nutrition Info:
- Per Serving: 127 calories, 15.1g protein, 5.8g carbohydrates, 3.7g fat, 0.7g fiber, 40mg cholesterol, 688mg sodium, 185mg potassium.

Chicken And Olives

Servings: 2 | Cooking Time: 5 Hours

Ingredients:
- 1 pound chicken breasts, skinless, boneless and sliced
- 1 cup black olives, pitted and halved
- ½ cup chicken stock
- ½ cup tomato sauce
- 1 tablespoon lime juice
- 1 tablespoon lime zest, grated
- 1 teaspoon chili powder
- 2 spring onions, chopped
- 1 tablespoon chives, chopped

Directions:
1. In your Slow Cooker, mix the chicken with the olives, stock and the other ingredients except the chives, toss, put the lid on and cook on High for 5 hours.
2. Divide the mix into bowls, sprinkle the chives on top and serve.

Nutrition Info:
- calories 200, fat 7, fiber 1, carbs 5, protein 12

Stuffed Chicken Breast

Servings:4 | Cooking Time: 6 Hours

Ingredients:
- 1-pound chicken breast, skinless, boneless
- 1 tomato, sliced
- 2 oz mozzarella, sliced
- 1 teaspoon fresh basil
- 1 teaspoon olive oil
- 1 teaspoon salt
- 1 cup of water

Directions:
1. Make the horizontal cut in the chicken breast in the shape of the pocket.
2. Then fill it with sliced mozzarella, tomato, and basil.
3. Secure the cut with the help of the toothpicks and sprinkle the chicken with olive oil and salt.
4. Place it in the Slow Cooker and add water.
5. Cook the chicken on low for 6 hours.

Nutrition Info:
- Per Serving: 182 calories, 28.2g protein, 1.1g carbohydrates, 6.5g fat, 0.2g fiber, 80mg cholesterol, 727mg sodium, 458mg potassium.

Maple Ginger Chicken

Servings: 4 | Cooking Time: 15 Hours

Ingredients:
- ½ cup of soy sauce
- 1 tsp maple syrup
- 1 tbsp fresh ginger, grated
- 1 tsp salt
- 1 lb. chicken breast, diced
- 1 tsp ground ginger
- ¼ tsp ground cinnamon
- 2 tbsp red wine

Directions:
1. Toss chicken with maple syrup and all other ingredients in the Slow Cooker.
2. Leave it for 10 minutes to marinate.
3. Put the cooker's lid on and set the cooking time to 15 hours on Low settings.
4. Serve warm.

Nutrition Info:
- Per Serving: Calories: 259, Total Fat: 13.5g, Fiber: 1g, Total Carbs: 6.71g, Protein: 26g

Chocolaty Chicken Mash

Servings: 7 | Cooking Time: 3 Hours 10 Minutes

Ingredients:
- 4 oz. milk chocolate
- ½ cup heavy cream
- 14 oz. ground chicken
- 1 tsp salt
- 1 tbsp tomato sauce
- 1 tsp hot chili sauce
- 1 cup of water
- 1 tbsp sesame oil
- 1 tsp cumin seeds
- ¼ cup baby carrot, chopped

Directions:
1. Mix the ground chicken with tomato sauce, salt, water, cumin seeds, sesame oil, and hot chili sauce in a bowl.
2. Spread the chicken in the Slow Cooker and top with baby carrots.
3. Put the cooker's lid on and set the cooking time to 3 hours on High settings.
4. Stir the chicken after 1 hour of cooking.
5. Melt the milk chocolate in a bowl by heating in the microwave.
6. Stir in cream and mix well, then add this mixture to the Slow Cooker.
7. Mix it with ground chicken.
8. Put the cooker's lid on and set the cooking time to 10 minutes on High settings.
9. Serve.

Nutrition Info:
- Per Serving: Calories: 219, Total Fat: 14.6g, Fiber: 1g, Total Carbs: 10.56g, Protein: 11g

Chicken And Lentils Meatballs

Servings:4 | Cooking Time: 2.5 Hours

Ingredients:
- ½ cup red lentils, cooked
- 10 oz ground chicken
- 1 teaspoon ground black pepper
- ½ teaspoon salt
- 2 tablespoons flour
- 1 teaspoon sesame oil
- ½ cup chicken stock

Directions:
1. Mix lentils with ground chicken.
2. Add ground black pepper, salt, and flour.
3. Make the meatballs and put them in the hot skillet.
4. Add sesame oil and roast the meatballs for 1 minute per side on high heat.
5. Pour chicken stock in the Slow Cooker.
6. Add meatballs and cook them on High for 2.5 hours.

Nutrition Info:
- Per Serving: 246 calories, 27.2g protein, 17.8g carbohydrates, 6.8g fat, 7.6g fiber, 63mg cholesterol, 449mg sodium, 414mg potassium.

Garlic Chipotle Lime Chicken

Servings:6 | Cooking Time: 8 Hours

Ingredients:
- 1 ½ pounds chicken breasts, bones and skin removed
- ½ cup organic tomato sauce
- 2 tablespoons olive oil
- 2 cloves of garlic
- 2 tablespoons mild green chilies, chopped
- 1 tablespoon apple cider vinegar
- 3 tablespoons lime juice
- 1/3 cup fresh cilantro
- 1 ½ teaspoon chipotle pepper, chopped
- Salt and pepper to taste

Directions:
1. Place all ingredients in the CrockPot.
2. Close the lid and cook on high for 5 hours or on low for 8 hours.
3. Serve with lime wedges.

Nutrition Info:
- Calories per serving:183; Carbohydrates: 2g; Protein: 22g; Fat: 9g; Sugar: 0g; Sodium: 527mg; Fiber: 1.2g

Chicken With Tomatillos

Servings: 6 | Cooking Time: 4 Hrs

Ingredients:
- 1 lb. chicken thighs, skinless and boneless
- 2 tbsp olive oil
- 1 yellow onion, chopped
- 1 garlic clove, minced
- 4 oz. canned green chilies, chopped
- Handful cilantro, chopped
- Salt and black pepper to the taste
- 15 oz. canned tomatillos, chopped
- 5 oz. canned garbanzo beans, drained
- 15 oz. rice, cooked
- 5 oz. tomatoes, chopped
- 15 oz. cheddar cheese, grated
- 4 oz. black olives, pitted and chopped

Directions:
1. Toss onion, chicken, garlic, chilies, salt, black pepper, tomatillos, and cilantro to the Slow Cooker.
2. Put the cooker's lid on and set the cooking time to 3 hours on High settings.
3. Shred the chicken and return to the cooker.
4. Stir in beans, cheese, rice, olives, and tomatoes.
5. Put the cooker's lid on and set the cooking time to 1 hour on High settings.
6. Serve.

Nutrition Info:
- Per Serving: Calories: 300, Total Fat: 11g, Fiber: 3g, Total Carbs: 14g, Protein: 30g

Chicken Chowder

Servings: 4 | Cooking Time: 6 Hours

Ingredients:
- 3 chicken breasts, skinless and boneless and cubed
- 4 cups chicken stock
- 1 sweet potato, cubed
- 8 ounces canned green chilies, chopped
- 1 yellow onion, chopped
- 15 ounces coconut cream
- 1 teaspoon garlic powder
- 4 bacon strips, cooked and crumbled
- A pinch of salt and black pepper
- 1 tablespoon parsley, chopped

Directions:
1. In your Slow Cooker, mix chicken with stock, sweet potato, green chilies, onion, garlic powder, salt and pepper, stir, cover and cook on Low for 5 hours and 40 minutes.
2. Add coconut cream and parsley, stir, cover and cook on Low for 20 minutes more.
3. Ladle chowder into bowls, sprinkle bacon on top and serve.

Nutrition Info:
- calories 232, fat 3, fiber 7, carbs 14, protein 7

Oregano Turkey And Tomatoes

Servings: 4 | Cooking Time: 7 Hours

Ingredients:
- 1 pound turkey breast, skinless, boneless and sliced
- 1 tablespoon oregano, chopped
- 1 cup chicken stock
- 1 cup cherry tomatoes, halved
- 1 teaspoon turmeric powder
- 2 tablespoons olive oil
- 1 cup scallions, chopped
- 1 teaspoon chili powder
- A pinch of salt and black pepper
- ½ cup tomato sauce

Directions:
1. In your Slow Cooker, mix the turkey with the oregano, stock and the other ingredients, toss, put the lid on and cook on Low for 7 hours.
2. Divide the mix between plates and serve.

Nutrition Info:
- calories 162, fat 8, fiber 2, carbs 5, protein 9

Creamy Chicken

Servings: 4 | Cooking Time: 4 Hrs

Ingredients:
- 4 chicken thighs
- Salt and black pepper to the taste
- 1 tsp onion powder
- ¼ cup sour cream
- 2 tbsp sweet paprika

Directions:
1. Add chicken, paprika, salt, black pepper, onion powder, and sour cream to the Slow Cooker.
2. Put the cooker's lid on and set the cooking time to 4 hours on High settings.
3. Serve warm.

Nutrition Info:
- Per Serving: Calories: 384, Total Fat: 31g, Fiber: 2g, Total Carbs: 11g, Protein: 33g

Crockpot Kalua Chicken

Servings:4 | Cooking Time: 8 Hours

Ingredients:
- 2 pounds chicken thighs, bones and skin removed
- 1 tablespoon salt
- 1 tablespoon liquid smoke
- ¼ cup water

Directions:
1. Place all ingredients in the CrockPot.
2. Close the lid and cook on high for 6 hours or on low for 8 hours.
3. Once cooked, serve with organic sour cream, avocado slices, and cilantro if desired.

Nutrition Info:
- Calories per serving: 501; Carbohydrates: 0.6g; Protein: 37.8g; Fat: 36.4g; Sugar: 0g; Sodium: 930mg; Fiber: 0g

Roasted Chicken With Lemon-parsley Butter

Servings:8 | Cooking Time: 8 Hours

Ingredients:
- 1 whole roasting chicken
- ½ teaspoon salt
- ¼ teaspoon black pepper
- 1 cup water
- 1 stick of grass-fed butter
- 2 tablespoons parsley, chopped
- 1 whole lemon, sliced

Directions:
1. Season the chicken with salt and pepper.
2. Place inside the CrockPot and pour in 1 cup of water.
3. Close the lid and cook on high for 6 hours or on low for 8 hours.
4. Meanwhile, heat the butter on a skillet over medium flame. Add in the parsley and cook for a minute.
5. Two hours before the cooking time, pour the butter mixture all over the chicken. Arrange lemon slices on top of the chicken.
6. Close the lid and continue cooking until the chicken is tender and cooked through.

Nutrition Info:
- Calories per serving:455; Carbohydrates: 0.5g; Protein: 46.4g; Fat: 29.1g; Sugar: 0g; Sodium: 1184mg; Fiber: 0g

African Chicken Meal

Servings: 6 | Cooking Time: 8 Hrs

Ingredients:
- 13 oz. chicken breast
- 1 tsp peanut oil
- 1 tsp ground black pepper
- 1 tsp oregano
- 1 chili pepper
- 1 carrot
- 1 tbsp tomato sauce
- 1 cup tomatoes, canned
- 1 tbsp kosher salt
- ¼ tsp ground cardamom
- ½ tsp ground anise

Directions:
1. Rub the chicken breast with peanut oil then and sear for 1 minute per side in the skillet.
2. Transfer the chicken to the Slow Cooker.
3. Add tomato sauce, salt, and all other ingredients to the cooker.
4. Put the cooker's lid on and set the cooking time to 8 hours on Low settings.
5. Serve.

Nutrition Info:
- Per Serving: Calories: 131, Total Fat: 6.6g, Fiber: 1g, Total Carbs: 4.14g, Protein: 14g

Saucy Chicken Thighs

Servings: 6 | Cooking Time: 5 Hrs And 20 Minutes

Ingredients:
- 6 garlic cloves, minced
- 4 scallions, sliced
- 1 cup veggie stock
- 1 tbsp olive oil
- 2 tsp sugar
- 1 tbsp soy sauce
- 1 tsp ginger, minced
- 2 lbs. chicken thighs, skinless and boneless
- 2 cups cabbage, shredded

Directions:
1. Add stock along with other ingredients except cabbage to the Slow Cooker.
2. Put the cooker's lid on and set the cooking time to 5 hours on Low settings.
3. Toss in cabbage and cook for another 30 minutes on the low setting.
4. Serve warm.

Nutrition Info:
- Per Serving: Calories 240, Total Fat 3g, Fiber 4g, Total Carbs 14g, Protein 10g

Zucchini Chicken

Servings: 4 | Cooking Time: Hours

Ingredients:
- 4 chicken drumsticks
- 3 large zucchinis, chopped
- 1 cup of water
- 1 teaspoon white pepper
- 1 carrot, grated
- 1 teaspoon salt

Directions:
1. Put all ingredients in the Slow Cooker.
2. Carefully mix the mixture and close the lid.
3. Cook the meal on Low for 6 hours.
4. When the time is finished, gently transfer the meal in the plates.

Nutrition Info:
- Per Serving: 124 calories, 15.8g protein, 10g carbohydrates, 3.1g fat, 3.2g fiber, 40mg cholesterol, 655mg sodium, 782mg potassium.

Ground Turkey Bowl

Servings: 4 | Cooking Time: 2.5 Hours

Ingredients:
- 2 tomatoes, chopped
- 10 oz ground turkey
- 1 cup Monterey Jack cheese, shredded
- ½ cup cream
- 1 teaspoon ground black pepper

Directions:
1. Put ground turkey in the Slow Cooker.
2. Add cheese, cream, and ground black pepper.
3. Close the lid and cook the meal on High for 2.5 hours.
4. Then carefully mix the mixture and transfer in the serving bowls.
5. Top the ground turkey with chopped tomatoes.

Nutrition Info:
- Per Serving: 275 calories, 27.2g protein, 3.9g carbohydrates, 18.1g fat, 0.9g fiber, 103mg cholesterol, 240mg sodium, 378mg potassium.

Stuffed Chicken Fillets

Servings: 6 | Cooking Time: 4 Hours

Ingredients:
- ½ cup green peas, cooked
- ½ cup long-grain rice, cooked
- 16 oz chicken fillets
- 1 cup of water
- 1 teaspoon Italian seasonings

Directions:
1. Make the horizontal cuts in chicken fillets.
2. After this, mix Italian seasonings with rice and green peas.
3. Fill the chicken fillet with rice mixture and secure them with toothpicks.
4. Put the chicken fillets in the Slow Cooker.
5. Add water and close the lid.
6. Cook the chicken on high for 4 hours.

Nutrition Info:
- Per Serving: 212 calories, 23.6g protein, 14.2g carbohydrates, 6g fat, 0.8g fiber, 68mg cholesterol, 68mg sodium, 232mg potassium.

Turkey Pepper Chili

Servings: 8 | Cooking Time: 4 Hrs

Ingredients:
- 1 red bell pepper, chopped
- 2 lbs. turkey meat, ground
- 28 oz. canned tomatoes, chopped
- 1 red onion, chopped
- 1 green bell pepper, chopped
- 4 tbsp tomato paste
- 1 tbsp oregano, dried
- 3 tbsp chili powder
- 3 tbsp cumin, ground
- Salt and black pepper to the taste

Directions:
1. Take a nonstick skillet and place it over medium-high heat.
2. Add turkey and sear it from both the sides until brown.
3. Transfer the turkey along with all other ingredients to the Slow Cooker.
4. Put the cooker's lid on and set the cooking time to 4 hours on High settings.
5. Serve warm.

Nutrition Info:
- Per Serving: Calories 225, Total Fat 6g, Fiber 4g, Total Carbs 15g, Protein 18g

Mediterranean Stuffed Chicken

Servings: 4 | Cooking Time: 8 Hours

Ingredients:
- 4 chicken breasts, bones and skin removed
- Salt and pepper to taste
- 1 cup feta cheese, crumbled
- 1/3 cup sun-dried tomatoes, chopped
- 2 tablespoons olive oil

Directions:
1. Create a slit in the chicken breasts to thin out the meat. Season with salt and pepper to taste
2. In a mixing bowl, combine the feta cheese and sun-dried tomatoes.
3. Spoon the feta cheese mixture into the slit created into the chicken.
4. Close the slit using toothpicks.
5. Brush the chicken with olive oil.
6. Place in the crockpot and cook on high for 6 hours or on low for 8 hours.

Nutrition Info:
- Calories per serving: 332; Carbohydrates: 3g; Protein:40 g; Fat: 17g; Sugar: 0g; Sodium: 621mg; Fiber:2.4 g

Chicken Mix

Servings:4 | Cooking Time: 8 Hours

Ingredients:
- 1 cup carrot, chopped
- 1-pound chicken wings
- 1 cup of water
- ½ cup tomato juice
- 1 teaspoon salt
- 1 teaspoon dried rosemary

Directions:
1. Put chicken wings in the Slow Cooker.
2. Add carrot, tomato juice, water, salt, and dried rosemary.
3. Close the lid and cook the meal on low for 8 hours.

Nutrition Info:
- Per Serving: 233 calories, 33.3g protein, 4.2g carbohydrates, 8.g 5fat, 0.9g fiber, 101mg cholesterol, 781mg sodium, 437mg potassium.

Cyprus Chicken

Servings:4 | Cooking Time: 4.5 Hours

Ingredients:
- 1-pound chicken breast, skinless, boneless
- 1 tablespoon sesame seeds
- ½ cup black olives, pitted and halved
- ½ cup pearl onions, peeled
- 1 teaspoon cumin seeds
- 1 cup of water

Directions:
1. Chop the chicken breast roughly and put it in the Slow Cooker.
2. Add sesame seeds, black olives, onions, cumin seeds, and water.
3. Close the lid and cook the meal on high for 4.5 hours.

Nutrition Info:
- Per Serving: 169 calories, 24.8g protein, 3.2g carbohydrates, 5.9g fat, 1.2g fiber, 73mg cholesterol, 208mg sodium, 463mg potassium.

Sun-dried Tomato Chicken

Servings:10 | Cooking Time: 8 Hours

Ingredients:
- 1 tablespoon butter
- 3 cloves of garlic, minced
- 4 pounds whole chicken, cut into pieces
- 1 cup sun-dried tomatoes in vinaigrette
- Salt and pepper to taste

Directions:
1. In a skillet, melt the butter and sauté the garlic until lightly browned.
2. Add the chicken pieces and cook for 3 minutes until slightly browned.
3. Transfer to the crockpot and stir in the sun-dried tomatoes including the vinaigrette.
4. Season with salt and pepper to taste.
5. Close the lid and cook on low for 8 hours or on high for 6 hours.

Nutrition Info:
- Calories per serving: 397; Carbohydrates:9.4 g; Protein: 30.26g; Fat:14.1 g; Sugar: 0.4g; Sodium: 472mg; Fiber: 5.8g

Chicken And Peppers

Servings: 2 | Cooking Time: 6 Hours

Ingredients:
- 1 pound chicken breasts, skinless, boneless and cubed
- ¼ cup tomato sauce
- 2 red bell peppers, cut into strips
- 1 teaspoon olive oil
- ½ teaspoon rosemary, dried
- ½ teaspoon coriander, ground
- 1 teaspoon Italian seasoning
- A pinch of cayenne pepper
- 1 cup chicken stock

Directions:
1. In your Slow Cooker, mix the chicken with the peppers, tomato sauce and the other ingredients, toss, put the lid on and cook on Low for 6 hours.
2. divide everything between plates and serve.

Nutrition Info:
- calories 282, fat 12, fiber 2, carbs 6, protein 18

Thai Peanut Chicken

Servings: 8 | Cooking Time: 4 Hours

Ingredients:
- 2 and ½ pounds chicken thighs and drumsticks
- 1 tablespoon soy sauce
- 1 tablespoon apple cider vinegar
- A pinch of red pepper flakes
- Salt and black pepper to the taste
- ½ teaspoon ginger, ground
- 1/3 cup peanut butter
- 1 garlic clove, minced
- ½ cup warm water

Directions:
1. In your blender mix peanut butter with water, soy sauce, salt, pepper, pepper flakes, ginger, garlic and vinegar and blend well.
2. Pat dry chicken pieces, arrange them in your Slow Cooker, cover and cook on High for 4 hours.
3. Divide between plates and serve.

Nutrition Info:
- calories 375, fat 12, fiber 1, carbs 10, protein 42

Chicken Pate

Servings:6 | Cooking Time: 8 Hours

Ingredients:
- 1 carrot, peeled
- 1 teaspoon salt
- 1-pound chicken liver
- 2 cups of water
- 2 tablespoons coconut oil

Directions:
1. Chop the carrot roughly and put it in the Slow Cooker.
2. Add chicken liver and water.
3. Cook the mixture for 8 hours on Low.
4. Then drain water and transfer the mixture in the blender.
5. Add coconut oil and salt.
6. Blend the mixture until smooth.
7. Store the pate in the fridge for up to 7 days.

Nutrition Info:
- Per Serving: 169 calories, 18.6g protein, 1.7g carbohydrates, 9.5g fat, 0.3g fiber, 426mg cholesterol, 454mg sodium, 232mg potassium.

Chicken Sausages In Jam

Servings:4 | Cooking Time: 6 Hours

Ingredients:
- ½ cup of strawberry jam
- ½ cup of water
- 1-pound chicken breast, skinless, boneless, chopped
- 1 teaspoon white pepper

Directions:
1. Sprinkle the chicken meat with white pepper and put it in the Slow Cooker.
2. Then mix jam with water and pour the liquid over the chicken.
3. Close the lid and cook it on Low for 6 hours.

Nutrition Info:
- Per Serving: 282 calories, 24.1g protein, 37.5g carbohydrates, 2.9g fat, 0.1g fiber, 73mg cholesterol, 59mg sodium, 427mg potassium.

Chicken, Peppers And Onions

Servings:4 | Cooking Time: 8 Hours

Ingredients:
- 1 tablespoon olive oil
- ½ cup shallots, peeled
- 1-pound boneless chicken breasts, sliced
- ½ cup green and red peppers, diced
- Salt and pepper to taste

Directions:
1. Heat oil in a skillet over medium flame.
2. Sauté the shallots until fragrant and translucent. Allow to cook so that the outer edges of the shallots turn slightly brown.
3. Transfer into the crockpot.
4. Add the chicken breasts and the peppers.
5. Season with salt and pepper to taste.
6. Add a few tablespoons of water.
7. Close the lid and cook on low for 8 hours or on high for 6 hours.

Nutrition Info:
- Calories per serving: 179; Carbohydrates: 3.05g; Protein:26.1 g; Fat: 10.4g; Sugar: 0g; Sodium: 538mg; Fiber:2.4 g

Lettuce And Chicken Salad

Servings:6 | Cooking Time: 7 Hours

Ingredients:
- ½ cup of soy sauce
- 2 oz scallions, chopped
- 2 cups lettuce, chopped
- 2 oz Mozzarella, chopped
- 1 tablespoon olive oil
- 8 oz chicken fillet, chopped

Directions:
1. Pour soy sauce in the Slow Cooker.
2. Add chicken and close the lid.
3. Cook the chicken on low for 7 hours.
4. Drain soy sauce and transfer the chicken in the salad bowl.
5. Add all remaining ingredients and stir the salad well.

Nutrition Info:
- Per Serving: 135 calories, 15.2g protein, 3.2g carbohydrates, 6.9g fat, 0.5g fiber, 39mg cholesterol, 1290mg sodium, 190mg potassium.

Chicken Pepper Chili

Servings: 4 | Cooking Time: 7 Hrs

Ingredients:
- 16 oz. salsa
- 8 chicken thighs
- 1 yellow onion, chopped
- 16 oz. canned tomatoes, chopped
- 1 red bell pepper, chopped
- 2 tbsp chili powder

Directions:
1. Add salsa and all other ingredients to the Slow Cooker.
2. Put the cooker's lid on and set the cooking time to 7 hours on Low settings.
3. Serve warm.

Nutrition Info:
- Per Serving: Calories 250, Total Fat 3g, Fiber 3g, Total Carbs 14g, Protein 8g

Chapter 7 Vegetable & Vegetarian Recipes

Chapter 7 Vegetable & Vegetarian Recipes

Mushroom Risotto

Servings:4 | Cooking Time: 6 Hours

Ingredients:
- ½ cup Arborio rice
- 2 cups brown mushrooms, chopped
- 1 yellow onion, diced
- 2 tablespoons avocado oil
- 1 teaspoon salt
- 1 teaspoon ground black pepper
- 4 cups vegetable stock

Directions:
1. Pour the vegetable stock in the Slow Cooker.
2. Add ground black pepper and salt.
3. After this, add avocado oil, diced onion, mushrooms, and Arborio rice.
4. Close the lid and cook the risotto on Low for 6 hours.

Nutrition Info:
- Per Serving: 127 calories, 2.9g protein, 25.7g carbohydrates, 3.1g fat, 1.9g fiber, 0mg cholesterol, 1307mg sodium, 248mg potassium.

Cream Of Mushroom Soup

Servings:4 | Cooking Time: 3 Hours

Ingredients:
- 1 tablespoons olive oil
- ½ cup onion, diced
- 20 ounces mushrooms, sliced
- 2 cups chicken broth
- 1 cup heavy cream

Directions:
1. In a skillet, heat the oil over medium flame and sauté the onions until translucent or slightly brown on the edges.
2. Transfer into the crockpot and add the mushrooms and chicken broth. Season with salt and pepper to taste.
3. Close the lid and cook on low for 6 hours or on high for 3 hours until the mushrooms are soft
4. Halfway before the cooking time ends, stir in the heavy cream.

Nutrition Info:
- Calories per serving: 229; Carbohydrates: 9g; Protein: 5g; Fat: 21g; Sugar:3 g; Sodium:214 mg; Fiber: 2g

Bulgur Sauté

Servings:4 | Cooking Time: 4 Hours

Ingredients:
- 1 cup bell pepper, chopped
- 1 white onion, diced
- 2 tablespoons tomato paste
- 1 cup bulgur
- 3 cups vegetable stock
- 1 tablespoon olive oil
- 1 teaspoon salt
- 1 teaspoon chili flakes

Directions:
1. Put all ingredients in the Slow Cooker and close the lid.

2. Cook the meal on low doe 4 hours or until the bulgur is tender.

Nutrition Info:
- Per Serving: 181 calories, 5.6g protein, 33.8g carbohydrates, 4.2g fat, 8g fiber, 0mg cholesterol, 747mg sodium, 322mg potassium.

Corn Pudding

Servings:4 | Cooking Time: 5 Hours

Ingredients:
- 3 cups corn kernels
- 2 cups heavy cream
- 3 tablespoons muffin mix
- 1 oz Parmesan, grated

Directions:
1. Mix heavy cream with muffin mix and pour the liquid in the Slow Cooker.
2. Add corn kernels and Parmesan. Stir the mixture well.
3. Close the lid and cook the pudding on Low for 5 hours.

Nutrition Info:
- Per Serving: 371 calories, 21.8g protein, 31.4g carbohydrates, 26.3g fat, 3.2g fiber, 87mg cholesterol, 180mg sodium, 378mg potassium.

Crockpot Mediterranean Eggplant Salad

Servings:2 | Cooking Time: 4 Hours

Ingredients:
- 1 red onion, sliced
- 2 bell peppers, sliced
- 3 extra virgin olive oil
- 1 eggplant, quartered
- 1 cup tomatoes, crushed
- 1 tablespoon smoked paprika
- 2 teaspoons cumin
- Juice from 1 lemon, freshly squeezed
- Salt and pepper to taste

Directions:
1. Place all ingredients in the CrockPot.
2. Give a good stir.
3. Close the lid and cook on high for 3 hours or on low for 4 hours.

Nutrition Info:
- Calories per serving: 312; Carbohydrates: 30.2g; Protein: 5.6g; Fat: 22g; Sugar: 0.4g; Sodium: 519mg; Fiber: 27.1g

Beet Salad

Servings:4 | Cooking Time: 5 Hours

Ingredients:
- 2 cups beet, peeled, chopped
- 3 oz goat cheese, crumbled
- 4 cups of water
- 1 tablespoon olive oil
- 1 teaspoon liquid honey
- 3 pecans, chopped

Directions:

1. Put beets in the Slow Cooker.
2. Add water and cook them on high for 5 hours.
3. The drain water and transfer the cooked beets in the bowl.
4. Add olive oil, honey, and pecans. Shake the vegetables well and transfer them to the serving plates.
5. Top every serving with crumbled goat cheese.

Nutrition Info:
• Per Serving: 242 calories, 9.1g protein, 11.9g carbohydrates, 18.7g fat, 2.8g fiber, 22mg cholesterol, 146mg sodium, 316mg potassium.

Chili Okra

Servings:6 | Cooking Time: 7 Hours

Ingredients:
• 6 cups okra, chopped
• 1 cup tomato juice
• 1 teaspoon salt
• ½ teaspoon chili powder
• ½ teaspoon cayenne pepper
• 1 tablespoon olive oil
• 1 cup vegetable stock

Directions:
1. Put all ingredients from the list above in the Slow Cooker.
2. Mix them gently and cook on Low for 7 hours.

Nutrition Info:
• Per Serving: 69 calories, 2.4g protein, 9.5g carbohydrates, 2.6g fat, 3.6g fiber, 0mg cholesterol, 514mg sodium, 399mg potassium.

White Beans Luncheon

Servings: 10 | Cooking Time: 4 Hrs

Ingredients:
• 2 lbs. white beans
• 3 celery stalks, chopped
• 2 carrots, chopped
• 1 bay leaf
• 1 yellow onion, chopped
• 3 garlic cloves, minced
• 1 tsp rosemary, dried
• 1 tsp oregano, dried
• 1 tsp thyme, dried
• 10 cups water
• Salt and black pepper to the taste
• 28 oz. canned tomatoes, chopped
• 6 cups chard, chopped

Directions:
1. Add beans, carrots, and all other ingredients to a Slow Cooker.
2. Put the cooker's lid on and set the cooking time to 4 hours on High settings.
3. Serve warm.

Nutrition Info:
• Per Serving: Calories 341, Total Fat 8, Fiber 12, Total Carbs 20, Protein 6

Vanilla Applesauce

Servings:4 | Cooking Time: 6 Hours

Ingredients:
• 4 cups apples, chopped, peeled
• 1 teaspoon vanilla extract
• ½ teaspoon ground cardamom
• 1 cup of water
• 1 tablespoon lemon juice
• 2 tablespoons sugar

Directions:
1. Put all ingredients in the Slow Cooker.
2. Close the lid and cook them on Low for 6 hours.
3. Then blend the mixture with the help of the immersion blender.
4. Transfer the smooth applesauce in the glass cans.

Nutrition Info:
• Per Serving: 143 calories, 0.7g protein, 37.2g carbohydrates, 0.5g fat, 5.5g fiber, 0mg cholesterol, 5mg sodium, 248mg potassium.

Teriyaki Kale

Servings:6 | Cooking Time: 30 Minutes

Ingredients:
• 5 cups kale, roughly chopped
• 1/2 cup teriyaki sauce
• 1 teaspoon sesame seeds
• 1 cup of water
• 1 teaspoon garlic powder
• 2 tablespoons coconut oil

Directions:
1. Melt the coconut oil and mix it with garlic powder, water, sesame seeds, and teriyaki sauce.
2. Pour the liquid in the Slow Cooker.
3. Add kale and close the lid.
4. Cook the kale on High for 30 minutes.
5. Serve the kale with a small amount of teriyaki liquid.

Nutrition Info:
• Per Serving: 92 calories, 3.3g protein, 10g carbohydrates, 4.8g fat, 1g fiber, 0mg cholesterol, 945mg sodium, 336mg potassium.

Hot Sauce Oysters Mushrooms

Servings:4 | Cooking Time: 2 Hours

Ingredients:
• 2 tablespoons hot sauce
• 2 cups oysters mushrooms, sliced
• ½ cup of water
• 1 tablespoon avocado oil
• 1 teaspoon dried dill
• 1 teaspoon salt

Directions:
1. Mix sliced oysters with avocado oil, dried dill, and salt.
2. Put them in the Slow Cooker.
3. Add water and cook the mushrooms on High for 2 hours.
4. After this, drain the mushrooms and mix them with hot sauce.

Nutrition Info:
• Per Serving: 15 calories, 1.1g protein, 2.2g carbohydrates, 0.6g fat, 0.9g fiber, 0mg cholesterol, 778mg sodium, 149mg potassium.

Corn Salad

Servings:4 | Cooking Time: 1.5 Hours

Ingredients:
- 2 cups corn kernels
- 1 cup of water
- 1 teaspoon vegan butter
- 1 cup lettuce, chopped
- 1 cup tomatoes, chopped
- 1 teaspoon chili flakes
- 1 teaspoon salt
- 1 tablespoon sunflower oil

Directions:
1. Pour water in the Slow Cooker, add corn kernels and cook them on high for 5 hours.
2. Then drain water and transfer the corn kernels in the salad bowl.
3. Add lettuce, tomatoes, chili flakes, salt, and sunflower oil.
4. Shake the salad gently.

Nutrition Info:
- Per Serving: 116 calories, 3.1g protein, 16.5g carbohydrates, 5.5g fat, 2.8g fiber, 3mg cholesterol, 604mg sodium, 317mg potassium.

Walnut Kale

Servings:4 | Cooking Time: 5 Hours

Ingredients:
- 5 cups kale, chopped
- 2 oz walnuts, chopped
- 1 cup of coconut milk
- 1 teaspoon vegan butter
- 1 cup of water
- 1 oz vegan Parmesan, grated

Directions:
1. Put all ingredients in the Slow Cooker and gently stir.
2. Then close the lid and cook the kale on Low for 5 hours.

Nutrition Info:
- Per Serving: 298 calories, 9.6g protein, 13.7g carbohydrates, 25.1g fat, 3.5g fiber, 8mg cholesterol, 120mg sodium, 644mg potassium.

Garlic Gnocchi

Servings:4 | Cooking Time: 3 Hours

Ingredients:
- 2 cups mozzarella, shredded
- 3 egg yolks, beaten
- 1 teaspoon garlic, minced
- ½ cup heavy cream
- Salt and pepper to taste

Directions:
1. In a mixing bowl, combine the mozzarella and egg yolks.
2. Form gnocchi balls and place in the fridge to set.
3. Boil a pot of water over high flame and drop the gnocchi balls for 30 seconds. Take them out and transfer to the crockpot.
4. Into the crockpot add the garlic and heavy cream.
5. Season with salt and pepper to taste.
6. Close the lid and cook on low for 3 hours or on high for 1 hour.

Nutrition Info:
- Calories per serving: 178; Carbohydrates: 4.1g; Protein:20.5 g;

Fat: 8.9g; Sugar:0.3g; Sodium: 421mg; Fiber: 2.1g

Spicy Okra

Servings:2 | Cooking Time: 1.5 Hours

Ingredients:
- 2 cups okra, sliced
- ½ cup vegetable stock
- 1 teaspoon chili powder
- ½ teaspoon ground turmeric
- 1 teaspoon chili flakes
- 1 teaspoon dried oregano
- 1 tablespoon butter

Directions:
1. Put okra in the Slow Cooker.
2. Add vegetable stock, chili powder, ground turmeric, chili flakes, and dried oregano.
3. Cook the okra on High for 1.5 hours.
4. Then add butter and stir the cooked okra well.

Nutrition Info:
- Per Serving: 102 calories, 2.5g protein, 9.2g carbohydrates, 6.4g fat, 4.1g fiber, 15mg cholesterol, 252mg sodium, 358mg potassium.

Fragrant Jackfruit

Servings:4 | Cooking Time: 2 Hours

Ingredients:
- 1-pound jackfruit, canned, chopped
- 1 teaspoon tomato paste
- 1 teaspoon taco seasoning
- 1 onion, diced
- ½ cup coconut cream
- 1 teaspoon chili powder

Directions:
1. In the mixing bowl mix taco seasoning, chili powder, tomato paste, and coconut cream.
2. Put the jackfruit and diced onion in the Slow Cooker.
3. Pour the tomato mixture over the vegetables and gently mix them.
4. Close the lid and cook the meal on High for 2 hours.

Nutrition Info:
- Per Serving: 145 calories, 2.4g protein, 32.4g carbohydrates, 2.2g fat, 2.7g fiber, 6mg cholesterol, 127mg sodium, 421mg potassium.

Cardamom Pumpkin Wedges

Servings:4 | Cooking Time: 6 Hours

Ingredients:
- 2-pound pumpkin, peeled
- 1 teaspoon ground cardamom
- 2 tablespoons lemon juice
- 1 teaspoon lemon zest, grated
- 2 tablespoons sugar
- 1 cup of water

Directions:
1. Cut the pumpkin into wedges and place them in the Slow Cooker.
2. Add water.
3. Then sprinkle the pumpkin with ground cardamom, lemon juice, lemon zest, and sugar.
4. Close the lid and cook the pumpkin on Low for 6 hours.

5. Serve the pumpkin wedges with sweet liquid from the Slow Cooker.

Nutrition Info:
• Per Serving: 103 calories, 2.6g protein, 25g carbohydrates, 0.7g fat, 6.8g fiber, 0mg cholesterol, 15mg sodium, 484mg potassium.

Parsnip Balls

Servings:4 | Cooking Time: 3 Hours

Ingredients:
• 8 oz parsnip, peeled, grated
• 1 tablespoon coconut cream
• 1/3 cup coconut flour
• 1 tablespoon coconut oil
• 1 carrot, boiled, peeled, mashed
• 1 teaspoon salt
• 1 teaspoon chili powder

Directions:
1. In the mixing bowl mix grated parsnip, coconut cream, coconut flour, mashed carrot, salt, and chili powder.
2. With the help of the scooper make the small balls and freeze them for 10-15 minutes.
3. Then put coconut oil in the Slow Cooker.
4. Add frozen parsnip balls and cook them on Low for 3 hours.

Nutrition Info:
• Per Serving: 129 calories, 2.3g protein, 18.9g carbohydrates, 5.6g fat, 7.5g fiber, 0mg cholesterol, 605mg sodium, 284mg potassium.

Mediterranean Veggies

Servings: 8 | Cooking Time: 7 Hrs

Ingredients:
• 1 zucchini, peeled and diced
• 2 eggplants, peeled and diced
• 2 red onion, diced
• 4 potatoes, peeled and diced
• 4 oz. asparagus, chopped
• 2 tbsp olive oil
• 1 tsp ground black pepper
• 1 tsp paprika
• 1 tsp salt
• 1 tbsp Mediterranean seasoning
• 1 tsp minced garlic

Directions:
1. Mix Mediterranean seasoning with olive oil, paprika, salt, garlic, and black pepper in a large bowl.
2. Toss in all the veggies to this mixture and mix well.
3. Spread all the seasoned veggies in the Slow Cooker.
4. Put the cooker's lid on and set the cooking time to 7 hours on Low settings.
5. Serve warm.

Nutrition Info:
• Per Serving: Calories 227, Total Fat 3.9g, Fiber 9g, Total Carbs 44.88g, Protein 6g

Cauliflower Mac And Cheese

Servings:6 | Cooking Time: 4 Hours

Ingredients:
• 1 large cauliflower, cut into small florets
• 2 tablespoons butter
• 1 cup heavy cream
• 2 ounces grass-fed cream cheese
• 1 ½ teaspoons Dijon mustard
• 1 ½ cup organic sharp cheddar cheese
• 1 tablespoon garlic powder
• ½ cup nutritional yeast
• Salt and pepper to taste

Directions:
1. Place all ingredients in the CrockPot.
2. Give a good stir.
3. Close the lid and cook on high for 3 hours or on low for 4 hours.

Nutrition Info:
• Calories per serving:329; Carbohydrates: 10.8g; Protein: 16.1g; Fat: 25.5g; Sugar: 0g; Sodium: 824mg; Fiber: 5.8g

Allspice Beans Stew

Servings: 6 | Cooking Time: 6 Hours And 20 Minutes

Ingredients:
• 1 yellow onion, chopped
• 1 tbsp olive oil
• 1 red bell pepper, chopped
• 1 jalapeno, chopped
• 2 garlic cloves, minced
• 1 tsp ginger, grated
• ½ tsp cumin
• ½ tsp allspice, ground
• ½ tsp oregano, dried
• 30 oz. canned black beans, drained
• ½ tsp sugar
• 1 cup chicken stock
• Salt and black pepper
• 3 cups brown rice, cooked
• 2 mangoes, peeled and chopped

Directions:
1. Take a non-stick skillet and heat oil in it.
2. Stir in onion and sauté for 4 minutes.
3. Toss in jalapeno, ginger, and garlic, then stir cook for 3 minutes.
4. Transfer the onion-jalapeno mixture to the Slow Cooker.
5. Add allspice, bell pepper, cumin, black beans, oregano, salt, black pepper, stock, and sugar.
6. Put the cooker's lid on and set the cooking time to 6 hours on Low settings.
7. Now add mangoes and rice then again cover the lid.
8. Slow cook for another 10 minutes.
9. Serve.

Nutrition Info:
• Per Serving: Calories 490, Total Fat 6g, Fiber 20g, Total Carbs 80g, Protein 17g

Zucchini Basil Soup

Servings:8 | Cooking Time: 3 Hours

Ingredients:
- 9 cups zucchini, diced
- 2 cups white onions, chopped
- 4 cups vegetable broth
- 8 cloves of garlic, minced
- 1 cup basil leaves
- 4 tablespoons olive oil
- Salt and pepper to taste

Directions:
1. Place the ingredients in the CrockPot.
2. Give a good stir.
3. Close the lid and cook on high for 2 hours or on low for 3 hours.
4. Once cooked, transfer into a blender and pulse until smooth.

Nutrition Info:
- Calories per serving: 93; Carbohydrates: 5.4g; Protein: 1.3g; Fat: 11.6g; Sugar: 0g; Sodium: 322mg; Fiber: 4.2g

Chili Dip

Servings:5 | Cooking Time: 5 Hours

Ingredients:
- 5 oz chilies, canned, chopped
- 3 oz Mozzarella, shredded
- 1 tomato, chopped
- ½ cup milk
- 1 teaspoon cornflour

Directions:
1. Mix milk with cornflour and whisk until smooth. Pour the liquid in the Slow Cooker.
2. Then add chilies, Mozzarella, and tomato.
3. Close the lid and cook the dip on low for 5 hours.

Nutrition Info:
- Per Serving: 156 calories, 8.7g protein, 22.5g carbohydrates, 5.2g fat, 8.3g fiber, 11mg cholesterol, 140mg sodium, 575mg potassium.

Brussel Sprouts

Servings:4 | Cooking Time: 2.5 Hours

Ingredients:
- 1-pound Brussel sprouts
- 2 oz tofu, chopped, cooked
- 1 teaspoon cayenne pepper
- 2 cups of water
- 1 tablespoon vegan butter

Directions:
1. Pour water in the Slow Cooker.
2. Add Brussel sprouts and cayenne pepper.
3. Cook the vegetables on high for 2.5 hours.
4. Then drain water and mix Brussel sprouts with butter and tofu.
5. Shake the vegetables gently.

Nutrition Info:
- Per Serving: 153 calories, 9.2g protein, 10.8g carbohydrates, 9.3g fat, 4.4g fiber, 23mg cholesterol, 380mg sodium, 532mg potassium

Creamy White Mushrooms

Servings:4 | Cooking Time: 8 Hours

Ingredients:
- 1-pound white mushrooms, chopped
- 1 cup cream
- 1 teaspoon chili flakes
- 1 teaspoon ground black pepper
- 1 tablespoon dried parsley

Directions:
1. Put all ingredients in the Slow Cooker.
2. Cook the mushrooms on low for 8 hours.
3. When the mushrooms are cooked, transfer them in the serving bowls and cool for 10-15 minutes.

Nutrition Info:
- Per Serving: 65 calories, 4.1g protein, 6g carbohydrates, 3.7g fat, 1.3g fiber, 11mg cholesterol, 27mg sodium, 396mg potassium.

Vegetable Korma

Servings:6 | Cooking Time: 6 Hours

Ingredients:
- 1 cup tomatoes, chopped
- 1 cup potatoes, chopped
- 1 cup green peas, frozen
- 1 teaspoon curry powder
- 1 teaspoon garam masala
- 6 oz green beans, chopped
- 2 cups of water
- 1 cup coconut cream

Directions:
1. Put all ingredients in the Slow Cooker and gently stir with the help of the spoon.
2. Close the lid and cook korma on Low for 6 hours.

Nutrition Info:
- Per Serving: 144 calories, 3.5g protein, 13g carbohydrates, 9.8g fat, 4.1g fiber, 0mg cholesterol, 15mg sodium, 402mg potassium.

Spaghetti Cheese Casserole

Servings: 8 | Cooking Time: 7 Hrs

Ingredients:
- 1 lb. cottage cheese
- 7 oz. spaghetti, cooked
- 5 eggs
- 1 cup heavy cream
- 5 tbsp semolina
- 3 tbsp white sugar
- 1 tsp vanilla extract
- 1 tsp marjoram
- 1 tsp lemon zest
- 1 tsp butter

Directions:
1. Start by blending cottage cheese in a blender jug for 1 minute.
2. Add eggs to the cottage cheese and blend again for 3 minutes.
3. Stir in semolina, cream, sugar, marjoram, vanilla extract, butter and lemon zest.
4. Blend again for 1 minute and keep the cheese-cream mixture aside.
5. Spread the chopped spaghetti layer in the Slow Cooker.
6. Top the spaghetti with 3 tbsp with the cheese-cream mixture.
7. Add another layer of spaghetti over the mixture.
8. Continue adding alternate layers in this manner until all ingre-

dients are used.

9. Put the cooker's lid on and set the cooking time to 7 hours on Low settings.

10. Slice and serve.

Nutrition Info:

- Per Serving: Calories 242, Total Fat 13.8g, Fiber 1g, Total Carbs 17.44g, Protein 12g

Curry Paneer

Servings:2 | Cooking Time: 2 Hours

Ingredients:

- 6 oz paneer, cubed
- 1 teaspoon garam masala
- ½ cup coconut cream
- 1 chili pepper, chopped
- 1 teaspoon olive oil
- ½ onion, diced
- 1 teaspoon garlic paste

Directions:

1. In the mixing bowl mix diced onion, garlic paste, olive oil, chili pepper, coconut cream, and garam masala.

2. Then mix the mixture with cubed paneer and put in the Slow Cooker.

3. Cook it on Low for 2 hours.

Nutrition Info:

- Per Serving: 309 calories, 7.1g protein, 22.5g carbohydrates, 22.4g fat, 3.5g fiber, 2mg cholesterol, 415mg sodium, 208mg potassium.

Potato Salad

Servings:2 | Cooking Time: 3 Hours

Ingredients:

- 1 cup potato, chopped
- 1 cup of water
- 1 teaspoon salt
- 2 oz celery stalk, chopped
- 2 oz fresh parsley, chopped
- ¼ onion, diced
- 1 tablespoon mayonnaise

Directions:

1. Put the potatoes in the Slow Cooker.

2. Add water and salt.

3. Cook the potatoes on High for 3 hours.

4. Then drain water and transfer the potatoes in the salad bowl.

5. Add all remaining ingredients and carefully mix the salad.

Nutrition Info:

- Per Serving: 129 calories, 5.5g protein, 12.4g carbohydrates, 6.7g fat, 2.5g fiber, 12mg cholesterol, 1479mg sodium, 465mg potassium.

Creamy Corn Chili

Servings: 6 | Cooking Time: 6 Hrs

Ingredients:

- 2 jalapeno chilies, chopped
- 1 cup yellow onion, chopped
- 1 tbsp olive oil
- 4 poblano chilies, chopped
- 4 Anaheim chilies, chopped
- 3 cups corn
- 6 cups veggie stock

- ½ bunch cilantro, chopped
- Salt and black pepper to the taste

Directions:

1. Add jalapenos, oil, onion, poblano, corn, stock, and Anaheim chilies to the Slow Cooker.

2. Put the cooker's lid on and set the cooking time to 6 hours on Low settings.

3. Puree the cooked mixture with the help of an immersion blender.

4. Stir in black pepper, salt and cilantro.

5. Serve warm.

Nutrition Info:

- Per Serving: Calories 209, Total Fat 5g, Fiber 5g, Total Carbs 33g, Protein 5g

Tofu Kebabs

Servings:4 | Cooking Time: 2 Hours

Ingredients:

- 2 tablespoons lemon juice
- 1 teaspoon ground turmeric
- 2 tablespoons coconut cream
- 1 teaspoon chili powder
- ¼ cup of water
- 1 teaspoon avocado oil
- 1-pound tofu, cubed

Directions:

1. Pour water in the Slow Cooker.

2. After this, in the mixing bowl mix lemon juice, ground turmeric, coconut cream, chili powder, and avocado oil.

3. Coat every tofu cube in the coconut cream mixture and string on the wooden skewers. Place them in the Slow Cooker.

4. Cook the tofu kebabs on Low for 2 hours.

Nutrition Info:

- Per Serving: 104 calories, 9.7g protein, 3.3g carbohydrates, 6.9g fat, 1.6g fiber, 0mg cholesterol, 24mg sodium, 227mg potassium.

Garlic Asparagus

Servings:5 | Cooking Time: 6 Hours

Ingredients:

- 1-pound asparagus, trimmed
- 1 teaspoon salt
- 1 teaspoon garlic powder
- 1 tablespoon vegan butter
- 1 ½ cup vegetable stock

Directions:

1. Chop the asparagus roughly and sprinkle with salt and garlic powder.

2. Put the vegetables in the Slow Cooker.

3. Add vegan butter and vegetable stock. Close the lid.

4. Cook the asparagus on Low for 6 hours.

Nutrition Info:

- Per Serving: 33 calories, 2.3g protein, 6.1g carbohydrates, 1g fat, 2g fiber, 0mg cholesterol, 687mg sodium, 190mg potassium.

Asian Broccoli Sauté

Servings:4 | Cooking Time: 3 Hours

Ingredients:
- 1 tablespoon coconut oil
- 1 head broccoli, cut into florets
- 1 tablespoon coconut aminos or soy sauce
- 1 teaspoon ginger, grated
- Salt and pepper to taste

Directions:
1. Place the ingredients in the crockpot.
2. Toss everything to combine.
3. Close the lid and cook on low for 3 hours or on high for an hour.
4. Once cooked, sprinkle with sesame seeds or sesame oil.

Nutrition Info:
- Calories per serving: 62; Carbohydrates:3.6 g; Protein: 1.8g; Fat: 4.3g; Sugar:0.3 g; Sodium: 87mg; Fiber: 2.1g

Broccoli Fritters

Servings:4 | Cooking Time: 40 Minutes

Ingredients:
- 2 cups broccoli, shredded
- 1 teaspoon chili flakes
- 1 teaspoon salt
- 2 tablespoons semolina
- 1 egg, beaten
- 1 tablespoon cornflour
- 1 tablespoon sunflower oil
- ¼ cup coconut cream

Directions:
1. In the mixing bowl mix shredded broccoli, chili flakes, salt, semolina, egg, and cornflour.
2. Make the small fritters from the broccoli mixture.
3. Then pour sunflower in the Slow Cooker.
4. Out the fritters in the Slow Cooker in one layer.
5. Add coconut cream.
6. Cook the fritters on High for 40 minutes.

Nutrition Info:
- Per Serving: 97 calories, 3.6g protein, 8.8g carbohydrates, 5.7g fat, 1.5g fiber, 44mg cholesterol, 617mg sodium, 181mg potassium.

Fragrant Appetizer Peppers

Servings:2 | Cooking Time: 1.5 Hours

Ingredients:
- 4 sweet peppers, seeded
- ¼ cup apple cider vinegar
- 1 red onion, sliced
- 1 teaspoon peppercorns
- ½ teaspoon sugar
- ¼ cup of water
- 1 tablespoon olive oil

Directions:
1. Slice the sweet peppers roughly and put in the Slow Cooker.
2. Add all remaining ingredients and close the lid.
3. Cook the peppers on high for 1.5 hours.
4. Then cool the peppers well and store them in the fridge for up to 6 days.

Nutrition Info:

- Per Serving: 171 calories, 3.1g protein, 25.1g carbohydrates, 7.7g fat, 4.7g fiber, 0mg cholesterol, 11mg sodium, 564mg potassium.

Spicy Eggplant With Red Pepper And Parsley

Servings:4 | Cooking Time: 3 Hours

Ingredients:
- 1 large eggplant, sliced
- 2 tablespoons parsley, chopped
- 1 big red bell pepper, chopped
- Salt and pepper to taste
- 2 tablespoons balsamic vinegar

Directions:
1. Place all ingredients in a mixing bowl.
2. Toss to coat ingredients.
3. Place in the crockpot and cook on low for 3 hours or on high for 1 hour.

Nutrition Info:
- Calories per serving: 52; Carbohydrates:11.67 g; Protein:1.8 g; Fat:0.31 g; Sugar: 0.2g; Sodium: 142mg; Fiber: 9.4g

Warming Butternut Squash Soup

Servings: 9 | Cooking Time: 8 Hrs

Ingredients:
- 2 lb. butternut squash, peeled and cubed
- 4 tsp minced garlic
- ½ cup onion, chopped
- 1 tsp salt
- ¼ tsp ground nutmeg
- 1 tsp ground black pepper
- 8 cups chicken stock
- 1 tbsp fresh parsley

Directions:
1. Spread the butternut squash in your Slow Cooker.
2. Add stock, garlic, and onion to the squash.
3. Put the cooker's lid on and set the cooking time to 8 hours on Low settings.
4. Add salt, black pepper, and nutmeg to the squash.
5. Puree the cooked squash mixture using an immersion blender until smooth.
6. Garnish with chopped parsley.
7. Enjoy.

Nutrition Info:
- Per Serving: Calories 129, Total Fat 2.7g, Fiber 2g, Total Carbs 20.85g, Protein 7g

Stuffed Okra

Servings:4 | Cooking Time: 5 Hours

Ingredients:
- 1-pound okra
- 1 cup cauliflower, shredded
- 1 teaspoon curry powder
- 1 teaspoon tomato paste
- 1 teaspoon dried dill
- 1/3 cup coconut milk
- 1 tablespoon coconut oil

Directions:
1. Make the cuts in the okra and remove seeds.
2. Then mix shredded cauliflower with curry powder, tomato

paste, and dried dill.
3. Fill every okra with cauliflower mixture and put in the Slow Cooker.
4. Add coconut oil and coconut milk in the Slow Cooker and close the lid.
5. Cook the okra on Low for 5 hours.

Nutrition Info:
• Per Serving: 130 calories, 3.3g protein, 11.6g carbohydrates, 8.5g fat, 5g fiber, 0mg cholesterol, 21mg sodium, 497mg potassium.

Onion Balls

Servings:4 | Cooking Time: 2 Hours

Ingredients:
• ½ cup red lentils, cooked
• ½ cup onion, minced
• 1 teaspoon ground black pepper
• ¼ cup flax meal
• 1 teaspoon cornflour
• ½ teaspoon salt
• ½ cup of water
• ½ cup ketchup

Directions:
1. In the mixing bowl mix red lentils with minced onion, ground black pepper, flax meal, cornflour, and salt.
2. Make the balls from the onion mixture and freeze them in the freezer for 20 minutes.
3. After this, mix water and ketchup in the Slow Cooker.
4. Add frozen balls and close the lid.
5. Cook the meal on High for 2 hours.

Nutrition Info:
• Per Serving: 153 calories, 8.5g protein, 26.1g carbohydrates, 2.9g fat, 9.9g fiber, 0mg cholesterol, 628mg sodium, 430mg potassium.

Mushroom Steaks

Servings:4 | Cooking Time: 2 Hours

Ingredients:
• 4 Portobello mushrooms
• 1 tablespoon avocado oil
• 1 tablespoon lemon juice
• 2 tablespoons coconut cream
• ½ teaspoon ground black pepper

Directions:
1. Slice Portobello mushrooms into steaks and sprinkle with avocado oil, lemon juice, coconut cream, and ground black pepper.
2. Then arrange the mushroom steaks in the Slow Cooker in one layer (you will need to cook all mushroom steaks by 2 times).
3. Cook the meal on High for 1 hour.

Nutrition Info:
• Per Serving: 43 calories, 3.3g protein, 3.9g carbohydrates, 2.3g fat, 1.4g fiber, 0mg cholesterol, 2mg sodium, 339mg potassium.

Crockpot Baked Tofu

Servings:4 | Cooking Time: 2 Hours

Ingredients:
• 1 small package extra firm tofu, sliced
• 3 tablespoons soy sauce
• 1 tablespoon sesame oil
• 2 teaspoons minced garlic
• Juice from ½ lemon, freshly squeezed

Directions:
1. In a deep dish, mix together the soy sauce, sesame oil, garlic, and lemon. Add a few tablespoons of water if the sauce is too thick.
2. Marinate the tofu slices for at least 2 hours.
3. Line the crockpot with foil and grease it with cooking spray.
4. Place the slices of marinated tofu into the crockpot.
5. Cook on low for 4 hours or on high for 2 hours.
6. Make sure that the tofu slices have a crispy outer texture.

Nutrition Info:
• Calories per serving:145; Carbohydrates: 4.1g; Protein: 11.6g; Fat: 10.8g; Sugar: 0.6g; Sodium: 142mg; Fiber:1.5 g

Marinated Poached Aubergines

Servings:6 | Cooking Time: 4 Hours

Ingredients:
• ½ cup apple cider vinegar
• 1-pound eggplants, chopped
• 1 cup of water
• ¼ cup avocado oil
• 3 garlic cloves, diced
• 1 teaspoon salt
• 1 teaspoon sugar

Directions:
1. Put all ingredients in the Slow Cooker.
2. Cook the meal on Low for 4 hours.
3. Cool the cooked aubergines well.

Nutrition Info:
• Per Serving: 40 calories, 1g protein, 6.3g carbohydrates, 1.3g fat, 3.1g fiber, 0mg cholesterol, 392mg sodium, 224mg potassium.

Rainbow Carrots

Servings:4 | Cooking Time: 3.5 Hours

Ingredients:
• 2-pound rainbow carrots, sliced
• 1 cup vegetable stock
• 1 cup bell pepper, chopped
• 1 onion, sliced
• 1 teaspoon salt
• 1 teaspoon chili powder

Directions:
1. Put all ingredients in the Slow Cooker.
2. Close the lid and cook the meal on High for 3.5 hours.
3. Then cool the cooked carrots for 5-10 minutes and transfer in the serving bowls.

Nutrition Info:
• Per Serving: 118 calories, 3.5g protein, 26.7g carbohydrates, 0.4g fat, 6.6g fiber, 0mg cholesterol, 954mg sodium, 112mg potassium.

Creamy Puree

Servings:4 | Cooking Time: 4 Hours

Ingredients:
- 2 cups potatoes, chopped
- 3 cups of water
- 1 tablespoon vegan butter
- ¼ cup cream
- 1 teaspoon salt

Directions:
1. Pour water in the Slow Cooker.
2. Add potatoes and salt.
3. Cook the vegetables on high for 4 hours.
4. Then drain water, add butter, and cream.
5. Mash the potatoes until smooth.

Nutrition Info:
- Per Serving: 87 calories, 1.4g protein, 12.3g carbohydrates, 3.8g fat, 1.8g fiber, 10mg cholesterol, 617mg sodium, 314mg potassium

Rice Cauliflower Casserole

Servings: 6 | Cooking Time: 8 Hrs 10 Minutes

Ingredients:
- 1 cup white rice
- 5 oz. broccoli, chopped
- 4 oz. cauliflower, chopped
- 1 cup Greek Yogurt
- 1 cup chicken stock
- 6 oz. Cheddar cheese, shredded
- 1 tsp onion powder
- 2 yellow onions, chopped
- 1 tsp paprika
- 1 tbsp salt
- 2 cups of water
- 1 tsp butter

Directions:
1. Add cauliflower, broccoli, water, chicken stock, salt, paprika, rice, and onion powder to the Slow Cooker.
2. Top the broccoli-cauliflower mixture with onion slices.
3. Put the cooker's lid on and set the cooking time to 8 hours on Low settings.
4. Add butter and cheese on top of the casserole.
5. Put the cooker's lid on and set the cooking time to 10 minutes on High settings.
6. Serve warm.

Nutrition Info:
- Per Serving: Calories 229, Total Fat 4.2g, Fiber 3g, Total Carbs 36.27g, Protein 12g

Cheddar Mushrooms

Servings:4 | Cooking Time: 6 Hours

Ingredients:
- 4 cups cremini mushrooms, sliced
- 1 teaspoon dried oregano
- 1 teaspoon ground black pepper
- ½ teaspoon salt
- 1 cup Cheddar cheese, shredded
- 1 cup heavy cream
- 1 cup of water

Directions:
1. Pour water and heavy cream in the Slow Cooker.
2. Add salt, ground black pepper, and dried oregano.
3. Then add sliced mushrooms, and Cheddar cheese.
4. Cook the meal on Low for 6 hours.
5. When the mushrooms are cooked, gently stir them and transfer in the serving plates.

Nutrition Info:
- Per Serving: 239 calories, 9.6g protein, 4.8g carbohydrates, 20.6g fat, 0.7g fiber, 71mg cholesterol, 484mg sodium, 386mg potassium.

Potato Parmesan Pie

Servings: 8 | Cooking Time: 6 Hrs

Ingredients:
- 2 sweet potatoes, peeled and sliced
- 2 red potatoes, peeled and sliced
- 6 oz. Parmesan, shredded
- 1 cup sweet corn
- 1 tsp salt
- 1 tsp paprika
- 1 tsp curry powder
- 2 red onions, sliced
- 1 cup flour
- 1 tsp baking soda
- ½ tsp apple cider vinegar
- 1 cup Greek Yogurt
- 3 tomatoes, sliced
- ¼ tsp butter

Directions:
1. Toss the vegetables with curry, salt, paprika, and curry powder for seasoning.
2. Coat the base of your Slow Cooker with butter.
3. At first, make a layer of red potatoes in the cooker.
4. Now add layers of sweet potatoes and onion.
5. Add corns and tomatoes on top.
6. Whisk yogurt with baking soda, flour, and apple cider vinegar in a bowl.
7. Add the yogurt-flour mixture on top of the layers of veggies.
8. Lastly, drizzle the shredded cheese over it.
9. Put the cooker's lid on and set the cooking time to 6 hours on High settings.
10. Slice and serve.

Nutrition Info:
- Per Serving: Calories 272, Total Fat 1.9g, Fiber 4g, Total Carbs 51.34g, Protein 14g

Bulgur Mushroom Chili

Servings: 4 | Cooking Time: 8 Hrs

Ingredients:
- 2 cups white mushrooms, sliced
- ¾ cup bulgur, soaked in 1 cup hot water for 15 minutes and drained
- 2 cups yellow onion, chopped
- ½ cup red bell pepper, chopped
- 1 cup veggie stock
- 2 garlic cloves, minced
- 1 cup strong brewed coffee
- 14 oz. canned kidney beans, drained
- 14 oz. canned pinto beans, drained
- 2 tbsp sugar
- 2 tbsp chili powder
- 1 tbsp cocoa powder
- 1 tsp oregano, dried
- 2 tsp cumin, ground
- 1 bay leaf
- Salt and black pepper to the taste

Directions:
1. Add bulgur with all other ingredients to the base of your Slow Cooker.
2. Put the cooker's lid on and set the cooking time to 12 hours on Low settings.
3. Remove the bay leaf from the chili and discard it.
4. Serve warm.

Nutrition Info:
- Per Serving: Calories 351, Total Fat 4g, Fiber 6g, Total Carbs 20g, Protein 4g

Vegetarian Red Coconut Curry

Servings:4 | Cooking Time: 3 Hours

Ingredients:
- 1 cup broccoli florets
- 1 large handful spinach, rinsed
- 1 tablespoon red curry paste
- 1 cup coconut cream
- 1 teaspoon garlic, minced

Directions:
1. Combine all ingredients in the crockpot.
2. Close the lid and cook on low for 3 hours or on high for 1 hour.

Nutrition Info:
- Calories per serving: 226; Carbohydrates: 8g; Protein: 5.2g; Fat:21.4 g; Sugar: 0.4g; Sodium: 341mg; Fiber:4.3 g

Braised Swiss Chard

Servings:4 | Cooking Time: 30 Minutes

Ingredients:
- 1-pound swiss chard, chopped
- 1 lemon
- 1 teaspoon garlic, diced
- 1 tablespoon sunflower oil
- 1 teaspoon salt
- 2 cups of water

Directions:
1. Put the swiss chard in the Slow Cooker.
2. Cut the lemon into halves and squeeze it over the swiss chard.
3. After this, sprinkle the greens with diced garlic, sunflower oil, salt, and water.
4. Mix the mixture gently with the help of the spoon and close the lid.
5. Cook the greens on High for 30 minutes.

Nutrition Info:
- Per Serving: 58 calories, 2.2g protein, 5.8g carbohydrates, 3.9g fat, 2.3g fiber, 0mg cholesterol, 828mg sodium, 455mg potassium.

Chapter 8 Side Dish Recipes

Chapter 8 Side Dish Recipes

Garlicky Black Beans

Servings: 8 | Cooking Time: 7 Hours

Ingredients:
- 1 cup black beans, soaked overnight, drained and rinsed
- 1 cup of water
- Salt and black pepper to the taste
- 1 spring onion, chopped
- 2 garlic cloves, minced
- ½ tsp cumin seeds

Directions:
1. Add beans, salt, black pepper, cumin seeds, garlic, and onion to the Slow Cooker.
2. Put the cooker's lid on and set the cooking time to 7 hours on Low settings.
3. Serve warm.

Nutrition Info:
- Per Serving: Calories: 300, Total Fat: 4g, Fiber: 6g, Total Carbs: 20g, Protein: 15g

Italian Eggplant

Servings: 2 | Cooking Time: 2 Hours

Ingredients:
- 2 small eggplants, roughly cubed
- ½ cup heavy cream
- Salt and black pepper to the taste
- 1 tablespoon olive oil
- A pinch of hot pepper flakes
- 2 tablespoons oregano, chopped

Directions:
1. In your Slow Cooker, mix the eggplants with the cream and the other ingredients, toss, put the lid on and cook on High for 2 hours.
2. Divide between plates and serve as a side dish.

Nutrition Info:
- calories 132, fat 4, fiber 6, carbs 12, protein 3

Rice And Veggies

Servings: 4 | Cooking Time: 5 Hours

Ingredients:
- 2 cups basmati rice
- 1 cup mixed carrots, peas, corn and green beans
- 2 cups water
- ½ teaspoon green chili, minced
- ½ teaspoon ginger, grated
- 3 garlic cloves, minced
- 2 tablespoons butter
- 1 cinnamon stick
- 1 tablespoon cumin seeds
- 2 bay leaves
- 3 whole cloves
- 5 black peppercorns
- 2 whole cardamoms
- 1 tablespoon sugar
- Salt to the taste

Directions:
1. Put the water in your Slow Cooker, add rice, mixed veggies, green chili, grated ginger, garlic, cinnamon stick, whole cloves, butter, cumin seeds, bay leaves, cardamoms, black peppercorns, salt and sugar, stir, cover and cook on Low for 5 hours.
2. Discard cinnamon, divide between plates and serve as a side dish.

Nutrition Info:
- calories 300, fat 4, fiber 3, carbs 40, protein 13

Thyme Mushrooms And Corn

Servings: 2 | Cooking Time: 4 Hours

Ingredients:
- 4 garlic cloves, minced
- 1 tablespoon olive oil
- 1 pound white mushroom caps, halved
- 1 cup corn
- 1 cup canned tomatoes, crushed
- ¼ teaspoon thyme, dried
- ½ cup veggie stock
- A pinch of salt and black pepper
- 2 tablespoons parsley, chopped

Directions:
1. Grease your Slow Cooker with the oil, and mix the garlic with the mushrooms, corn and the other ingredients inside.
2. Toss, put the lid on and cook on Low for 4 hours.
3. Divide between plates and serve as a side dish.

Nutrition Info:
- calories 122, fat 6, fiber 1, carbs 8, protein 5

Kale And Ham Mix

Servings: 6 | Cooking Time: 6 Hours

Ingredients:
- 8 ounces ham hock slices
- 1 and ½ cups water
- 1 cup chicken stock
- 12 cups kale leaves, torn
- A pinch of salt and cayenne pepper
- 2 tablespoons olive oil
- 1 yellow onion, chopped
- 2 tablespoons apple cider vinegar
- Cooking spray

Directions:
1. Put ham in a heatproof bowl, add the water and the stock, cover and microwave for 3 minutes.
2. Heat up a pan with the oil over medium-high heat, add onion, stir and cook for 5 minutes.
3. Drain ham and add it to your Slow Cooker, add onions, kale, salt, cayenne and vinegar, toss, cover and cook on Low for 6 hours.
4. Divide between plates and serve as a side dish.

Nutrition Info:
- calories 200, fat 4, fiber 7, carbs 10, protein 3

Creamy Chipotle Sweet Potatoes

Servings: 10 | Cooking Time: 4 Hours

Ingredients:
- 1 sweet onion, chopped
- 2 tablespoons olive oil
- ¼ cup parsley, chopped
- 2 shallots, chopped
- 2 teaspoons chipotle pepper, crushed
- Salt and black pepper
- 4 big sweet potatoes, shredded
- 8 ounces coconut cream
- 16 ounces bacon, cooked and chopped
- ½ teaspoon sweet paprika
- Cooking spray

Directions:
1. Heat up a pan with the oil over medium-high heat, add shallots and onion, stir, cook for 6 minutes and transfer to a bowl.
2. Add parsley, chipotle pepper, salt, pepper, sweet potatoes, coconut cream, paprika and bacon, stir, pour everything in your Slow Cooker after you've greased it with some cooking spray, cover, cook on Low for 4 hours, leave aside to cool down a bit, divide between plates and serve as a side dish.

Nutrition Info:
- calories 260, fat 14, fiber 6, carbs 20, protein 15

Tarragon Sweet Potatoes

Servings: 4 | Cooking Time: 3 Hours

Ingredients:
- 1 pound sweet potatoes, peeled and cut into wedges
- 1 cup veggie stock
- ½ teaspoon chili powder
- ½ teaspoon cumin, ground
- Salt and black pepper to the taste
- 1 tablespoon olive oil
- 1 tablespoon tarragon, dried
- 2 tablespoons balsamic vinegar

Directions:
1. In your Slow Cooker, mix the sweet potatoes with the stock, chili powder and the other ingredients, toss, put the lid on and cook on High for 3 hours.
2. Divide the mix between plates and serve as a side dish.

Nutrition Info:
- calories 80, fat 4, fiber 4, carbs 8, protein 4

Asparagus Mix

Servings: 4 | Cooking Time: 6 Hours

Ingredients:
- 10 ounces cream of celery
- 12 ounces asparagus, chopped
- 2 eggs, hard-boiled, peeled and sliced
- 1 cup cheddar cheese, shredded
- 1 teaspoon olive oil

Directions:
1. Grease your Slow Cooker with the oil, add cream of celery and cheese to the Slow Cooker and stir.
2. Add asparagus and eggs, cover and cook on Low for 6 hours.
3. Divide between plates and serve as a side dish.

Nutrition Info:
- calories 241, fat 5, fiber 4, carbs 5, protein 12

Bean Medley

Servings: 12 | Cooking Time: 5 Hours

Ingredients:
- 2 celery ribs, chopped
- 1 and ½ cups ketchup
- 1 green bell pepper, chopped
- 1 yellow onion, chopped
- 1 sweet red pepper, chopped
- ½ cup brown sugar
- ½ cup Italian dressing
- ½ cup water
- 1 tablespoon cider vinegar
- 2 bay leaves
- 16 ounces kidney beans, drained
- Salt and black pepper to the taste
- 15 ounces canned black-eyed peas, drained
- 15 ounces canned northern beans, drained
- 15 ounces canned corn, drained
- 15 ounces canned lima beans, drained
- 15 ounces canned black beans, drained

Directions:
1. In your Slow Cooker, mix celery with ketchup, red and green bell pepper, onion, sugar, Italian dressing, water, vinegar, bay leaves, kidney beans, black-eyed peas, northern beans, corn, lima beans and black beans, stir, cover and cook on Low for 5 hours.
2. Divide between plates and serve as a side dish.

Nutrition Info:
- calories 255, fat 4, fiber 9, carbs 45, protein 6

Rice With Artichokes

Servings: 4 | Cooking Time: 4 Hrs

Ingredients:
- 1 tbsp olive oil
- 5 oz. Arborio rice
- 2 garlic cloves, minced
- 1 and ¼ cups chicken stock
- 1 tbsp white wine
- 6 oz. graham crackers, crumbled
- 1 and ¼ cups of water
- 15 oz. canned artichoke hearts, chopped
- 16 oz. cream cheese
- 1 tbsp parmesan, grated
- 1 and ½ tbsp thyme, chopped
- Salt and black pepper to the taste

Directions:
1. Add oil, rice, artichokes, garlic, water, wine, crackers, and stock to the Slow Cooker.
2. Put the cooker's lid on and set the cooking time to 4 hours on Low settings.
3. Stir in cream cheese, salt, parmesan, thyme, and black pepper.
4. Mix well and serve warm.

Nutrition Info:
- Per Serving: Calories: 230, Total Fat: 3g, Fiber: 5g, Total Carbs: 30g, Protein: 4g

Savoy Cabbage Mix

Servings: 2 | Cooking Time: 2 Hours

Ingredients:
- 1 pound Savoy cabbage, shredded
- 1 red onion, sliced
- 1 tablespoon olive oil
- ½ cup veggie stock
- A pinch of salt and black pepper
- 1 carrot, grated
- ½ cup tomatoes, cubed
- ½ teaspoon sweet paprika
- ½ inch ginger, grated

Directions:
1. In your Slow Cooker, mix the cabbage with the onion, oil and the other ingredients, toss, put the lid on and cook on High for 2 hours.
2. Divide the mix between plates and serve as a side dish.

Nutrition Info:
- calories 100, fat 3, fiber 4, carbs 5, protein 2

Mango Rice

Servings: 2 | Cooking Time: 2 Hours

Ingredients:
- 1 cup rice
- 2 cups chicken stock
- ½ cup mango, peeled and cubed
- Salt and black pepper to the taste
- 1 teaspoon olive oil

Directions:
1. In your Slow Cooker, mix the rice with the stock and the other ingredients, toss, put the lid on and cook on High for 2 hours.
2. Divide between plates and serve as a side dish.

Nutrition Info:
- calories 152, fat 4, fiber 5, carbs 18, protein 4

Nut And Berry Side Salad

Servings: 4 | Cooking Time: 1 Hour

Ingredients:
- 2 cups strawberries, halved
- 2 tablespoons mint, chopped
- 1/3 cup raspberry vinegar
- 2 tablespoons honey
- 1 tablespoon canola oil
- Salt and black pepper to the taste
- 4 cups spinach, torn
- ½ cup blueberries
- ¼ cup walnuts, chopped
- 1 ounce goat cheese, crumbled

Directions:
1. In your Slow Cooker, mix strawberries with mint, vinegar, honey, oil, salt, pepper, spinach, blueberries and walnuts, cover and cook on High for 1 hour.
2. Divide salad on plates, sprinkle cheese on top and serve as a side dish.

Nutrition Info:
- calories 200, fat 12, fiber 4, carbs 17, protein 15

Tamale Side Dish

Servings: 5 | Cooking Time: 7 Hours

Ingredients:
- 12 oz. masa harina
- 1 cup chicken stock
- ½ tsp salt
- 1 tsp onion powder
- 1 onion, chopped
- 5 tbsp olive oil
- 5 corn husks
- 5 cups of water

Directions:
1. Chicken Mix masa harina with chicken salt, salt, onion powder.
2. Stir in the chopped onion, and olive oil, then knead this dough.
3. Soak corn husks for 15 minutes in water then drain.
4. Spread the corn husks on the working surface.
5. Divide the masa harina mixture over the corn husks.
6. Roll the corn husk around the filling, then place these rolls in the Slow Cooker.
7. Put the cooker's lid on and set the cooking time to 7 hours on Low settings.
8. Serve fresh.

Nutrition Info:
- Per Serving: Calories: 214, Total Fat: 14.8g, Fiber: 2g, Total Carbs: 18g, Protein: 3g

Cheesy Rice

Servings: 6 | Cooking Time: 4 Hrs.

Ingredients:
- 2 garlic cloves, minced
- 2 tbsp olive oil
- ¾ cup yellow onion, chopped
- 1 and ½ cups Arborio rice
- ½ cup white wine
- 12 oz. spinach, chopped
- 3 and ½ cups hot veggie stock
- Salt and black pepper to the taste
- 4 oz. goat cheese, soft and crumbled
- 2 tbsp lemon juice
- 1/3 cup pecans, toasted and chopped

Directions:
1. Add spinach, garlic, oil, onion, rice, salt, black, stock, and wine to the Slow Cooker.
2. Put the cooker's lid on and set the cooking time to 4 hours on Low settings.
3. Stir in goat cheese and lemon juice.
4. Serve warm.

Nutrition Info:
- Per Serving: Calories: 300, Total Fat: 12g, Fiber: 4g, Total Carbs: 20g, Protein: 15g

Jalapeno Meal

Servings: 6 | Cooking Time: 6 Hrs.

Ingredients:
- 12 oz. jalapeno pepper, cut in half and deseeded
- 2 tbsp olive oil
- 1 tbsp balsamic vinegar
- 1 onion, sliced
- 1 garlic clove, sliced
- 1 tsp ground coriander
- 4 tbsp water

Directions:
1. Place the jalapeno peppers in the Slow Cooker.
2. Top the pepper with olive oil, balsamic vinegar, onion, garlic, coriander, and water.
3. Put the cooker's lid on and set the cooking time to 6 hours on Low settings.
4. Serve warm.

Nutrition Info:
- Per Serving: Calories: 67, Total Fat: 4.7g, Fiber: 2g, Total Carbs: 6.02g, Protein: 1g

Saucy Macaroni

Servings: 6 | Cooking Time: 3.5 Hours

Ingredients:
- 8 oz. macaroni
- 1 cup tomatoes, chopped
- 1 garlic clove, peeled
- 1 tsp butter
- 1 cup heavy cream
- 3 cups of water
- 1 tbsp salt
- 6 oz. Parmesan, shredded
- 1 tbsp dried basil

Directions:
1. Add macaroni, salt, and water to the Slow Cooker.
2. Put the cooker's lid on and set the cooking time to 3 hours on High settings.
3. Meanwhile, puree tomatoes in a blender then add cheese, cream, butter, and dried basil.
4. Drain the cooked macaroni and return them to the Slow Cooker.
5. Pour in the tomato-cream mixture.
6. Put the cooker's lid on and set the cooking time to 30 minutes on High settings.
7. Serve warm.

Nutrition Info:
- Per Serving: Calories: 325, Total Fat: 10.1g, Fiber: 2g, Total Carbs: 41.27g, Protein: 17g

Goat Cheese Rice

Servings: 6 | Cooking Time: 4 Hours

Ingredients:
- 2 garlic cloves, minced
- 2 tablespoons olive oil
- ¾ cup yellow onion, chopped
- 1 and ½ cups Arborio rice
- ½ cup white wine
- 12 ounces spinach, chopped
- 3 and ½ cups hot veggie stock
- Salt and black pepper to the taste
- 4 ounces goat cheese, soft and crumbled
- 2 tablespoons lemon juice
- 1/3 cup pecans, toasted and chopped

Directions:
1. In your Slow Cooker, mix oil with garlic, onion, rice, wine, salt, pepper and stock, stir, cover and cook on Low for 4 hours.
2. Add spinach, toss and leave aside for a few minutes
3. Add lemon juice and goat cheese, stir, divide between plates and serve with pecans on top as a side dish.

Nutrition Info:
- calories 300, fat 12, fiber 4, carbs 20, protein 15

Turmeric Potato Strips

Servings: 8 | Cooking Time: 5 Hours

Ingredients:
- 3 lbs. potato, peeled and cut into strips
- 2 tomatoes, chopped
- 1 tbsp paprika
- 1 sweet pepper, chopped
- 1 tsp salt
- ½ tsp turmeric
- 2 tbsp sesame oil

Directions:
1. Season the potato strips with salt, paprika, and turmeric.
2. Add oil and seasoned potatoes to the Slow Cooker and toss them well.
3. Put the cooker's lid on and set the cooking time to 3 hours on High settings.
4. Meanwhile, you can blend tomatoes with sweet pepper in a blender jug.
5. Pour this puree into the Slow Cooker.
6. Put the cooker's lid on and set the cooking time to 2 hours on High settings.
7. Serve warm.

Nutrition Info:
- Per Serving: Calories: 176, Total Fat: 3.8g, Fiber: 5g, Total Carbs: 32.97g, Protein: 4g

Lemon Kale Mix

Servings: 2 | Cooking Time: 2 Hours

Ingredients:
- 1 yellow bell pepper, chopped
- 1 red bell pepper, chopped
- 1 tablespoon olive oil
- 1 red onion, sliced
- 4 cups baby kale
- 1 teaspoon lemon zest, grated
- 1 tablespoon lemon juice
- ½ cup veggie stock
- 1 garlic clove, minced
- A pinch of salt and black pepper
- 1 tablespoon basil, chopped

Directions:
1. In your Slow Cooker, mix the kale with the oil, onion, bell peppers and the other ingredients, toss, put the lid on and cook on Low for 2 hours.
2. Divide the mix between plates and serve as a side dish.

Nutrition Info:
- calories 251, fat 9, fiber 6, carbs 7, protein 8

Squash Side Salad

Servings: 8 | Cooking Time: 4 Hours

Ingredients:
- 1 tablespoon olive oil
- 1 cup carrots, chopped
- 1 yellow onion, chopped
- 1 teaspoon sugar
- 1 and ½ teaspoons curry powder
- 1 garlic clove, minced
- 1 big butternut squash, peeled and cubed
- A pinch of sea salt and black pepper
- ¼ teaspoon ginger, grated
- ½ teaspoon cinnamon powder
- 3 cups coconut milk

Directions:
1. In your Slow Cooker, mix oil with carrots, onion, sugar, curry powder, garlic, squash, salt, pepper, ginger, cinnamon and coconut milk, stir well, cover and cook on Low for 4 hours.
2. Stir, divide between plates and serve as a side dish.

Nutrition Info:
- calories 200, fat 4, fiber 4, carbs 17, protein 4

Mexican Avocado Rice

Servings: 8 | Cooking Time: 4 Hrs

Ingredients:
- 1 cup long-grain rice
- 1 and ¼ cups veggie stock
- ½ cup cilantro, chopped
- ½ avocado, pitted, peeled and chopped
- Salt and black pepper to the taste
- ¼ cup green hot sauce

Directions:
1. Add rice and stock to the Slow Cooker.
2. Put the cooker's lid on and set the cooking time to 4 hours on Low settings.
3. Meanwhile, blend avocado flesh with hot sauce, cilantro, salt, and black pepper.
4. Serve the cooked rice with avocado sauce on top.

Nutrition Info:
- Per Serving: Calories: 100, Total Fat: 3g, Fiber: 6g, Total Carbs: 18g, Protein: 4g

Spinach Rice

Servings: 2 | Cooking Time: 2 Hours

Ingredients:
- 2 scallions, chopped
- 1 tablespoon olive oil
- 1 cup Arborio rice
- 1 cup chicken stock
- 6 ounces spinach, chopped
- Salt and black pepper to the taste
- 2 ounces goat cheese, crumbled

Directions:
1. In your Slow Cooker, mix the rice with the stock and the other ingredients, toss, put the lid on and cook on High for 2 hours.
2. Divide between plates and serve as a side dish.

Nutrition Info:
- calories 300, fat 10, fiber 6, carbs 20, protein 14

Cauliflower Carrot Gratin

Servings: 12 | Cooking Time: 7 Hours

Ingredients:
- 16 oz. baby carrots
- 6 tbsp butter, soft
- 1 cauliflower head, florets separated
- Salt and black pepper to the taste
- 1 yellow onion, chopped
- 1 tsp mustard powder
- 1 and ½ cups of milk
- 6 oz. cheddar cheese, grated
- ½ cup breadcrumbs

Directions:
1. Add carrots, cauliflower, and rest of the ingredients to the Slow Cooker.
2. Put the cooker's lid on and set the cooking time to 7 hours on Low settings.
3. Serve warm.

Nutrition Info:
- Per Serving: Calories: 182, Total Fat: 4g, Fiber: 7g, Total Carbs: 9g, Protein: 4g

Italian Black Beans Mix

Servings: 2 | Cooking Time: 5 Hours

Ingredients:
- 2 tablespoons tomato paste
- Cooking spray
- 2 cups black beans
- ¼ cup veggie stock
- 1 red onion, sliced
- Cooking spray
- 1 teaspoon Italian seasoning
- ½ celery rib, chopped
- ½ red bell pepper, chopped
- ½ sweet red pepper, chopped
- ¼ teaspoon mustard seeds
- Salt and black pepper to the taste
- 2 ounces canned corn, drained
- 1 tablespoon cilantro, chopped

Directions:
1. Grease the Slow Cooker with the cooking spray, and mix the beans with the stock, onion and the other ingredients inside.
2. Put the lid on, cook on Low for 5 hours, divide between plates and serve as a side dish.

Nutrition Info:
- calories 255, fat 6, fiber 7, carbs 38, protein 7

Scalloped Potatoes

Servings: 6 | Cooking Time: 6 Hours

Ingredients:
- Cooking spray
- 2 and ½ pounds gold potatoes, sliced
- 10 ounces canned cream of potato soup
- 1 yellow onion, roughly chopped
- 8 ounces sour cream
- 1 cup Gouda cheese, shredded
- ½ cup blue cheese, crumbled
- ½ cup parmesan, grated
- ½ cup chicken stock
- Salt and black pepper to the taste
- 1 tablespoon chives, chopped

Directions:
1. Grease your Slow Cooker with cooking spray and arrange potato slices on the bottom.
2. Add cream of potato soup, onion, sour cream, Gouda cheese, blue cheese, parmesan, stock, salt and pepper, cover and cook on Low for 6 hours.
3. Add chives, divide between plates and serve as a side dish.

Nutrition Info:
- calories 306, fat 14, fiber 4, carbs 33, protein 12

Mexican Rice

Servings: 8 | Cooking Time: 4 Hours

Ingredients:
- 1 cup long grain rice
- 1 and ¼ cups veggie stock
- ½ cup cilantro, chopped
- ½ avocado, pitted, peeled and chopped
- Salt and black pepper to the taste
- ¼ cup green hot sauce

Directions:
1. Put the rice in your Slow Cooker, add stock, stir, cover, cook on Low for 4 hours, fluff with a fork and transfer to a bowl.
2. In your food processor, mix avocado with hot sauce and cilantro, blend well, pour over rice, toss well, add salt and pepper, divide between plates and serve as a side dish.

Nutrition Info:
- calories 100, fat 3, fiber 6, carbs 18, protein 4

Coconut Bok Choy

Servings: 2 | Cooking Time: 1 Hour

Ingredients:
- 1 pound bok choy, torn
- ½ cup chicken stock
- ½ teaspoon chili powder
- 1 garlic clove, minced
- 1 teaspoon ginger, grated
- 1 tablespoon coconut oil
- Salt to the taste

Directions:
1. In your Slow Cooker, mix the bok choy with the stock and the other ingredients, toss, put the lid on and cook on High for 1 hour.
2. Divide between plates and serve as a side dish.

Nutrition Info:
- calories 100, fat 1, fiber 2, carbs 7, protein 4

Hot Zucchini Mix

Servings: 2 | Cooking Time: 2 Hours

Ingredients:
- ¼ cup carrots, grated
- 1 pound zucchinis, roughly cubed
- 1 teaspoon hot paprika
- ½ teaspoon chili powder
- 2 spring onions, chopped
- ½ tablespoon olive oil
- ½ teaspoon curry powder
- 1 garlic clove, minced
- ½ teaspoon ginger powder
- A pinch of salt and black pepper
- 1 tablespoon cilantro, chopped

Directions:
1. In your Slow Cooker, mix the carrots with the zucchinis, paprika and the other ingredients, toss, put the lid on and cook on Low for 2 hours.
2. Divide between plates and serve as a side dish.

Nutrition Info:
- calories 200, fat 5, fiber 7, carbs 28, protein 4

Baked Potato

Servings: 6 | Cooking Time: 8 Hours

Ingredients:
- 6 large potatoes, peeled and cubed
- 3 oz. mushrooms, chopped
- 1 onion, chopped
- 1 tsp butter
- ½ tsp salt
- ½ tsp minced garlic
- 1 tsp sour cream
- ½ tsp turmeric
- 1 tsp olive oil

Directions:
1. Grease the insert of the Slow Cooker with olive oil.
2. Toss in potatoes, onion, mushrooms, and rest of the ingredients.
3. Put the cooker's lid on and set the cooking time to 8 hours on Low settings.
4. Serve warm.

Nutrition Info:
- Per Serving: Calories: 309, Total Fat: 1.9g, Fiber: 9g, Total Carbs: 66.94g, Protein: 8g

Summer Squash Mix

Servings: 4 | Cooking Time: 2 Hours

Ingredients:
- ¼ cup olive oil
- 2 tablespoons basil, chopped
- 2 tablespoons balsamic vinegar
- 2 garlic cloves, minced
- 2 teaspoons mustard
- Salt and black pepper to the taste
- 3 summer squash, sliced
- 2 zucchinis, sliced

Directions:
1. In your Slow Cooker, mix squash with zucchinis, salt, pepper, mustard, garlic, vinegar, basil and oil, toss a bit, cover and cook on High for 2 hours.
2. Divide between plates and serve as a side dish.

Nutrition Info:
- calories 179, fat 13, fiber 2, carbs 10, protein 4

Beans Risotto

Servings: 6 | Cooking Time: 5 Hours

Ingredients:
- 1 lb. red kidney beans, soaked overnight and drained
- Salt to the taste
- 1 tsp olive oil
- 1 lb. smoked sausage, roughly chopped
- 1 yellow onion, chopped
- 1 celery stalk, chopped
- 4 garlic cloves, chopped
- 1 green bell pepper, chopped
- 1 tsp thyme, dried
- 2 bay leaves
- 5 cups of water
- 2 green onions, minced
- 2 tbsp parsley, minced

Directions:
1. Add red beans, oil, sausage, and rest of the ingredients to the Slow Cooker.
2. Put the cooker's lid on and set the cooking time to 5 hours on Low settings.
3. Serve warm.

Nutrition Info:
- Per Serving: Calories: 200, Total Fat: 5g, Fiber: 6g, Total Carbs: 20g, Protein: 5g

Mustard Brussels Sprouts

Servings: 2 | Cooking Time: 3 Hours

Ingredients:
- 1 pound Brussels sprouts, trimmed and halved
- 1 tablespoon olive oil
- 1 tablespoon mustard
- 1 tablespoon balsamic vinegar
- Salt and black pepper to the taste
- ¼ cup veggie stock
- A pinch of red pepper, crushed
- 2 tablespoons chives, chopped

Directions:
1. In your Slow Cooker, mix the Brussels sprouts with the oil, mustard and the other ingredients, toss, put the lid on and cook on High for 3 hours.

2. Divide the mix between plates and serve as a side dish.

Nutrition Info:
- calories 256, fat 12, fiber 6, carbs 8, protein 15

Green Beans And Red Peppers

Servings: 2 | Cooking Time: 2 Hours

Ingredients:
- 2 cups green beans, halved
- 1 red bell pepper, cut into strips
- Salt and black pepper to the taste
- 1 tablespoon olive oil
- 1 and ½ tablespoon honey mustard

Directions:
1. In your Slow Cooker, mix green beans with bell pepper, salt, pepper, oil and honey mustard, toss, cover and cook on High for 2 hours.
2. Divide between plates and serve as a side dish.

Nutrition Info:
- calories 50, fat 0, fiber 4, carbs 8, protein 2

Buttery Artichokes

Servings: 5 | Cooking Time: 6 Hrs.

Ingredients:
- 13 oz. artichoke heart halved
- 1 tsp salt
- 4 cups chicken stock
- 1 tsp turmeric
- 1 garlic clove, peeled
- 4 tbsp butter
- 4 oz. Parmesan, shredded

Directions:
1. Add artichoke, stock, salt, and turmeric to the Slow Cooker.
2. Put the cooker's lid on and set the cooking time to 6 hours on Low settings.
3. Drain and transfer the cooked artichoke to the serving plates.
4. Drizzle, cheese, and butter over the artichoke.
5. Serve warm.

Nutrition Info:
- Per Serving: Calories: 272, Total Fat: 12.8g, Fiber: 4g, Total Carbs: 24.21g, Protein: 17g

Garlic Squash Mix

Servings: 2 | Cooking Time: 3 Hours

Ingredients:
- 1 pound butternut squash, peeled and cubed
- 2 spring onions, chopped
- 1 cup veggie stock
- ½ teaspoon red pepper flakes, crushed
- ½ teaspoon turmeric powder
- A pinch of salt and black pepper
- 3 garlic cloves, minced

Directions:
1. In your Slow Cooker, mix the squash with the garlic, stock and the other ingredients, toss, put the lid on and cook on Low for 3 hours.
2. Divide squash mix between plates and serve as a side dish.

Nutrition Info:
- calories 196, fat 3, fiber 7, carbs 8, protein 7

Okra Side Dish

Servings: 4 | Cooking Time: 3 Hours

Ingredients:
- 2 cups okra, sliced
- 1 and ½ cups red onion, roughly chopped
- 1 cup cherry tomatoes, halved
- 2 and ½ cups zucchini, sliced
- 2 cups red and yellow bell peppers, sliced
- 1 cup white mushrooms, sliced
- ½ cup olive oil
- ½ cup balsamic vinegar
- 2 tablespoons basil, chopped
- 1 tablespoon thyme, chopped

Directions:
1. In your Slow Cooker, mix okra with onion, tomatoes, zucchini, bell peppers, mushrooms, basil and thyme.
2. In a bowl mix oil with vinegar, whisk well, add to the Slow Cooker, cover and cook on High for 3 hours.
3. Divide between plates and serve as a side dish.

Nutrition Info:
- calories 233, fat 12, fiber 4, carbs 8, protein 4

Okra Mix

Servings: 4 | Cooking Time: 8 Hours

Ingredients:
- 2 garlic cloves, minced
- 1 yellow onion, chopped
- 14 ounces tomato sauce
- 1 teaspoon sweet paprika
- 2 cups okra, sliced
- Salt and black pepper to the taste

Directions:
1. In your Slow Cooker, mix garlic with the onion, tomato sauce, paprika, okra, salt and pepper, cover and cook on Low for 8 hours.
2. Divide between plates and serve as a side dish.

Nutrition Info:
- calories 200, fat 6, fiber 5, carbs 10, protein 4

Zucchini Mix

Servings: 2 | Cooking Time: 6 Hours

Ingredients:
- 1 pound zucchinis, sliced
- ½ teaspoon Italian seasoning
- ½ teaspoon sweet paprika
- Salt and black pepper
- ½ cup heavy cream
- ½ teaspoon garlic powder
- 1 tablespoon olive oil

Directions:
1. In your Slow Cooker, mix the zucchinis with the seasoning, paprika and the other ingredients, toss, put the lid on and cook on Low for 6 hours.
2. Divide between plates and serve as a side dish.

Nutrition Info:
- calories 170, fat 2, fiber 4, carbs 8, protein 5

Veggie Side Salad

Servings: 4 | Cooking Time: 2 Hours

Ingredients:
- 2 garlic cloves, minced
- ½ cup olive oil
- ¼ cup basil, chopped
- Salt and black pepper to the taste
- 1 red bell pepper, chopped
- 1 eggplant, roughly chopped
- 1 summer squash, cubed
- 1 Vidalia onion, cut into wedges
- 1 zucchini, sliced
- 1 green bell pepper, chopped

Directions:
1. In your Slow Cooker, mix red bell pepper with green one, squash, zucchini, eggplant, onion, salt, pepper, basil, oil and garlic, toss gently, cover and cook on High for 2 hours.
2. Divide between plates and serve as a side dish.

Nutrition Info:
- calories 165, fat 11, fiber 3, carbs 15, protein 2

Creamy Red Cabbage

Servings: 9 | Cooking Time: 8 Hours

Ingredients:
- 17 oz. red cabbage, sliced
- 1 cup fresh cilantro, chopped
- 3 red onions, diced
- 1 tbsp sliced almonds
- 1 cup sour cream
- ½ cup chicken stock
- 1 tsp salt
- 1 tbsp tomato paste
- 1 tsp ground black pepper
- 1 tsp cumin
- ½ tsp thyme
- 2 tbsp butter
- 1 cup green peas

Directions:
1. Add cabbage, onion and all other ingredients to the Slow Cooker.
2. Put the cooker's lid on and set the cooking time to 8 hours on Low settings.
3. Serve warm.

Nutrition Info:
- Per Serving: Calories: 112, Total Fat: 5.9g, Fiber: 3g, Total Carbs: 12.88g, Protein: 4g

Chicken With Sweet Potato

Servings: 6 | Cooking Time: 3 Hours

Ingredients:
- 16 oz. sweet potato, peeled and diced
- 3 cups chicken stock
- 1 tbsp salt
- 3 tbsp margarine
- 2 tbsp cream cheese

Directions:
1. Add sweet potato, chicken stock, and salt to the Slow Cooker.
2. Put the cooker's lid on and set the cooking time to 5 hours on High settings.
3. Drain the slow-cooked potatoes and transfer them to a suitable

bowl.
4. Mash the sweet potatoes and stir in cream cheese and margarine.
5. Serve fresh.

Nutrition Info:
- Per Serving: Calories: 472, Total Fat: 31.9g, Fiber: 6.7g, Total Carbs: 43.55g, Protein: 3g

Squash And Peppers Mix
Servings: 4 | Cooking Time: 1 Hr 30 Minutes

Ingredients:
- 12 small squash, peeled and cut into wedges
- 2 red bell peppers, cut into wedges
- 2 green bell peppers, cut into wedges
- 1/3 cup Italian dressing
- 1 red onion, cut into wedges
- Salt and black pepper to the taste
- 1 tbsp parsley, chopped

Directions:
1. Add squash, peppers, and rest of the ingredients to the Slow Cooker.
2. Put the cooker's lid on and set the cooking time to 1.5 hours on High settings.
3. Garnish with parsley.
4. Serve warm.

Nutrition Info:
- Per Serving: Calories: 80, Total Fat: 2g, Fiber: 3g, Total Carbs: 11g, Protein: 2g

Veggies Rice Pilaf
Servings: 4 | Cooking Time: 5 Hours

Ingredients:
- 2 cups basmati rice
- 1 cup mixed carrots, peas, corn, and green beans
- 2 cups of water
- ½ tsp green chili, minced
- ½ tsp ginger, grated
- 3 garlic cloves, minced
- 2 tbsp butter
- 1 cinnamon stick
- 1 tbsp cumin seeds
- 2 bay leaves
- 3 whole cloves
- 5 black peppercorns
- 2 whole cardamoms
- 1 tbsp sugar
- Salt to the taste

Directions:
1. Add water, rice, veggies and all other ingredients to the Slow Cooker.
2. Put the cooker's lid on and set the cooking time to 5 hours on Low settings.
3. Discard the cinnamon and serve warm.

Nutrition Info:
- Per Serving: Calories: 300, Total Fat: 4g, Fiber: 3g, Total Carbs: 40g, Protein: 13g

Pumpkin Rice
Servings: 4 | Cooking Time: 5 Hours

Ingredients:
- 2 ounces olive oil
- 1 small yellow onion, chopped
- 2 garlic cloves, minced
- 12 ounces risotto rice
- 4 cups chicken stock
- 6 ounces pumpkin puree
- ½ teaspoon nutmeg, ground
- 1 teaspoon thyme, chopped
- ½ teaspoon ginger, grated
- ½ teaspoon cinnamon powder
- ½ teaspoon allspice, ground
- 4 ounces heavy cream

Directions:
1. In your Slow Cooker, mix oil with onion, garlic, rice, stock, pumpkin puree, nutmeg, thyme, ginger, cinnamon and allspice, stir, cover and cook on Low for 4 hours and 30 minutes.
2. Add cream, stir, cover, cook on Low for 30 minutes more, divide between plates and serve as a side dish.

Nutrition Info:
- calories 251, fat 4, fiber 3, carbs 30, protein 5

Classic Veggies Mix
Servings: 4 | Cooking Time: 3 Hours

Ingredients:
- 1 and ½ cups red onion, cut into medium chunks
- 1 cup cherry tomatoes, halved
- 2 and ½ cups zucchini, sliced
- 2 cups yellow bell pepper, chopped
- 1 cup mushrooms, sliced
- 2 tablespoons basil, chopped
- 1 tablespoon thyme, chopped
- ½ cup olive oil
- ½ cup balsamic vinegar

Directions:
1. In your Slow Cooker, mix onion pieces with tomatoes, zucchini, bell pepper, mushrooms, basil, thyme, oil and vinegar, toss to coat everything, cover and cook on High for 3 hours.
2. Divide between plates and serve as a side dish.

Nutrition Info:
- calories 150, fat 2, fiber 2, carbs 6, protein 5

Cider Dipped Farro
Servings: 6 | Cooking Time: 5 Hours

Ingredients:
- 1 tbsp apple cider vinegar
- 1 cup whole-grain farro
- 1 tsp lemon juice
- Salt to the taste
- 3 cups of water
- 1 tbsp olive oil
- ½ cup cherries, dried and chopped
- ¼ cup green onions, chopped
- 10 mint leaves, chopped
- 2 cups cherries, pitted and halved

Directions:
1. Add water and farro to the Slow Cooker.
2. Put the cooker's lid on and set the cooking time to 5 hours on

Low settings.
3. Toss the cooker farro with salt, cherries, mint, green onion, lemon juice, and oil in a bowl.
4. Serve fresh.

Nutrition Info:
• Per Serving: Calories: 162, Total Fat: 3g, Fiber: 6g, Total Carbs: 12g, Protein: 4g

Dill Mixed Fennel
Servings: 7 | Cooking Time: 3 Hour

Ingredients:
• 10 oz. fennel bulbs, diced
• 2 tbsp olive oil
• 1 tsp ground black pepper
• 1 tsp paprika
• 1 tsp cilantro
• 1 tsp oregano
• 1 tsp basil
• 3 tbsp white wine
• 1 tsp salt
• 2 garlic cloves
• 1 tsp dried dill

Directions:
1. Add fennel bulbs and all other ingredients to the Slow Cooker.
2. Put the cooker's lid on and set the cooking time to 3.5 hours on High settings.
3. Serve warm.

Nutrition Info:
• Per Serving: Calories: 53, Total Fat: 4.1g, Fiber: 2g, Total Carbs: 4g, Protein: 1g

Pumpkin Nutmeg Rice
Servings: 4 | Cooking Time: 5 Hours

Ingredients:
• 2 oz. olive oil
• 1 small yellow onion, chopped
• 2 garlic cloves, minced
• 12 oz. risotto rice
• 4 cups chicken stock
• 6 oz. pumpkin puree
• ½ tsp nutmeg, ground
• 1 tsp thyme, chopped
• ½ tsp ginger, grated
• ½ tsp cinnamon powder
• ½ tsp allspice, ground
• 4 oz. heavy cream

Directions:
1. Add rice, pumpkin puree, and all other ingredients except the cream to the Slow Cooker.
2. Put the cooker's lid on and set the cooking time to 4 hours 30 minutes on Low settings.
3. Stir in cream and cover again to the cook for 30 minutes on the low setting.
4. Serve warm.

Nutrition Info:
• Per Serving: Calories: 251, Total Fat: 4g, Fiber: 3g, Total Carbs: 30g, Protein: 5g

Cauliflower And Almonds Mix
Servings: 2 | Cooking Time: 3 Hours

Ingredients:
• 2 cups cauliflower florets
• 2 ounces tomato paste
• 1 small yellow onion, chopped
• 1 tablespoon chives, chopped
• Salt and black pepper to the taste
• 1 tablespoon almonds, sliced

Directions:
1. In your Slow Cooker, mix the cauliflower with the tomato paste and the other ingredients, toss, put the lid on and cook on High for 3 hours.
2. Divide between plates and serve as a side dish.

Nutrition Info:
• calories 177, fat 12, fiber 7, carbs 20, protein 7

Chapter 9 Soups & Stews Recipes

Chapter 9 Soups & Stews Recipes

Curried Turkey Soup

Servings: 8 | Cooking Time: 6 1/2 Hours

Ingredients:
- 2 tablespoons olive oil
- 1 1/2 pounds turkey breast, cubed
- 2 carrots, diced
- 1 sweet onion, chopped
- 1 celery stalk, sliced
- 2 garlic cloves, chopped
- 1 teaspoon grated ginger
- 1 cup coconut milk
- 3 cups chicken stock
- 1 cup water
- 1 tablespoon curry powder
- Salt and pepper to taste

Directions:
1. Heat the oil in a skillet and stir in the turkey. Cook on all sides for a few minutes until golden then transfer in your Slow Cooker.
2. Add the carrots, onion, celery, garlic, ginger, coconut milk, stock, water and curry powder.
3. Season with salt and pepper and cook on low settings for 6 hours.
4. Serve the soup warm.

Curried Lentil Soup

Servings: 8 | Cooking Time: 4 1/4 Hours

Ingredients:
- 4 bacon slices, chopped
- 1 sweet onion, chopped
- 2 garlic cloves, chopped
- 1 cup dried lentils, rinsed
- 1 carrot, diced
- 1 celery stalk, sliced
- 1 parsnip, diced
- 1 cup diced tomatoes
- 2 cups chicken stock
- 4 cups water
- 1 teaspoon curry powder
- 1/4 teaspoon ground ginger
- Salt and pepper to taste
- 1 lime, juiced
- 2 tablespoons chopped parsley

Directions:
1. Heat a skillet over medium flame and stir in the bacon. Cook for a few minutes until crisp.
2. Transfer the bacon in a Slow Cooker and stir in the onion, garlic, lentils, carrot, celery, parsnip, tomatoes, stock, water, curry powder and ginger.
3. Add salt and pepper to taste and cook on low settings for 4 hours.
4. When done, stir in the lime juice and chopped parsley and serve the soup warm or chilled.

Spiced Creamy Pumpkin Soup

Servings: 6 | Cooking Time: 5 1/4 Hours

Ingredients:
- 1 shallot, chopped
- 2 carrots, sliced
- 2 garlic cloves, chopped
- 2 tablespoons olive oil
- 1 medium sugar pumpkin, peeled and cubed
- 2 cups chicken stock
- 2 cups water
- 1 thyme sprig
- Salt and pepper to taste
- 1/2 cinnamon stick
- 1 star anise
- 1/2 teaspoon cumin powder
- 1/4 teaspoon chili powder

Directions:
1. Combine the shallot, carrots, garlic and olive oil in a skillet. Cook for 5 minutes until softened.
2. Transfer in your Slow Cooker and add the remaining ingredients, including the spices.
3. Cook on low settings for 5 hours then remove the cinnamon, thyme sprig and star anise and puree the soup with an immersion blender.
4. The soup can be served either warm or chilled.

Ginger And Sweet Potato Stew

Servings:3 | Cooking Time: 7 Hours

Ingredients:
- 1 cup sweet potatoes, chopped
- ½ teaspoon ground ginger
- 1 cup bell pepper, cut into the strips
- 1 apple, chopped
- 1 teaspoon ground cumin
- 2 cups beef broth

Directions:
1. Mix ingredients in the Slow Cooker.
2. Close the lid and cook the stew on Low for 7 hours.

Nutrition Info:
- Per Serving: 140 calories, 4.8g protein, 28.3g carbohydrates, 1.4g fat, 4.5g fiber, 0mg cholesterol, 516mg sodium, 716mg potassium.

Celery Stew

Servings:4 | Cooking Time: 6 Hours

Ingredients:
- 3 cups of water
- 1-pound beef stew meat, cubed
- 2 cups celery, chopped
- ½ cup cremini mushrooms, sliced
- 2 tablespoons sour cream
- 1 teaspoon smoked paprika
- 1 teaspoon cayenne pepper
- 1 tablespoon sesame oil

Directions:
1. Mix beef stew meat with cayenne pepper and put in the hot skillet.
2. Add sesame oil and roast the meat for 1 minute per side on high heat.
3. Transfer the meat in the Slow Cooker.
4. Add celery, cremini mushrooms, sour cream, smoked paprika, and water.
5. Close the lid and cook the stew on high for 6 hours.

Nutrition Info:
- Per Serving: 267 calories, 35.3g protein, 2.7g carbohydrates, 12g fat, 1.2g fiber, 104g cholesterol, 124mg sodium, 660mg potassium.

Summer Squash Chickpea Soup

Servings: 6 | Cooking Time: 2 1/2 Hours

Ingredients:
- 1 sweet onion, chopped
- 1 garlic clove, chopped
- 1 carrot, diced
- 1 celery stalk, sliced
- 2 summer squashes, cubed
- 1 can (15 oz.) chickpeas, drained
- 2 cups chicken stock
- 3 cups water
- 1 cup diced tomatoes
- 1 bay leaf
- 1 thyme sprig
- Salt and pepper to taste
- 1 lemon, juiced
- 1 tablespoon chopped cilantro
- 1 tablespoon chopped parsley

Directions:
1. Combine the onion, garlic, celery, carrot, summer squash, chickpeas, stock and water in your Slow Cooker.
2. Add the tomatoes, bay leaf, thyme, salt and pepper and cook on high settings for 2 hours.
3. When done, stir in the lemon juice, parsley and cilantro and serve the soup warm.

Snow Peas Soup

Servings:4 | Cooking Time: 3.5 Hours

Ingredients:
- 1 tablespoon chives, chopped
- 1 teaspoon ground ginger
- 8 oz salmon fillet, chopped
- 5 oz bamboo shoots, canned, chopped
- 2 cups snow peas
- 1 teaspoon hot sauce
- 5 cups of water

Directions:
1. Put bamboo shoots in the Slow Cooker.
2. Add ground ginger, salmon, snow peas, and water.
3. Close the lid and cook the soup for 3 hours on high.
4. Then add hot sauce and chives. Stir the soup carefully and cook for 30 minutes on high.

Nutrition Info:
- Per Serving: 120 calories, 14.6g protein, 7.9g carbohydrates, 3.8g fat, 3.1g fiber, 25mg cholesterol, 70mg sodium, 612mg potassium

Tomato And Turkey Chili

Servings:6 | Cooking Time: 7 Hours

Ingredients:
- 1-pound turkey fillet, chopped
- 2 cup tomatoes, chopped
- 1 jalapeno pepper, chopped
- 1 onion, diced
- 1 cup chicken stock

Directions:
1. Put turkey and tomatoes in the Slow Cooker.
2. Add jalapeno pepper, onion, and chicken stock.
3. Close the lid and cook the chili on low for 7 hours.

Nutrition Info:
- Per Serving: 164 calories, 22.7g protein, 4.3g carbohydrates, 5.8g fat, 1.2g fiber, 67mg cholesterol, 196mg sodium, 360mg potassium.

Ham And White Bean Soup

Servings: 8 | Cooking Time: 6 1/4 Hours

Ingredients:
- 2 tablespoons olive oil
- 1 sweet onion, chopped
- 1 garlic clove, chopped
- 1 yellow bell pepper, cored and diced
- 1 celery stalk, diced
- 1 cup diced ham
- 2 cans (15 oz.) white beans, drained
- 2 cups chicken stock
- 3 cups water
- Salt and pepper to taste
- 2 tablespoons chopped parsley

Directions:
1. Heat the oil in a skillet and stir in the onion, garlic, celery and bell pepper. Sauté for 5 minutes until softened and transfer in your Slow Cooker.
2. Add the ham, white beans, stock and water and season with salt and pepper.
3. Cook on low settings for 6 hours.
4. To serve, pour the soup into bowls and top with parsley. The soup can be served both warm and chilled.

Sweet Corn Chowder

Servings: 8 | Cooking Time: 6 1/4 Hours

Ingredients:
- 2 shallots, chopped
- 4 medium size potatoes, peeled and cubed1
- 1 celery stalk, sliced
- 1 can (15 oz.) sweet corn, drained
- 2 cups chicken stock
- 2 cups water
- Salt and pepper to taste

Directions:
1. Combine the shallot, potatoes, celery, corn, stock and water in a Slow Cooker.
2. Add salt and pepper to taste and cook on low settings for 6 hours.
3. When done, remove a few tablespoons of corn from the pot then puree the remaining soup in the pot.
4. Pour the soup into serving bowls and top with the reserved corn.
5. Serve warm.

Swedish Split Pea Soup

Servings: 8 | Cooking Time: 6 1/4 Hours

Ingredients:
- 2 cups yellow split peas, rinsed
- 4 cups chicken stock
- 4 cups water
- 1 large sweet onion, chopped
- 2 carrots, diced
- 1 celery stalk, diced
- 2 cups diced ham
- 1/2 teaspoon dried oregano
- 1/2 teaspoon dried marjoram
- Salt and pepper to taste

Directions:
1. Combine the split peas, stock, water, onion, carrots and celery stalk in your Slow Cooker.
2. Add the ham, herbs, salt and pepper and cook on low settings for 6 hours.
3. Serve the soup warm.

Creamy Carrot Lentil Soup

Servings: 6 | Cooking Time: 2 1/4 Hours

Ingredients:
- 2 tablespoons olive oil
- 4 carrots, sliced
- 1 shallot, chopped
- 1 small fennel bulb, sliced
- 1/2 cup red lentils
- 2 cups chicken stock
- 2 cups water
- 1/4 teaspoon cumin powder
- Salt and pepper to taste
- 1 thyme sprig
- 1 rosemary sprig

Directions:
1. Heat the oil in a skillet and add the shallot and carrots. Sauté for 5 minutes then transfer the mixture in your Slow Cooker.
2. Add the remaining ingredients and cook on high settings for 2 hours.

3. When done, remove the thyme and rosemary and puree the soup with an immersion blender.
4. Serve the soup warm.

Lasagna Soup

Servings: 8 | Cooking Time: 8 1/2 Hours

Ingredients:
- 1 pound ground beef
- 2 tablespoons olive oil
- 1 large sweet onion, chopped
- 2 garlic cloves, chopped
- 1 teaspoon dried oregano
- 1 1/2 cups tomato sauce
- 1 cup diced tomatoes
- 2 cups beef stock
- 6 cups water
- 1 1/2 cups uncooked pasta shells
- Salt and pepper to taste
- Grated Cheddar for serving

Directions:
1. Heat the oil in a skillet and add the ground beef. Cook for 5 minutes then transfer in your Slow Cooker.
2. Add the remaining ingredients and season with salt and pepper.
3. Cook on low settings for 8 hours.
4. When done, pour into serving bowls and top with cheese.
5. Serve the soup warm and fresh.

Beans Stew

Servings:3 | Cooking Time: 5 Hours

Ingredients:
- ½ cup sweet pepper, chopped
- ¼ cup onion, chopped
- 1 cup edamame beans
- 1 cup tomatoes
- 1 teaspoon cayenne pepper
- 5 cups of water
- 2 tablespoons cream cheese

Directions:
1. Mix water with cream cheese and pour the liquid in the Slow Cooker.
2. Add cayenne pepper, edamame beans, and onion.
3. Then chop the tomatoes roughly and add in the Slow Cooker.
4. Close the lid and cook the stew on high for 5 hours.

Nutrition Info:
- Per Serving: 74 calories, 3.4g protein, 7.9g carbohydrates, 3.6g fat, 2.4g fiber, 7mg cholesterol, 109mg sodium, 218mg potassium.

Creamy White Bean Soup

Servings: 6 | Cooking Time: 4 1/4 Hours

Ingredients:
- 1 tablespoon olive oil
- 1 sweet onion, chopped
- 2 garlic cloves, chopped
- 1/2 celery root, peeled and cubed
- 1 parsnip, diced
- 1 can (15 oz.) white beans, drained
- 2 cups chicken stock
- 3 cups water
- 1/2 teaspoon dried thyme

• Salt and pepper to taste

Directions:
1. Heat the oil in a skillet and stir in the onion, garlic, celery and parsnip. Cook for 5 minutes until softened then transfer the mix in your Slow Cooker.
2. Add the rest of the ingredients and cook on low settings for 4 hours.
3. When done, puree the soup with an immersion blender and pulse until smooth and creamy.
4. Serve the soup warm and fresh.

Herbed Spinach Lentil Soup

Servings: 8 | Cooking Time: 3 1/4 Hours

Ingredients:
• 1 cup green lentils, rinsed
• 1 celery stalk, sliced
• 1 carrot, sliced
• 1 sweet onion, chopped
• 2 sweet potatoes, peeled and cubed
• 2 cups chicken stock
• 6 cups water
• 1 bay leaf
• 1 thyme sprig
• Salt and pepper to taste
• 4 cups fresh spinach, shredded

Directions:
1. Combine the lentils, celery, carrot, onion, potatoes, stock and water in your Slow Cooker.
2. Add the bay leaf and thyme and season with salt and pepper.
3. Cook on high settings for 2 hours then add the spinach and cook one more hour.
4. Serve the soup warm or chilled.

Lamb Stew

Servings:5 | Cooking Time: 5 Hours

Ingredients:
• 1 pound lamb meat, cubed
• 1 red onion, sliced
• 1 teaspoon cayenne pepper
• 1 teaspoon dried rosemary
• ½ teaspoon dried thyme
• 1 cup potatoes, chopped
• 4 cups of water

Directions:
1. Sprinkle the lamb meat with cayenne pepper, dried rosemary, and dried thyme.
2. Transfer the meat in the Slow Cooker.
3. Add water, onion, and potatoes.
4. Close the lid and cook the stew on high for 5 hours.

Nutrition Info:
• Per Serving: 216 calories, 17.7g protein, 7.2g carbohydrates, 12.2g fat, 1.4g fiber, 64mg cholesterol, 73mg sodium, 166mg potassium.

Chicken Sausage Rice Soup

Servings: 6 | Cooking Time: 6 1/4 Hours

Ingredients:
• 2 fresh chicken sausages, sliced
• 1 shallot, chopped
• 1 carrot, sliced
• 1 celery stalk, sliced
• 1 yellow bell pepper, cored and diced
• 1 cup diced tomatoes
• 2 large potatoes, peeled and cubed
• 1/4 cup jasmine rice
• 2 cups chicken stock
• 4 cups water
• Salt and pepper to taste

Directions:
1. Combine the chicken, shallot and the rest of the ingredients in your Slow Cooker.
2. Add salt and pepper to taste and cook on low settings for 6 hours.
3. The soup is best served warm.

Kale Potato Soup

Servings: 6 | Cooking Time: 2 1/4 Hours

Ingredients:
• 1 shallot, chopped
• 1 garlic clove, chopped
• 1 celery stalk, sliced
• 2 carrots, sliced
• 1 1/2 pounds potatoes, peeled and cubed
• 1/2 cup diced tomatoes
• 1/4 pound kale, chopped
• 2 cups chicken stock
• 4 cups water
• Salt and pepper to taste
• 1/4 teaspoon chili flakes
• 2 tablespoons lemon juice

Directions:
1. Combine the shallot, garlic, celery, carrots, potatoes and tomatoes in your Slow Cooker.
2. Add the kale, chili flakes, lemon juice, water and stock and season with salt and pepper.
3. Cook on high settings for 2 hours.
4. Serve the soup warm.

Cheesy Broccoli Soup

Servings: 8 | Cooking Time: 4 1/4 Hours

Ingredients:
• 1 shallot, chopped
• 2 garlic cloves, chopped
• 2 tablespoons olive oil
• 1 head broccoli, cut into florets
• 1 large potato, peeled and cubed
• 1 can condensed chicken soup
• 2 cups water1/2 teaspoon dried oregano
• 1 cup grated Cheddar soup
• Salt and pepper to taste

Directions:
1. Heat the olive oil in a skillet and stir in the shallot and garlic. Cook for 2 minutes until softened.
2. Transfer the shallot and garlic in your Slow Cooker and add

the remaining ingredients.
3. Cook on low settings for 4 hours then puree the soup with an immersion blender.
4. Serve the soup warm.

Meatball Soup

Servings: 8 | Cooking Time: 6 1/2 Hours

Ingredients:
- 1 pound ground pork
- 1/4 cup white rice
- 1/2 teaspoon dried oregano
- 1/2 teaspoon dried basil
- Salt and pepper to taste
- 1 sweet onion, chopped
- 2 celery stalk, sliced
- 1 carrot, sliced
- 1 fennel bulb, sliced
- 1 cup diced tomatoes
- 2 cups chicken stock
- 4 cups water
- Salt and pepper to taste

Directions:
1. Mix the pork, rice, oregano, basil, salt and pepper in a bowl.
2. Combine the onion, celery stalk, carrot, fennel, tomatoes, stock and water in your Slow Cooker.
3. Adjust the taste with salt and pepper then form small meatballs and place them in the Slow Cooker.
4. Cook on low settings for 6 hours.
5. Serve the soup warm.

Yogurt Soup

Servings:4 | Cooking Time: 5 Hours

Ingredients:
- 1 cup Greek yogurt
- ½ teaspoon dried mint
- ½ teaspoon ground black pepper
- 1 onion, diced
- 1 tablespoon coconut oil
- 3 cups chicken stock
- 7 oz chicken fillet, chopped

Directions:
1. Melt the coconut oil in the skillet.
2. Add onion and roast it until light brown.
3. After this, transfer the roasted onion in the Slow Cooker.
4. Add dried mint, ground black pepper, chicken stock, and chicken fillet.
5. Add Greek yogurt and carefully mix the soup ingredients.
6. Close the lid and cook the soup on High for 5 hours.

Nutrition Info:
- Per Serving: 180 calories, 20.2g protein, 5.3g carbohydrates, 8.6g fat, 0.7g fiber, 47mg cholesterol, 633mg sodium, 247mg potassium.

Three Cheese Broccoli Soup

Servings: 6 | Cooking Time: 2 1/2 Hours

Ingredients:
- 2 tablespoons butter
- 1 sweet onion, chopped
- 1 garlic clove, chopped
- 1 tablespoon all-purpose flour
- 1 1/2 cups evaporated milk
- 4 cups chicken stock
- 10 oz. broccoli florets
- Salt and pepper to taste
- 1 cup grated Cheddar cheese
- 1 cup grated Monterey Jack
- 1/2 cup grated Parmesan

Directions:
1. Heat the butter in a skillet and stir in the onion and garlic. Sauté for 2 minutes until softened then add the flour and cook 1 additional minute.
2. Transfer the mixture in your Slow Cooker and add the milk, stock, broccoli and cheeses.
3. Season with salt and pepper if needed and cook on high settings for 2 hours.
4. Serve the soup warm.

Okra Vegetable Soup

Servings: 8 | Cooking Time: 7 1/4 Hours

Ingredients:
- 1 pound ground beef
- 2 tablespoons canola oil
- 2 shallots, chopped
- 1 carrot, sliced
- 1 can fire roasted tomatoes, chopped
- 2 cups chopped okra
- 1/2 cup green peas
- 2 potatoes, peeled and cubed
- 1/2 cup sweet corn, drained
- Salt and pepper to taste
- 2 cups water
- 2 cups chicken stock
- 1 lemon, juiced

Directions:
1. Heat the oil in a skillet and stir in the beef. Cook for a few minutes then transfer the meat in your Slow Cooker.
2. Add the shallots, carrot, tomatoes, okra, peas, potatoes, corn, water and stock, as well as lemon juice, salt and pepper.
3. Cook the soup on low settings for 7 hours.
4. Serve the soup warm and fresh.

Rabbit Stew

Servings: 5 | Cooking Time: 8 Hours 15 Minutes

Ingredients:
- ½ cup celery, diced
- 1 sausage, cubed
- 1 bay leaf
- 1 garlic clove, diced
- 1 cup Swiss chards, stalks
- ½ can water chestnuts, diced
- 1 piece of bacon
- ½ cup apple cider vinegar
- 3 cups chicken broth

- ½ cup olive oil
- 1 pound rabbit, cubed
- Salt and black pepper, to taste

Directions:
1. Marinate rabbit in olive oil and apple cider vinegar and keep aside overnight.
2. Put chicken broth in the slow cooker and warm it up.
3. Meanwhile, sear bacon and sausage in a pan and transfer it to the slow cooker.
4. Stir in rest of the ingredients and cover the lid.
5. Cook on LOW for about 8 hours and dish out to serve hot.

Nutrition Info:
- Calories: 418 Fat: 30.7g Carbohydrates: 2.7g

Tuscan White Bean Soup
Servings: 6 | Cooking Time: 6 1/2 Hours

Ingredients:
- 1 cup dried white beans
- 2 cups chicken stock
- 4 cups water
- 1 carrot, diced
- 1 celery stalk, diced
- 4 garlic cloves, chopped
- 2 tablespoons tomato paste
- 1 bay leaf
- 2 cups spinach, shredded
- Salt and pepper to taste
- 1 teaspoon dried oregano
- 1 teaspoon dried basil
- 1/2 lemon, juiced

Directions:
1. Combine the beans, stock, water, carrot, celery, garlic and tomato paste in your Slow Cooker.
2. Add the bay leaf, dried herbs and lemon juice, as well as salt and pepper.
3. Cook on low settings for 4 hours then add the spinach and cook for 2 additional hours on low settings.
4. Serve the soup warm or chilled.

Spinach Sweet Potato Soup
Servings: 6 | Cooking Time: 3 1/2 Hours

Ingredients:
- 1 shallot, chopped
- 1 garlic clove, chopped
- 1/2 pound ground chicken
- 2 tablespoons olive oil
- 2 medium size sweet potatoes, peeled and cubed
- 2 cups chicken stock
- 4 cups water
- Salt and pepper to taste
- 4 cups fresh spinach, shredded
- 1/2 teaspoon dried oregano
- 1/2 teaspoon dried basil
- 1 tablespoon chopped parsley

Directions:
1. Heat the oil in a skillet and add the ground chicken, shallot and garlic. Cook for about 5 minutes, stirring often.
2. Transfer the meat mix in your Slow Cooker and add the potatoes, stock, water, salt and pepper.
3. Cook on high settings for 2 hours then stir in the spinach, oregano, basil and parsley and cook one additional hour on high.
4. Serve the soup warm.

Lentil Stew
Servings:4 | Cooking Time: 6 Hours

Ingredients:
- 2 cups chicken stock
- ½ cup red lentils
- 1 eggplant, chopped
- 1 tablespoon tomato paste
- 1 cup of water
- 1 teaspoon Italian seasonings

Directions:
1. Mix chicken stock with red lentils and tomato paste.
2. Pour the mixture in the Slow Cooker.
3. Add eggplants and Italian seasonings.
4. Cook the stew on low for 6 hours.

Nutrition Info:
- Per Serving: 125 calories, 7.8g protein, 22.4g carbohydrates, 1.1g fat, 11.5g fiber, 1mg cholesterol, 392mg sodium, 540mg potassium.

Portobello Mushroom Soup
Servings: 6 | Cooking Time: 6 1/4 Hours

Ingredients:
- 4 Portobello mushrooms, sliced
- 1 shallot, chopped
- 2 garlic cloves, chopped
- 1 cup diced tomatoes
- 1 tablespoon tomato paste
- 2 cups chicken stock
- 1 can condensed cream of mushroom soup
- Salt and pepper to taste
- 1/2 teaspoon cumin seeds
- 1 tablespoon chopped parsley
- 1 tablespoon chopped cilantro

Directions:
1. Combine the mushrooms, shallot, garlic, tomatoes, tomato paste, stock and mushroom soup in your Slow Cooker.
2. Add the cumin seeds then season with salt and pepper.
3. Cook on low settings for 6 hours.
4. When done, stir in the chopped parsley and cilantro.
5. Serve the soup warm.

Cabbage Stew
Servings:2 | Cooking Time: 3 Hours

Ingredients:
- 2 cups white cabbage, shredded
- ½ cup tomato juice
- 1 teaspoon ground white pepper
- 1 cup cauliflower, chopped
- ½ cup potato, chopped
- 1 cup of water

Directions:
1. Put cabbage, potato, and cauliflower in the Slow Cooker.
2. Add tomato juice, ground white pepper, and water. Stir the stew ingredients and close the lid.
3. Cook the stew on high for 3 hours.

Nutrition Info:
- Per Serving: 57 calories, 2.8g protein, 13.3g carbohydrates, 0.2g fat, 3.9g fiber, 0mg cholesterol, 196mg sodium, 503mg potassium.

Butternut Squash Chili

Servings:4 | Cooking Time: 3.5 Hours

Ingredients:
- 1 cup butternut squash, chopped
- 2 tablespoons pumpkin puree
- ½ cup red kidney beans, canned
- 1 teaspoon smoked paprika
- ½ teaspoon chili flakes
- 1 tablespoon cocoa powder
- ½ teaspoon salt
- 2 cups chicken stock

Directions:
1. Mix cocoa powder with chicken stock and stir it until smooth.
2. Then pour the liquid in the Slow Cooker.
3. Add all remaining ingredients and carefully mix the chili.
4. Close the lid and cook the chili on high for 3.5 hours.

Nutrition Info:
- Per Serving: 105 calories, 6.3g protein, 20.2g carbohydrates, 0.8g fat, 5g fiber, 0mg cholesterol, 678mg sodium, 506mg potassium.

Beef Vegetable Soup

Servings: 8 | Cooking Time: 7 1/4 Hours

Ingredients:
- 1 pound beef roast, cubed
- 2 tablespoons canola oil
- 1 celery stalk, sliced
- 1 sweet onion, chopped
- 1 carrot, sliced
- 1 garlic clove, chopped
- 1/2 head cauliflower, cut into florets
- 2 large potatoes, peeled and cubed
- 1 cup diced tomatoes
- 1/2 teaspoon dried basil
- 2 cups beef stock
- 4 cups water
- Salt and pepper to taste

Directions:
1. Heat the oil in a skillet and add the beef. Cook on all sides for a few minutes then transfer the beef in your Slow Cooker.
2. Add the remaining ingredients and season with salt and pepper.
3. Cover and cook on low settings for 7 hours.
4. The soup is delicious either warm or chilled.

Crab Stew

Servings:4 | Cooking Time: 5 Hours

Ingredients:
- 8 oz crab meat, chopped
- ½ cup mango, chopped
- 1 teaspoon dried lemongrass
- 1 teaspoon ground turmeric
- 1 potato, peeled chopped
- 1 cup of water
- ½ cup of coconut milk

Directions:
1. Put all ingredients in the Slow Cooker.
2. Gently stir them with the help of the spoon and close the lid.
3. Cook the stew on low for 5 hours.
4. Then leave the cooked stew for 10-15 minutes to rest.

Nutrition Info:

- Per Serving: 167 calories, 8.9g protein, 13.6g carbohydrates, 8.3g fat, 2.1g fiber, 30mg cholesterol, 364mg sodium, 310mg potassium.

Basil Tomato Soup

Servings: 6 | Cooking Time: 6 1/2 Hours

Ingredients:
- 2 tablespoons olive oil
- 2 red onions, sliced
- 1 teaspoon dried basil
- 1 1/2 pound fresh tomatoes, peeled and cubed
- 1 celery stalk, sliced
- 1/2 red chili, seeded and chopped
- 2 cups vegetable stock
- 2 cups water
- 1/2 cup half and half
- Salt and pepper to taste

Directions:
1. Heat the oil in a skillet and add the red onions. Cook on low heat for 10 minutes until softened.
2. Transfer in your Slow Cooker and add the remaining ingredients, except the half and half.
3. Season with salt and pepper and cook on low settings for 6 hours.
4. When done, puree the soup with an immersion blender, adding the half and half as well.
5. Serve the soup warm.

Cream Of Chicken Soup

Servings: 6 | Cooking Time: 7 1/2 Hours

Ingredients:
- 6 chicken thighs
- 6 cups water
- 1/4 cup all-purpose flour
- 1 cup chicken stock
- 1/4 teaspoon garlic powder
- 1 pinch chili flakes
- Salt and pepper to taste

Directions:
1. Combine the chicken with water and cook on low settings for 6 hours.
2. When done, remove the meat from the liquid and shred it off the bone.
3. Combine the flour with stock and mix well. Add the garlic powder and chili flakes and give it a good mix.
4. Pour this mixture over the liquid in the slow cooker.
5. Add the meat and cook for 1 additional hour on high settings.
6. Serve the soup warm and fresh.

Thick Green Lentil Soup

Servings: 8 | Cooking Time: 6 1/4 Hours

Ingredients:
- 1 cup dried green lentils, rinsed
- 1/2 cup red lentils, rinsed
- 2 cups chicken stock
- 4 cups water
- 1/2 teaspoon cumin powder
- 1/4 teaspoon chili powder
- 1/2 teaspoon dried oregano
- 1 celery stalk, chopped
- 1 shallot, chopped

- Salt and pepper to taste
- 2 tablespoons lemon juice
- 1 tablespoon chopped parsley

Directions:
1. Combine the lentils, stock, water, cumin powder, chili, oregano, celery and shallot in your Slow Cooker.
2. Add salt and pepper to taste and cook on low settings for 6 hours.
3. When done, stir in the lemon juice and parsley and serve right away.

Curried Prawn Soup

Servings: 6 | Cooking Time: 6 1/4 Hours

Ingredients:
- 2 tablespoons olive oil
- 2 shallots, chopped
- 1 carrot, sliced
- 1/2 head cauliflower, cut into florets
- 2 cups cherry tomatoes, halved
- 2 cups chicken stock
- 4 cups water
- 2 tablespoons lemon juice
- 1 tablespoon red curry paste
- Salt and pepper to taste
- 1 pound fresh shrimps, peeled and deveined

Directions:
1. Combine the olive oil, shallots, carrot, cauliflower and tomatoes in your Slow Cooker.
2. Add the stock, water, curry paste and lemon juice and season with salt and pepper.
3. Place the shrimps on top and cook on high settings for 2 hours.
4. Serve the soup warm.

Coconut Squash Soup

Servings: 6 | Cooking Time: 2 1/4 Hours

Ingredients:
- 1 tablespoon olive oil
- 1 shallot, chopped
- 1/2 teaspoon grated ginger
- 2 garlic cloves, minced
- 1 tablespoon curry paste
- 1 teaspoon brown sugar
- 1 teaspoon Worcestershire sauce
- 3 cups butternut squash cubes
- 2 cups chicken stock
- 2 cups water
- 1 cup coconut milk
- 1 tablespoon tomato paste
- Salt and pepper to taste

Directions:
1. Heat the oil in a skillet and stir in the shallot, garlic, ginger and curry paste. Sauté for 1 minute then transfer the mixture in your Slow Cooker.
2. Add the remaining ingredients and season with salt and pepper.
3. Cover with its lid and cook on high settings for 2 hours.
4. When done, puree the soup with an immersion blender until smooth.
5. Pour the soup into serving bowls and serve it warm.

Tuscan Kale And White Bean Soup

Servings: 8 | Cooking Time: 8 1/2 Hours

Ingredients:
- 1 1/2 cups dried white beans, rinsed
- 1 sweet onion, chopped
- 2 carrots, diced
- 1 celery stalk, sliced
- 1 teaspoon dried oregano
- 2 cups chicken stock
- 6 cups water
- 1 bay leaf
- 1 teaspoon dried basil
- 1 bunch kale, shredded
- Salt and pepper to taste
- 1 lemon, juiced

Directions:
1. Combine the beans, onion, carrots, celery, dried herbs, stock and water in your Slow Cooker.
2. Add salt and pepper to taste and throw in the bay leaf as well.
3. Cook on low settings for 4 hours then add the kale and lemon juice and cook for 4 additional hours.
4. Serve the soup warm or chilled.

Orange Sweet Potato Soup

Servings: 8 | Cooking Time: 3 1/2 Hours

Ingredients:
- 2 tablespoons olive oil
- 1 shallot, chopped
- 2 carrots, sliced
- 1/2 celery stalk
- 2 large sweet potatoes, peeled and cubed
- 2 oranges, juiced
- 1 teaspoon orange zest
- 2 cups chicken stick
- 1 bay leaf
- 1/2 cinnamon stalk
- Salt and pepper to taste
- 1 teaspoon pumpkin seeds oil
- 2 tablespoons pumpkin seeds

Directions:
1. Heat the olive oil in a skillet and add the shallot and carrots. Sauté for 5 minutes then transfer in your Slow Cooker.
2. Add the celery stalk, potatoes, orange juice, orange zest, stock, bay leaf, cinnamon, salt and pepper.
3. Cook the soup on high settings for 2 hours then on low settings for 1 additional hour.
4. When done, remove the bay leaf and cinnamon stick and puree the soup with an immersion blender.
5. To serve, pour the soup into bowls and top with pumpkin seeds drizzle of pumpkin seed oil. Serve right away.

Southwestern Turkey Stew

Servings: 6 | Cooking Time: 7 Hours 15 Minutes

Ingredients:
- ½ cup red kidney beans
- ½ cup corn
- 2 cups diced canned tomatoes
- 15 oz ground turkey
- 1 cup red bell peppers, sliced
- ½ medium onion, diced
- ½ cup sour cream
- ½ cup cheddar cheese, shredded
- 1 garlic clove, minced
- 1½ medium red potatoes, cubed

Directions:
1. Put all the ingredients in a bowl except sour cream and cheddar cheese.
2. Transfer into the slow cooker and cook on LOW for about 7 hours.
3. Stir in the sour cream and cheddar cheese.
4. Dish out in a bowl and serve hot.

Nutrition Info:
- Calories: 332 Fat: 15.5g Carbohydrates: 17.1g Protein: 27.7g

Hungarian Goulash Soup

Servings: 8 | Cooking Time: 8 1/2 Hours

Ingredients:
- 2 sweet onions, chopped
- 1 pound beef roast, cubed
- 2 tablespoons canola oil
- 2 carrots, diced
- 1/2 celery stalk, diced
- 2 red bell peppers, cored and diced
- 1 1/2 pounds potatoes, peeled and cubed
- 2 tablespoons tomato paste
- 1 cup diced tomatoes
- 1/2 cup beef stock
- 5 cups water
- 1/2 teaspoon cumin seeds
- 1/2 teaspoon smoked paprika
- Salt and pepper to taste

Directions:
1. Heat the oil in a skillet and stir in the beef. Cook for 5 minutes on all sides then stir in the onion. Sauté for 2 additional minutes then transfer in your Slow Cooker.
2. Add the remaining ingredients and season with salt and pepper.
3. Cook on low settings for 8 hours.
4. Serve the soup warm.

Moroccan Lamb Soup

Servings: 6 | Cooking Time: 7 1/2 Hours

Ingredients:
- 1 pound lamb shoulder
- 1 teaspoon turmeric powder
- 1/2 teaspoon cumin powder
- 1/2 teaspoon chili powder
- 2 tablespoons canola oil
- 2 cups chicken stock
- 3 cups water
- 1 cup fire roasted tomatoes
- 1 cup canned chickpeas, drained

- 1 thyme sprig
- 1/2 teaspoon dried sage
- 1/2 teaspoon dried oregano
- Salt and pepper to taste
- 1 lemon, juiced

Directions:
1. Sprinkle the lamb with salt, pepper, turmeric, cumin powder and chili powder.
2. Heat the oil in a skillet and add the lamb. Cook on all sides for a few minutes then transfer it in a Slow Cooker.
3. Add the remaining ingredients and season with salt and pepper.
4. Cook the soup on low settings for 7 hours.
5. Serve the soup warm.

Red Kidney Beans Soup

Servings:6 | Cooking Time: 5 Hours

Ingredients:
- 2 cups red kidney beans, canned
- 1 cup cauliflower, chopped
- 1 cup carrot, diced
- 1 teaspoon chili powder
- 1 teaspoon Italian seasonings
- 1 cup tomatoes, canned
- 4 cups chicken stock

Directions:
1. Put all ingredients except red kidney beans in the Slow Cooker.
2. Close the lid and cook the soup on High for 4 hours.
3. Then add red kidney beans and stir the soup carefully with the help of the spoon.
4. Close the lid and cook it on high for 1 hour more.

Nutrition Info:
- Per Serving: 234 calories, 15.1g protein, 42.3g carbohydrates, 1.4g fat, 10.7g fiber, 1mg cholesterol, 540mg sodium, 1032mg potassium.

Creamy Tortellini Soup

Servings: 6 | Cooking Time: 6 1/4 Hours

Ingredients:
- 1 shallot, chopped
- 1 garlic clove, chopped
- 1/2 pound mushrooms, sliced
- 1 can condensed cream of mushroom soup
- 2 cups chicken stock
- 1 cup water
- 1/2 teaspoon dried oregano
- 1/2 teaspoon dried basil
- 1 cup evaporated milk
- 7 oz. cheese tortellini
- Salt and pepper to taste

Directions:
1. Combine the shallot, garlic, mushrooms, cream of mushroom soup, stock, water, dried herbs and milk in your Slow Cooker.
2. Add the cheese tortellini and season with salt and pepper.
3. Cook on low settings for 6 hours.
4. Serve the soup warm.

Comforting Chicken Soup

Servings: 8 | Cooking Time: 8 1/2 Hours

Ingredients:

- 1 whole chicken, cut into pieces
- 2 carrots, cut into sticks
- 1 celery stalk, sliced
- 4 potatoes, peeled and cubed
- 8 cups water
- 6 oz. egg noodles
- 2 garlic cloves, chopped
- Salt and pepper to taste
- 1 whole onion
- 1 bay leaf

Directions:
1. Combine all the ingredients in your Slow Cooker.
2. Add salt and pepper to taste and cook on low settings for 8 hours.
3. Serve the soup warm.

Crock-pot Buffalo Chicken Soup

Servings: 5 | Cooking Time: 6 Hours

Ingredients:
- 3 medium chicken thighs, deboned, sliced
- 1 teaspoon garlic powder
- 1 teaspoon onion powder
- ½ teaspoon celery seed
- ¼ cup butter
- ½ cup Frank's hot sauce or to taste, depending on how hot you like it
- 3 cups beef broth
- 1 cup heavy cream
- 2 ounces cream cheese
- ¼ teaspoon Xanthan gum
- Salt and pepper to taste

Directions:
1. Cut up chicken into chunks and place in Crock-Pot. Add all the other ingredients except the cream cheese and Xanthan gum. Set to Crock-Pot on LOW for 6 hours and allow to cook completely. Once cooking is done, remove the chicken from pot and shred with fork. Add the cream cheese and Xanthan gum to Crock-Pot. Using an immersion blender, emulsify all the liquids together. Add chicken back to Crock-Pot and stir. Season with salt and pepper to taste. Serve hot.

Nutrition Info:
- Calories: 523.2, Total Fats: 44.2 g, Carbs: 3.4 g, Fiber: 0 g, Net Carbs: 3.4 g, Protein: 20.8 g

Garlicky Spinach Soup With Herbed Croutons

Servings: 6 | Cooking Time: 2 1/4 Hours

Ingredients:
- 1 pound fresh spinach, shredded
- 1/2 teaspoon dried oregano
- 1 shallot, chopped
- 4 garlic cloves, chopped
- 1/2 celery stalk, sliced
- 2 cups water
- 2 cups chicken stock
- Salt and pepper to taste
- 1 lemon, juiced
- 1/2 cup half and half
- 10 oz. one-day old bread, cubed
- 3 tablespoons olive oil
- 1 teaspoon dried basil

- 1 teaspoon dried marjoram

Directions:
1. Combine the spinach, oregano, shallot, garlic and celery in your Slow Cooker.
2. Add the water, stock and lemon juice, as well as salt and pepper to taste and cook on high settings for 2 hours.
3. While the soup is cooking, place the bread cubes in a large baking tray and drizzle with olive oil. Sprinkle with salt and pepper and cook in the preheated oven at 375F for 10-12 minutes until crispy and golden.
4. When the soup is done, puree it with an immersion blender, adding the half and half while doing so.
5. Serve the soup warm, topped with herbed croutons.

Vegetable Chickpea Soup

Servings: 6 | Cooking Time: 6 1/2 Hours

Ingredients:
- 2/3 cup dried chickpeas, rinsed
- 2 cups chicken stock
- 4 cups water
- 1 celery stalk, sliced
- 1 carrot, diced
- 1 shallot, chopped
- 2 ripe tomatoes, peeled and diced
- 1 red bell pepper, cored and diced
- 1 potato, peeled and diced
- 1 tablespoon lemon juice
- Salt and pepper to taste

Directions:
1. Combine all the ingredients in your Slow Cooker.
2. Add salt and pepper to taste and cook on low settings for 6 hours.
3. Serve the soup warm and fresh.

Beef Chili

Servings: 8 | Cooking Time: 3 Hours 15 Minutes

Ingredients:
- 29 ounces canned diced tomatoes, not drained
- 3 tablespoons chili powder
- 1 yellow onion, chopped
- 2 pounds lean ground beef
- ¼ cup tomato paste
- ½ cup saltine cracker crumbs, finely ground
- 1 jalapeno, minced
- 3 garlic cloves, minced
- 2 (16-ounce) cans red kidney beans, rinsed and drained
- 1 teaspoon Kosher salt
- 1 teaspoon ground cumin
- 1 teaspoon black pepper

Directions:
1. Cook onions and beef over medium high heat in a pot until brown.
2. Transfer to the slow cooker along with the rest of the ingredients.
3. Cover and cook on HIGH for about 3 hours and dish out to serve.

Nutrition Info:
- Calories: 638 Fat: 9.1g Carbohydrates: 78.9g

Chapter 10 Snack Recipes

Chapter 10 Snack Recipes

"pumpkin Pie" With Almond Meal

Servings: 8 (2.8 Ounces Per Serving)

Cooking Time: 3 Hours And 15 Minutes

Ingredients:
- 4 tablespoons coconut oil
- 1 ¾ cups almond meal
- 2 cups pure pumpkin
- 1 teaspoon pumpkin pie spice
- Natural sweetener of your choice, to taste
- 3 eggs
- ½ teaspoon of cloves, ground
- 1 ¼ teaspoon baking powder
- 1 ¼ teaspoon baking soda
- 1 teaspoon cinnamon, ground
- Sea salt to taste

Nutrition Info:
- Calories: 233.2, Total Fat: 17.36 g, Saturated Fat: 7.15 g, Cholesterol: 69.75 mg, Sodium: 354.61 mg, Potassium: 237.81 mg, Total Carbohydrates: 9.41 g, Sugar: 6.59 g, Protein: 6.6 g

Creamy Mushroom Bites

Servings: 10 | Cooking Time: 5 Hours

Ingredients:
- 7 oz. shiitake mushroom, chopped
- 2 eggs
- 1 tbsp cream cheese
- 3 tbsp panko bread crumbs
- 2 tbsp flour
- 1 tsp minced garlic
- 1 tsp salt
- ½ tsp chili flakes
- 1 tsp olive oil
- 1 tsp ground coriander
- ½ tsp nutmeg
- 1 tbsp almond flour
- 1 tsp butter, melted

Directions:
1. Toss the mushrooms with salt, chili flakes, olive oil, ground coriander, garlic, and nutmeg in a skillet.
2. Stir cook for 5 minutes approximately on medium heat.
3. Whisk eggs with flour, cream cheese, and bread crumbs in a suitable bowl.
4. Stir in sauteed mushrooms and butter then mix well.
5. Knead this mushroom dough and divide it into golf ball-sized balls.
6. Pour the oil from the skillet in the Slow Cooker.
7. Add the mushroom dough balls to the cooker.
8. Put the cooker's lid on and set the cooking time to 3 hours on High settings.
9. Flip the balls and cook for another 2 hours on high heat.
10. Serve.

Nutrition Info:
- Per Serving: Calories: 65, Total Fat: 3.5g, Fiber: 1g, Total Carbs: 6.01g, Protein: 3g

Jalapeno Chorizo Poppers

Servings: 4 | Cooking Time: 3 Hours

Ingredients:
- ½ lb. chorizo, chopped
- 10 jalapenos, tops cut off and deseeded
- 1 small white onion, chopped
- ½ lb. beef, ground
- ¼ tsp garlic powder
- 1 tbsp maple syrup
- 1 tbsp mustard
- 1/3 cup water

Directions:
1. Mix beef with onion, garlic powder, and chorizo in a bowl.
2. Divide this beef filling into the jalapenos.
3. Add water and stuffed jalapenos to the base of the Slow Cooker.
4. Put the cooker's lid on and set the cooking time to 3 hours on High settings.
5. Meanwhile, mix maple syrup with mustard in a bowl.
6. Serve the jalapeno popper with maple sauce on top.

Nutrition Info:
- Per Serving: Calories: 214, Total Fat: 2g, Fiber: 3g, Total Carbs: 8g, Protein: 3g

Jalapeno Salsa Snack

Servings: 6 | Cooking Time: 3 Hours

Ingredients:
- 10 Roma tomatoes, chopped
- 2 jalapenos, chopped
- 1 sweet onion, chopped
- 28 oz. canned plum tomatoes
- 3 garlic cloves, minced
- 1 bunch cilantro, chopped
- Salt and black pepper to the taste

Directions:
1. Add Roma tomatoes, onion, and all other ingredients to the Slow Cooker.
2. Put the cooker's lid on and set the cooking time to 3 hours on High settings.
3. Mix well and serve.

Nutrition Info:
- Per Serving: Calories: 162, Total Fat: 4g, Fiber: 6g, Total Carbs: 12g, Protein: 3g

Potato Onion Salsa

Servings: 6 | Cooking Time: 8 Hrs

Ingredients:
- 1 sweet onion, chopped
- ¼ cup white vinegar
- 2 tbsp mustard
- Salt and black pepper to the taste
- 1 and ½ lbs. gold potatoes, cut into medium cubes
- ¼ cup dill, chopped
- 1 cup celery, chopped
- Cooking spray

Directions:
1. Grease the base of the Slow Cooker with cooking spray.
2. Add onion, potatoes and all other ingredients to the cooker.
3. Put the cooker's lid on and set the cooking time to 8 hours on Low settings.
4. Mix well and serve.

Nutrition Info:
- Per Serving: Calories: 251, Total Fat: 6g, Fiber: 7g, Total Carbs: 12g, Protein: 7g

Peas Dip

Servings: 4 | Cooking Time: 5 Hours

Ingredients:
- 1 and ½ cups black-eyed peas
- 3 cups water
- 1 teaspoon Cajun seasoning
- ½ cup pecans, toasted
- ½ teaspoon garlic powder
- ½ teaspoon jalapeno powder
- Salt and black pepper to the taste
- ¼ teaspoon liquid smoke
- ½ teaspoon Tabasco sauce

Directions:
1. In your Slow Cooker, mix black-eyed pea with Cajun seasoning, salt, pepper and water, stir, cover and cook on High for 5 hours.
2. Drain, transfer to a blender, add pecans, garlic powder, jalapeno powder, Tabasco sauce, liquid smoke, more salt and pepper, pulse well and serve.

Nutrition Info:
- calories 221, fat 4, fiber 7, carbs 16, protein 4

Bulgur And Beans Salsa

Servings: 2 | Cooking Time: 8 Hours

Ingredients:
- 1 cup veggie stock
- ½ cup bulgur
- 1 small yellow onion, chopped
- 1 red bell pepper, chopped
- 1 garlic clove, minced
- 5 ounces canned kidney beans, drained
- ½ cup salsa
- 1 tablespoon chili powder
- ¼ teaspoon oregano, dried
- Salt and black pepper to the taste

Directions:
1. In your Slow Cooker, mix the bulgur with the stock and the other ingredients, toss, put the lid on and cook on Low for 8 hours.

2. Divide into bowls and serve cold as an appetizer.

Nutrition Info:
- calories 351, fat 4, fiber 6, carbs 12, protein 4

Spinach Dip

Servings: 2 | Cooking Time: 1 Hour

Ingredients:
- 2 tablespoons heavy cream
- ½ cup Greek yogurt
- ½ pound baby spinach
- 2 garlic cloves, minced
- Salt and black pepper to the taste

Directions:
1. In your Slow Cooker, mix the spinach with the cream and the other ingredients, toss, put the lid on and cook on High for 1 hour.
2. Blend using an immersion blender, divide into bowls and serve as a party dip.

Nutrition Info:
- calories 221, fat 5, fiber 7, carbs 12, protein 5

Eggplant Salsa

Servings: 2 | Cooking Time: 4 Hours

Ingredients:
- 1 cup cherry tomatoes, cubed
- 2 cups eggplant, cubed
- 1 tablespoon capers, drained
- 1 tablespoon black olives, pitted and sliced
- 1 tablespoon lemon juice
- 1 tablespoon olive oil
- ¼ cup mild salsa
- 2 teaspoons balsamic vinegar
- 1 tablespoon basil, chopped
- 1 tablespoon chives, chopped
- Salt and black pepper to the taste

Directions:
1. In your Slow Cooker, mix the eggplant with the cherry tomatoes, capers, olives and the other ingredients, toss, put the lid on and cook on High for 4 hours.
2. Divide salsa into small bowls and serve.

Nutrition Info:
- calories 200, fat 6, fiber 5, carbs 9, protein 2

Spaghetti Squash

Servings: 6 (6.8 Ounces)

Cooking Time: 6 Hours

Ingredients:
- 1 spaghetti squash (vegetable spaghetti)
- 4 tablespoon olive oil
- 1 ¾ cups water
- Sea salt

Directions:
1. Slice the squash in half lengthwise and scoop out the seeds. Drizzle the halves with olive oil and season with sea salt. Place the squash in Crock-Pot and add the water. Close the lid and cook on LOW for 4-6 hours. Remove the squash and allow it to cool for about 30 minutes. Use a fork to scrape out spaghetti squash.

Nutrition Info:
- Calories: 130.59, Total Fat: 9.11 g, Saturated Fat: 1.27 g, Cholesterol: 0 mg, Sodium: 6.79 mg, Potassium: 399.95 mg, To-

tal Carbohydrates: 13.26 g, Fiber: 2.27 g, Sugar: 2.49 g, Protein: 1.13 g

Chickpeas Spread

Servings: 2 | Cooking Time: 8 Hours

Ingredients:
- ½ cup chickpeas, dried
- 1 tablespoons olive oil
- 1 tablespoon lemon juice
- 1 cup veggie stock
- 1 tablespoon tahini
- A pinch of salt and black pepper
- 1 garlic clove, minced
- ½ tablespoon chives, chopped

Directions:
1. In your Slow Cooker, combine the chickpeas with the stock, salt, pepper and the garlic, stir, put the lid on and cook on Low for 8 hours.
2. Drain chickpeas, transfer them to a blender, add the rest of the ingredients, pulse well, divide into bowls and serve as a party spread.

Nutrition Info:
- calories 211, fat 6, fiber 7, carbs 8, protein 4

Cashew Dip

Servings: 10 | Cooking Time: 3 Hours

Ingredients:
- 1 cup water
- 1 cup cashews
- 10 ounces hummus
- ¼ teaspoon garlic powder
- ¼ teaspoon onion powder
- A pinch of salt and black pepper
- ¼ teaspoon mustard powder
- 1 teaspoon apple cider vinegar

Directions:
1. In your Slow Cooker, mix water with cashews, salt and pepper, stir, cover and cook on High for 3 hours.
2. Transfer to your blender, add hummus, garlic powder, onion powder, mustard powder and vinegar, pulse well, divide into bowls and serve.

Nutrition Info:
- calories 192, fat 7, fiber 7, carbs 12, protein 4

Garlicky Bacon Slices

Servings: 9 | Cooking Time: 4 Hrs

Ingredients:
- 10 oz. Canadian bacon, sliced
- 2 tbsp garlic powder
- 2 garlic cloves, peeled and sliced
- 2 tbsp whipped cream
- 1 tsp dried dill
- 1 tsp chili flakes
- ½ tsp salt

Directions:
1. Season the bacon with garlic powder and spread it in the Slow Cooker.
2. Whisk the cream with garlic, dill, salt, and chili flakes in a bowl.
3. Spread this cream mixture over the bacon strips and leave for

10 minutes.
4. Put the cooker's lid on and set the cooking time to 3 hours on High settings.
5. Flip the bacon slices and remove excess liquid out of the cooker.
6. Put the cooker's lid on and set the cooking time to 1 hour on High settings.
7. Serve.

Nutrition Info:
- Per Serving: Calories: 51, Total Fat: 1.6g, Fiber: 0g, Total Carbs: 2.59g, Protein: 7g

Chickpeas Salsa

Servings: 2 | Cooking Time: 6 Hours

Ingredients:
- 1 cup canned chickpeas, drained
- 1 cup veggie stock
- ½ cup black olives, pitted and halved
- 1 small yellow onion, chopped
- ¼ tablespoon ginger, grated
- 4 garlic cloves, minced
- ¼ tablespoons coriander, ground
- ¼ tablespoons red chili powder
- ¼ tablespoons garam masala
- 1 tablespoon lemon juice

Directions:
1. In your Slow Cooker, mix the chickpeas with the stock, olives and the other ingredients, toss, put the lid on and cook on Low for 6 hours.
2. Divide into bowls and serve as an appetizer.

Nutrition Info:
- calories 355, fat 5, fiber 14, carbs 16, protein 11

Cheeseburger Cream Dip

Servings: 10 | Cooking Time: 3 Hours

Ingredients:
- 1 lb. beef, ground
- 1 tsp garlic powder
- Salt and black pepper to the taste
- 2 tbsp Worcestershire sauce
- 8 bacon strips, chopped
- 3 garlic cloves, minced
- 1 yellow onion, chopped
- 12 oz. cream cheese, soft
- 1 cup sour cream
- 2 tbsp ketchup
- 2 tbsp mustard
- 10 oz. canned tomatoes and chilies, chopped
- 1 and ½ cup cheddar cheese, shredded
- 1 cup mozzarella, shredded

Directions:
1. Add beef, Worcestershire sauce and all other ingredients to the Slow Cooker.
2. Put the cooker's lid on and set the cooking time to 3 hours on Low settings.
3. Serve fresh.

Nutrition Info:
- Per Serving: Calories: 251, Total Fat: 5g, Fiber: 8g, Total Carbs: 16g, Protein: 4g

Calamari Rings Bowls

Servings: 2 | Cooking Time: 6 Hours

Ingredients:
- ½ pound calamari rings
- 1 tablespoon balsamic vinegar
- ½ tablespoon soy sauce
- 1 tablespoon sugar
- 1 cup veggie stock
- ½ teaspoon turmeric powder
- ½ teaspoon sweet paprika
- ½ cup chicken stock

Directions:
1. In your Slow Cooker, mix the calamari rings with the vinegar, soy sauce and the other ingredients, toss, put the lid on and cook on High for 6 hours.
2. Divide into bowls and serve right away as an appetizer.

Nutrition Info:
- calories 230, fat 2, fiber 4, carbs 7, protein 5

Crab Dip

Servings: 6 | Cooking Time: 2 Hours

Ingredients:
- 12 ounces cream cheese
- ½ cup parmesan, grated
- ½ cup mayonnaise
- ½ cup green onions, chopped
- 2 garlic cloves, minced
- Juice of 1 lemon
- 1 and ½ tablespoon Worcestershire sauce
- 1 and ½ teaspoons old bay seasoning
- 12 ounces crabmeat

Directions:
1. In your Slow Cooker, mix cream cheese with parmesan, mayo, green onions, garlic, lemon juice, Worcestershire sauce, old bay seasoning and crabmeat, stir, cover and cook on Low for 2 hours.
2. Divide into bowls and serve as a dip.

Nutrition Info:
- calories 200, fat 4, fiber 6, carbs 12, protein 3

Turkey Meatballs

Servings: 2 | Cooking Time: 7 Hours

Ingredients:
- 1 pound turkey breast, skinless, boneless and ground
- 1 egg, whisked
- 6 ounces canned tomato puree
- 2 tablespoons parsley, chopped
- 1 tablespoon oregano, chopped
- 1 garlic clove, minced
- 1 small yellow onion, chopped
- Salt and black pepper to the taste

Directions:
1. In a bowl, mix the meat with the egg, parsley and the other ingredients except the tomato puree, stir well and shape medium meatballs out of it.
2. Put the meatballs in the Slow Cooker, add the tomato puree, put the lid on and cook on Low for 7 hours
3. Arrange the meatballs on a platter and serve as an appetizer.

Nutrition Info:
- calories 170, fat 5, fiber 3, carbs 10, protein 7

Mussels Salad

Servings: 4 | Cooking Time: 1 Hour

Ingredients:
- 2 pounds mussels, cleaned and scrubbed
- 1 radicchio, cut into thin strips
- 1 white onion, chopped
- 1 pound baby spinach
- ½ cup dry white wine
- 1 garlic clove, crushed
- ½ cup water
- A drizzle of olive oil

Directions:
1. Divide baby spinach and radicchio in salad bowls and leave aside for now.
2. In your Slow Cooker, mix mussels with onion, wine, garlic, water and oil, toss, cover and cook on High for 1 hour.
3. Divide mussels on top of spinach and radicchio, add cooking liquid all over and serve.

Nutrition Info:
- calories 59, fat 4, fiber 1, carbs 1, protein 1

Almond Buns

Servings: 6 (1.9 Ounces Per Serving)

Cooking Time: 20 Minutes

Ingredients:
- 3 cups almond flour
- 5 tablespoons butter
- 1 ½ teaspoons sweetener of your choice (optional)
- 2 eggs
- 1 ½ teaspoons baking powder

Directions:
1. In a mixing bowl, combine the dry ingredients. In another bowl, whisk the eggs. Add melted butter to mixture and mix well. Divide almond mixture equally into 6 parts. Grease the bottom of Crock-Pot and place in 6 almond buns. Cover and cook on HIGH for 2 to 2 ½ hours or LOW for 4 to 4 ½ hours. Serve hot.

Nutrition Info:
- Calories: 219.35, Total Fat: 20.7 g, Saturated Fat: 7.32 g, Cholesterol: 87.44 mg, Sodium: 150.31 mg, Potassium: 145.55 mg, Total Carbohydrates: 4.59 g, Fiber: 1.8 g, Sugar: 1.6 g, Protein: 6.09 g

Queso Dip

Servings: 10 | Cooking Time: 1 Hour

Ingredients:
- 16 ounces Velveeta
- 1 cup whole milk
- ½ cup cotija
- 2 jalapenos, chopped
- 2 teaspoons sweet paprika
- 2 garlic cloves, minced
- A pinch of cayenne pepper
- 1 tablespoon cilantro, chopped

Directions:
1. In your Slow Cooker, mix Velveeta with milk, cotija, jalapenos, paprika, garlic and cayenne, stir, cover and cook on High for 1 hour.
2. Stir the dip, add cilantro, divide into bowls and serve as a dip.

Nutrition Info:
- calories 233, fat 4, fiber 7, carbs 10, protein 4

Dill Potato Salad

Servings: 2 | Cooking Time: 8 Hours

Ingredients:
- 1 red onion, sliced
- 1 pound gold potatoes, peeled and roughly cubed
- 2 tablespoons balsamic vinegar
- ½ cup heavy cream
- 1 tablespoons mustard
- A pinch of salt and black pepper
- 1 tablespoon dill, chopped
- ½ cup celery, chopped

Directions:
1. In your Slow Cooker, mix the potatoes with the cream, mustard and the other ingredients, toss, put the lid on and cook on Low for 8 hours.
2. Divide salad into bowls, and serve as an appetizer.

Nutrition Info:
- calories 251, fat 6, fiber 7, carbs 8, protein 7

Rice Snack Bowls

Servings: 2 | Cooking Time: 6 Hours

Ingredients:
- ½ cup wild rice
- 1 red onion, sliced
- ½ cup brown rice
- 2 cups veggie stock
- ½ cup baby spinach
- ½ cup cherry tomatoes, halved
- 2 tablespoons pine nuts, toasted
- 1 tablespoon raisins
- 1 tablespoon chives, chopped
- 1 tablespoon dill, chopped
- ½ tablespoon olive oil
- A pinch of salt and black pepper

Directions:
1. In your Slow Cooker, mix the rice with the onion, stock and the other ingredients, toss, put the lid on and cook on Low for 6 hours.
2. Divide in to bowls and serve as a snack.

Nutrition Info:
- calories 301, fat 6, fiber 6, carbs 12, protein 3

Cheese Stuffed Meat Balls

Servings: 9 | Cooking Time: 9 Hours

Ingredients:
- 10 oz. ground pork
- 1 tbsp minced garlic
- 1 tsp ground black pepper
- 1 tsp salt
- 1 tsp paprika
- 1 tsp oregano
- 6 oz. Romano cheese, cut into cubes
- 1 cup panko bread crumbs
- 1 tsp chili flakes
- 1 egg
- 2 tsp milk
- 1 tsp olive oil

Directions:
1. Mix ground pork with oregano, chili flakes, paprika, salt, garlic, and black pepper in a bowl.
2. Stir in beaten egg and milk, then mix well with your hands.
3. Make golf ball-sized meatballs out of this beef mixture and insert one cheese cubes into each ball.
4. Roll each meatball in the bread crumbs to coat well.
5. Place these cheese-stuffed meatballs in the Slow Cooker.
6. Put the cooker's lid on and set the cooking time to 9 hours on Low settings.
7. Serve warm.

Nutrition Info:
- Per Serving: Calories: 167, Total Fat: 9.2g, Fiber: 0g, Total Carbs: 3.92g, Protein: 17g

Artichoke Dip

Servings: 6 | Cooking Time: 2 Hours

Ingredients:
- 10 ounces spinach
- 30 ounces canned artichoke hearts
- 5 ounces boursin
- 1 and ½ cup cheddar cheese, shredded
- ½ cup parmesan, grated
- 2 garlic cloves, minced
- 1 teaspoon red pepper flakes, crushed
- A pinch of salt

Directions:
1. In your Slow Cooker mix spinach with artichokes, boursin, cheddar, parmesan, garlic, pepper flakes and salt, stir, cover and cook on High for 1 hour.
2. Stir the dip, cover and cook on Low for 1 more hour.
3. Divide into bowls and serve.

Nutrition Info:
- calories 251, fat 6, fiber 8, carbs 16, protein 5

Lasagna Dip

Servings: 10 | Cooking Time: 1 Hour

Ingredients:
- 8 ounces cream cheese
- ¾ cup parmesan, grated
- 1 and ½ cups ricotta
- ½ teaspoon red pepper flakes, crushed
- 2 garlic cloves, minced
- 3 cups marinara sauce
- 1 and ½ cups mozzarella, shredded
- 1 and ½ teaspoon oregano, chopped

Directions:
1. In your Slow Cooker, mix cream cheese with parmesan, ricotta, pepper flakes, garlic, marinara, mozzarella and oregano, stir, cover and cook on High for 1 hour.
2. Stir, divide into bowls and serve as a dip.

Nutrition Info:
- calories 231, fat 4, fiber 7, carbs 21, protein 5

Beer And Cheese Dip

Servings: 10 | Cooking Time: 1 Hour

Ingredients:
- 12 ounces cream cheese
- 6 ounces beer
- 4 cups cheddar cheese, shredded
- 1 tablespoon chives, chopped

Directions:
1. In your Slow Cooker, mix cream cheese with beer and cheddar, stir, cover and cook on Low for 1 hour.
2. Stir your dip, add chives, divide into bowls and serve.

Nutrition Info:
- calories 212, fat 4, fiber 7, carbs 16, protein 5

Pesto Pitta Pockets

Servings: 6 | Cooking Time: 4 Hrs

Ingredients:
- 6 pita bread
- 2 sweet peppers, deseeded and chopped
- 1 chili pepper, chopped
- 1 red onion, chopped
- 1 tsp salt
- 2 tbsp vinegar
- 1 tbsp olive oil
- 1 tbsp garlic, sliced
- 2 tbsp pesto

Directions:
1. Add sweet peppers and all other ingredients, except for pesto and pita bread to the Slow Cooker.
2. Put the cooker's lid on and set the cooking time to 4 hours on Low settings.
3. Layer the pocket of each pita bread with pesto.
4. Mix the cooked sweet peppers filling and divide in the pita bread pockets.
5. Serve.

Nutrition Info:
- Per Serving: Calories: 153, Total Fat: 6.1g, Fiber: 3g, Total Carbs: 22.42g, Protein: 4g

Fajita Chicken Dip

Servings: 6 | Cooking Time: 4 Hrs

Ingredients:
- 3 chicken breasts, skinless and boneless
- 8 oz. root beer
- 3 red bell peppers, chopped
- 1 yellow onion, chopped
- 8 oz. cream cheese
- 8 oz. pepper jack cheese, shredded
- 16 oz. sour cream
- 2 fajita seasoning mix packets
- 1 tbsp olive oil
- Salt and black pepper to the taste

Directions:
1. Add root beer, chicken and all other ingredients to the Slow Cooker.
2. Put the cooker's lid on and set the cooking time to 4 hours on High settings.
3. Shred the slow-cooked chicken with the help of two forks.
4. Mix well with its sauce and serve.

Nutrition Info:
- Per Serving: Calories: 261, Total Fat: 4g, Fiber: 6g, Total Carbs: 17g, Protein: 5g

Beef And Chipotle Dip

Servings: 10 | Cooking Time: 2 Hours

Ingredients:
- 8 ounces cream cheese, soft
- 2 tablespoons yellow onion, chopped
- 2 tablespoons mayonnaise
- 2 ounces hot pepper Monterey Jack cheese, shredded
- ¼ teaspoon garlic powder
- 2 chipotle chilies in adobo sauce, chopped
- 2 ounces dried beef, chopped
- ¼ cup pecans, chopped

Directions:
1. In your Slow Cooker, mix cream cheese with onion, mayo, Monterey Jack cheese, garlic powder, chilies and dried beef, stir, cover and cook on Low for 2 hours.
2. Add pecans, stir, divide into bowls and serve.

Nutrition Info:
- calories 130, fat 11, fiber 1, carbs 3, protein 4

Paprika Cod Sticks

Servings: 2 | Cooking Time: 2 Hours

Ingredients:
- 1 eggs whisked
- ½ pound cod fillets, cut into medium strips
- ½ cup almond flour
- ½ teaspoon cumin, ground
- ½ teaspoon coriander, ground
- ½ teaspoon turmeric powder
- A pinch of salt and black pepper
- ¼ teaspoon sweet paprika
- Cooking spray

Directions:
1. In a bowl, mix the flour with cumin, coriander and the other ingredients except the fish, eggs and cooking spray.
2. Put the egg in another bowl and whisk it.
3. Dip the fish sticks in the egg and then dredge them in the flour mix.
4. Grease the Slow Cooker with cooking spray, add fish sticks, put the lid on, cook on High for 2 hours, arrange on a platter and serve.

Nutrition Info:
- calories 200, fat 2, fiber 4, carbs 13, protein 12

Shrimp Salad

Servings: 2 | Cooking Time: 2 Hours

Ingredients:
- ½ pound shrimp, peeled and deveined
- 1 green bell pepper, chopped
- ½ cup kalamata olives, pitted and halved
- 4 spring onions, chopped
- 1 red bell pepper, chopped
- ½ cup mild salsa
- 1 tablespoon olive oil
- 1 garlic clove, minced
- ¼ teaspoon oregano, dried
- ¼ teaspoon basil, dried
- Salt and black pepper to the taste
- A pinch of red pepper, crushed
- 1 tablespoon parsley, chopped

Directions:
1. In your Slow Cooker, mix the shrimp with the peppers and the other ingredients, toss, put the lid on and cook on High for 2 hours.
2. Divide into bowls and serve as an appetizer.

Nutrition Info:
- calories 240, fat 2, fiber 5, carbs 7, protein 2

Lentils Hummus

Servings: 2 | Cooking Time: 4 Hours

Ingredients:
- 1 cup chicken stock
- 1 cup canned lentils, drained
- 2 tablespoons tahini paste
- ¼ teaspoon onion powder
- ¼ cup heavy cream
- A pinch of salt and black pepper
- ¼ teaspoon turmeric powder
- 1 teaspoon lemon juice

Directions:
1. In your Slow Cooker, mix the lentils with the stock, onion powder, salt and pepper, toss, put the lid on and cook on High for 4 hours.
2. Drain the lentils, transfer to your blender, add the rest of the ingredients, pulse well, divide into bowls and serve.

Nutrition Info:
- calories 192, fat 7, fiber 7, carbs 12, protein 4

Caramel Milk Dip

Servings: 4 | Cooking Time: 2 Hours

Ingredients:
- 1 cup butter
- 12 oz. condensed milk
- 2 cups brown sugar
- 1 cup of corn syrup

Directions:
1. Add butter, milk, corn syrup, and sugar to the Slow Cooker.
2. Put the cooker's lid on and set the cooking time to 2 hours on High settings.
3. Serve warm.

Nutrition Info:
- Per Serving: Calories: 172, Total Fat: 2g, Fiber: 6g, Total Carbs: 12g, Protein: 4g

Candied Pecans

Servings: 4 | Cooking Time: 3 Hours

Ingredients:
- 1 cup white sugar
- 1 and ½ tablespoons cinnamon powder
- ½ cup brown sugar
- 1 egg white, whisked
- 4 cups pecans
- 2 teaspoons vanilla extract
- ¼ cup water

Directions:
1. In a bowl, mix white sugar with cinnamon, brown sugar and vanilla and stir.
2. Dip pecans in egg white, then in sugar mix and put them in your Slow Cooker, also add the water, cover and cook on Low for 3 hours.
3. Divide into bowls and serve as a snack.

Nutrition Info:
- calories 152, fat 4, fiber 7, carbs 16, protein 6

Cheesy Mix

Servings: 24 | Cooking Time: 2 Hours

Ingredients:
- 2 cups small pretzels
- 2 cups wheat cereal
- 3 cups rice cereal
- 3 cups corn cereal
- 2 cups small cheese crackers
- 1/3 cup parmesan, grated
- 1/3 cup bacon flavor chips
- ½ cup melted butter
- 1/3 cup canola oil
- 1 ounce ranch dressing

Directions:
1. In your Slow Cooker, mix pretzels with wheat cereal, rice cereal, corn cereal, crackers, chips and parmesan, cover and cook on High for 2 hours stirring every 20 minutes.
2. In a bowl, mix butter with oil and ranch dressing and whisk well.
3. Divide the mix from the Slow Cooker into bowls and serve them with the ranch dressing on the side.

Nutrition Info:
- calories 182, fat 2, fiber 6, carbs 12, protein 4

Almond Bowls

Servings: 2 | Cooking Time: 4 Hours

Ingredients:
- 1 tablespoon cinnamon powder
- 1 cup sugar
- 2 cups almonds
- ½ cup water
- ½ teaspoons vanilla extract

Directions:
1. In your Slow Cooker, mix the almonds with the cinnamon and the other ingredients, toss, put the lid on and cook on Low for 4 hours.
2. Divide into bowls and serve as a snack.

Nutrition Info:
- calories 260, fat 3, fiber 4, carbs 12, protein 8

Bean Pesto Dip

Servings: 8 | Cooking Time: 6 Hrs

Ingredients:
- 10 oz. refried beans
- 1 tbsp pesto sauce
- 1 tsp salt
- 7 oz. Cheddar cheese, shredded
- 1 tsp paprika
- 1 cup of salsa
- 4 tbsp sour cream
- 2-oz. cream cheese
- 1 tsp dried dill

Directions:
1. Mix pesto with salt, salsa, sour cream, dill, beans, cheese, paprika, and cream cheese in the Slow Cooker.
2. Put the cooker's lid on and set the cooking time to 6 hours on Low settings.
3. Once Slow Cooker, blend the mixture using a hand blender.
4. Serve fresh.

Nutrition Info:
- Per Serving: Calories: 102, Total Fat: 6.3g, Fiber: 1g, Total Carbs: 7.43g, Protein: 5g

Almond Spread

Servings: 2 | Cooking Time: 8 Hours

Ingredients:
- ¼ cup almonds
- 1 cup heavy cream
- ½ teaspoon nutritional yeast flakes
- A pinch of salt and black pepper

Directions:
1. In your Slow Cooker, mix the almonds with the cream and the other ingredients, toss, put the lid on and cook on Low for 8 hours.
2. Transfer to a blender, pulse well, divide into bowls and serve.

Nutrition Info:
- calories 270, fat 4, fiber 4, carbs 8, protein 10

Black Eyes Peas Dip

Servings: 4 | Cooking Time: 5 Hours

Ingredients:
- 1 ½ cups black-eyed peas
- 3 cups of water
- 1 tsp Cajun seasoning
- ½ cup pecans, toasted
- ½ tsp garlic powder
- ½ tsp jalapeno powder
- Salt and black pepper to the taste
- ¼ tsp liquid smoke
- ½ tsp Tabasco sauce

Directions:
1. Add water, salt, Cajun seasoning, black pepper, and black eye peas to the Slow Cooker.
2. Put the cooker's lid on and set the cooking time to 5 hours on High settings.
3. Drain and transfer the black-eyed peas to a blender jug.
4. Add jalapeno powder, tabasco sauce, pecans, garlic, liquid smoke, salt and black pepper, to taste.
5. Blend this black-eyes pea dip until smooth.
6. Serve.

Nutrition Info:
- Per Serving: Calories: 221, Total Fat: 4g, Fiber: 7g, Total Carbs: 16g, Protein: 4g

Italian Mussels Salad

Servings: 4 | Cooking Time: 1 Hour

Ingredients:
- 28 ounces canned tomatoes, crushed
- ½ cup white onion, chopped
- 2 jalapeno peppers, chopped
- ¼ cup dry white wine
- ¼ cup extra virgin olive oil
- ¼ cup balsamic vinegar
- 2 pounds mussels, cleaned and scrubbed
- 2 tablespoons red pepper flakes
- 2 garlic cloves, minced
- Salt to the taste
- ½ cup basil, chopped
- Lemon wedges for serving

Directions:
1. In your Slow Cooker, mix tomatoes with onion, jalapenos, wine, oil, vinegar, garlic, pepper flakes, salt, basil and mussels, cover and cook on High for 1 hour.
2. Discard unopened mussels, divide everything into bowls and serve with lemon wedges.

Nutrition Info:
- calories 100, fat 1, fiber 1, carbs 7, protein 2

Artichoke Dip

Servings: 2 | Cooking Time: 2 Hours

Ingredients:
- 2 ounces canned artichoke hearts, drained and chopped
- 2 ounces heavy cream
- 2 tablespoons mayonnaise
- ¼ cup mozzarella, shredded
- 2 green onions, chopped
- ½ teaspoon garam masala
- Cooking spray

Directions:
1. Grease your Slow Cooker with the cooking spray, and mix the artichokes with the cream, mayo and the other ingredients inside.
2. Stir, cover, cook on Low for 2 hours, divide into bowls and serve as a party dip.

Nutrition Info:
- calories 100, fat 3, fiber 2, carbs 7, protein 3

Macadamia Nuts Snack

Servings: 2 | Cooking Time: 2 Hours

Ingredients:
- ½ pound macadamia nuts
- 1 tablespoon avocado oil
- ¼ cup water
- ½ tablespoon chili powder
- ½ teaspoon oregano, dried
- ½ teaspoon onion powder

Directions:
1. In your Slow Cooker, mix the macadamia nuts with the oil and the other ingredients, toss, put the lid on, cook on Low for 2 hours, divide into bowls and serve as a snack.

Nutrition Info:
- calories 108, fat 3, fiber 2, carbs 9, protein 2

Mushroom Salsa

Servings: 4 | Cooking Time: 5 Hours

Ingredients:
- 2 cups white mushrooms, sliced
- 1 cup cherry tomatoes halved
- 1 cup spring onions, chopped
- ½ teaspoon chili powder
- ½ teaspoon rosemary, dried
- ½ teaspoon oregano, dried
- ½ cup black olives, pitted and sliced
- 3 garlic cloves, minced
- 1 cup mild salsa
- Salt and black pepper to the taste

Directions:
1. In your Slow Cooker, mix the mushrooms with the cherry tomatoes and the other ingredients, toss, put the lid on and cook on Low for 5 hours.
2. Divide into bowls and serve as a snack.

Nutrition Info:
- calories 205, fat 4, fiber 7, carbs 9, protein 3

Basic Pepper Salsa

Servings: 6 | Cooking Time: 5 Hours

Ingredients:
- 7 cups tomatoes, chopped
- 1 green bell pepper, chopped
- 1 red bell pepper, chopped
- 2 yellow onions, chopped
- 4 jalapenos, chopped
- ¼ cup apple cider vinegar
- 1 tsp coriander, ground
- 1 tbsp cilantro, chopped
- 3 tbsp basil, chopped
- Salt and black pepper to the taste

Directions:
1. Add jalapenos, tomatoes and all other ingredients to the Slow Cooker.
2. Put the cooker's lid on and set the cooking time to 5 hours on Low settings.
3. Mix gently and serve.

Nutrition Info:
- Per Serving: Calories: 172, Total Fat: 3g, Fiber: 5g, Total Carbs: 8g, Protein: 4g

Bean Salsa Salad

Servings: 6 | Cooking Time: 4 Hrs

Ingredients:
- 1 tbsp soy sauce
- ½ tsp cumin, ground
- 1 cup canned black beans
- 1 cup of salsa
- 6 cups romaine lettuce leaves
- ½ cup avocado, peeled, pitted and mashed

Directions:
1. Add black beans, cumin, soy sauce, and salsa to the Slow Cooker.
2. Put the cooker's lid on and set the cooking time to 4 hours on Low settings.
3. Transfer the beans to a salad bowl and toss in lettuce leaves, and mashed avocado.
4. Mix well then serve.

Nutrition Info:
- Per Serving: Calories: 221, Total Fat: 4g, Fiber: 7g, Total Carbs: 12g, Protein: 3g

Zucchini Sticks

Servings: 13 | Cooking Time: 2 Hours

Ingredients:
- 9 oz. green zucchini, cut into thick sticks
- 4 oz. Parmesan, grated
- 1 egg
- 1 tsp salt
- 1 tsp ground white pepper
- 1 tsp olive oil
- 2 tbsp milk

Directions:
1. Grease of the base of your Slow Cooker with olive oil.
2. Whisk egg with milk, white pepper, and salt in a bowl.
3. Dip the prepared zucchini sticks in the egg mixture then place them in the Slow Cooker.
4. Put the cooker's lid on and set the cooking time to 2 hours on High settings.
5. Spread the cheese over the zucchini sticks evenly.
6. Put the cooker's lid on and set the cooking time to 2 hours on High settings.
7. Serve.

Nutrition Info:
- Per Serving: Calories: 51, Total Fat: 1.7g, Fiber: 0g, Total Carbs: 4.62g, Protein: 5g

Jalapeno Poppers

Servings: 4 | Cooking Time: 3 Hours

Ingredients:
- ½ pound chorizo, chopped
- 10 jalapenos, tops cut off and deseeded
- 1 small white onion, chopped
- ½ pound beef, ground
- ¼ teaspoon garlic powder
- 1 tablespoon maple syrup
- 1 tablespoon mustard
- 1/3 cup water

Directions:
1. In a bowl, mix beef with chorizo, garlic powder and onion and stir.
2. Stuff your jalapenos with the mix, place them in your Slow Cooker, add the water, cover and cook on High for 3 hours.
3. Transfer jalapeno poppers to a lined baking sheet.
4. In a bowl, mix maple syrup with mustard, whisk well, brush poppers with this mix, arrange on a platter and serve.

Nutrition Info:
- calories 214, fat 2, fiber 3, carbs 8, protein 3

Maple Glazed Turkey Strips

Servings: 8 | Cooking Time: 3.5 Hours

Ingredients:
- 15 oz. turkey fillets, cut into strips
- 2 tbsp honey
- 1 tbsp maple syrup
- 1 tsp cayenne pepper
- 1 tbsp butter
- 1 tsp paprika
- 1 tsp oregano
- 1 tsp dried dill
- 2 tbsp mayo

Directions:
1. Place the turkey strips in the Slow Cooker.
2. Add all other spices, herbs, and mayo on top of the turkey.
3. Put the cooker's lid on and set the cooking time to 3 hours on High settings.
4. During this time, mix honey with maples syrup and melted butter in a bowl.
5. Pour this honey glaze over the turkey evenly.
6. Put the cooker's lid on and set the cooking time to 30 minutes on High settings.
7. Serve warm.

Nutrition Info:
- Per Serving: Calories: 295, Total Fat: 25.2g, Fiber: 0g, Total Carbs: 6.82g, Protein: 10g

Crab Dip

Servings: 2 | Cooking Time: 1 Hour

Ingredients:
- 2 ounces crabmeat
- 1 tablespoon lime zest, grated
- ½ tablespoon lime juice
- 2 tablespoons mayonnaise
- 2 green onions, chopped
- 2 ounces cream cheese, cubed
- Cooking spray

Directions:
1. Grease your Slow Cooker with the cooking spray, and mix the crabmeat with the lime zest, juice and the other ingredients inside.
2. Put the lid on, cook on Low for 1 hour, divide into bowls and serve as a party dip.

Nutrition Info:
- calories 100, fat 3, fiber 2, carbs 9, protein 4

Chapter 11 Lunch & Dinner Recipes

Green Pea Tomato Stew

Servings: 6 | Cooking Time: 2 1/4 Hours

Ingredients:
- 2 shallots, chopped
- 2 garlic cloves, chopped
- 2 tablespoons olive oil
- 1 celery stalk, sliced
- 1 red bell pepper, cored and diced
- 1 carrot, diced
- 1 pound frozen green peas
- 1 cup diced tomatoes
- 1 bay leaf
- Salt and pepper to taste

Directions:
1. Heat the oil in a skillet and stir in the shallots and garlic. Cook for 2 minutes until softened then transfer in your Slow Cooker.
2. Add the remaining ingredients and season with salt and pepper.
3. Cook on high for 2 hours.
4. Serve the stew warm or chilled.

Beer Braised Beef

Servings: 6 | Cooking Time: 8 1/4 Hours

Ingredients:
- 2 pounds beef sirloin
- 1/2 pound baby carrots
- 2 large potatoes, peeled and cubed
- 1 celery stalk, sliced
- 1 large sweet onion, chopped
- 4 garlic cloves, chopped
- 1 thyme sprig
- 1 cup dark beer
- 1/4 cup beef stock
- Salt and pepper to taste

Directions:
1. Mix all the ingredients in your slow cooker, adding salt and pepper to taste.
2. Cover the pot with its lid and cook on low settings for 8 hours.
3. Serve the beef and veggies warm and fresh.

Five-spice Beef Short Ribs

Servings: 6 | Cooking Time: 8 1/4 Hours

Ingredients:
- 4 pounds beef short ribs
- 1/4 cup molasses
- 1 tablespoon five-spice powder
- 1 teaspoon garlic powder
- 1 teaspoon chili powder
- 2 tablespoons peanut oil
- 2 tablespoons soy sauce
- 1 teaspoon fish sauce
- 8 green onions, chopped
- 1/2 cup beef stock

Directions:
1. Mix the molasses, five-spice powder, garlic powder, chili, pea-

nut oil, soy sauce and fish sauce in a bowl. Spread this mix over the beef ribs and rub it well into the meat and bone. Place the ribs in your Slow Cooker.
2. Add the green onions and stock and cover the pot with a lid.
3. Cook on low settings for 8 hours.
4. Serve the ribs warm and fresh.

Leek Potato Stew

Servings: 6 | Cooking Time: 4 1/2 Hours

Ingredients:
- 2 tablespoons olive oil
- 2 leeks, sliced
- 2 celery stalks, sliced
- 2 carrots, diced
- 1 1/2 pounds potatoes, peeled and cubed
- 2 tablespoons tomato paste
- 1/2 cup diced tomatoes
- 1 bay leaf
- 1 thyme sprig
- Salt and pepper to taste

Directions:
1. Heat the oil in your Slow Cooker and add the leeks. Cook for 5 minutes until softened then transfer the mix in your Slow Cooker.
2. Add the remaining ingredients and season with salt and pepper.
3. Cook on low settings for 4 hours.
4. The stew is best served warm.

Hard Cider Beef Pot Roast

Servings: 6 | Cooking Time: 6 1/2 Hours

Ingredients:
- 6 small shallots, peeled
- 2 pounds beef sirloin roast
- 6 oz. button mushrooms
- 1 pound small new potatoes, washed
- 1/2 pound baby carrots
- 1 thyme sprig
- 1 1/2 cups hard cider
- 1 bay leaf
- Salt and pepper to taste

Directions:
1. Combine the shallots, beef, mushrooms, potatoes, baby carrots, thyme, hard cider, bay leaf, salt and pepper in your slow cooker.
2. Cover the pot and cook on low settings for 6 hours.
3. Serve the pot roast warm.

Coconut Ginger Chicken

Servings: 8 | Cooking Time: 7 1/4 Hours

Ingredients:
- 4 chicken breasts, halved
- 2 teaspoons grated ginger
- 4 garlic cloves, chopped
- 1 shallot, chopped
- 2 tablespoons butter
- 1 1/2 cups coconut milk
- 1/2 cup chicken stock
- 1 can baby corn, drained
- 1 cup green peas
- 1/2 cup green beans, chopped
- 1 pound new potatoes
- 1 bay leaf
- Salt and pepper to taste
- 1 lemongrass stalk, crushed

Directions:
1. Melt the butter in a skillet and add the chicken. Cook for a few minutes on all sides then transfer in your slow cooker.
2. Add the rest of the ingredients and adjust the taste with salt and pepper.
3. Cook on low settings for 7 hours.
4. Serve the chicken warm.

Bacon Brussels Sprouts

Servings: 6 | Cooking Time: 6 1/4 Hours

Ingredients:
- 2 pounds Brussels sprouts, halved
- 6 bacon slices, chopped
- 1/2 cup vegetable stock
- Salt and pepper to taste

Directions:
1. Cook the bacon in a skillet until crisp.
2. Combine all the ingredients in your slow cooker, adding salt and pepper to taste.
3. Cook on low settings for 6 hours.
4. Serve the sprouts warm or chilled.

Indian Spiced Quinoa Stew

Servings: 6 | Cooking Time: 7 1/4 Hours

Ingredients:
- 2 tablespoons olive oil
- 2 shallots, chopped
- 2 garlic cloves, chopped
- 1/2 cup red quinoa, rinsed
- 1/2 cup red lentils, rinsed
- 1 large sweet potato, peeled and cubed
- 1 turnip, peeled and cubed
- 1/2 teaspoon turmeric powder
- 1/2 teaspoon garam masala
- Salt and pepper to taste
- 3 cups vegetable stock

Directions:
1. Combine all the ingredients in your slow cooker.
2. Add salt and pepper as needed and cook on low settings for 7 hours.
3. Serve the stew warm or chilled.

Layered Sweet Potatoes

Servings: 8 | Cooking Time: 6 1/2 Hours

Ingredients:
- 2 tablespoons olive oil
- 2 large sweet potatoes, peeled and finely sliced
- 2 onions, finely sliced
- 1 pinch nutmeg
- 2 cups whole milk
- 1/2 cup cream cheese
- 2 eggs, beaten
- 1/2 teaspoon garlic powder
- Salt and pepper to taste

Directions:
1. Grease your Slow Cooker then layer the potatoes and onions in your Slow Cooker.
2. Mix the nutmeg, milk, eggs and garlic powder in a bowl. Add salt and pepper to taste then pour over the veggies.
3. Cook on low settings for 6 hours.
4. Serve the dish warm.

Lemon Chicken

Servings: 6 | Cooking Time: 5 Hours

Ingredients:
- 6 chicken breast halves, skinless and bone in
- Salt and black pepper to the taste
- 1 teaspoon oregano, dried
- ¼ cup water
- 2 tablespoons butter
- 3 tablespoons lemon juice
- 2 garlic cloves, minced
- 1 teaspoon chicken bouillon granules
- 2 teaspoons parsley, chopped

Directions:
1. In your Slow Cooker, mix chicken with salt, pepper, water, butter, lemon juice, garlic and chicken granules, stir, cover and cook on Low for 5 hours.
2. Add parsley, stir, divide between plates and serve for lunch.

Nutrition Info:
- calories 336, fat 10, fiber 1, carbs 1, protein 46

Beef And Artichokes Stew

Servings: 2 | Cooking Time: 4 Hours

Ingredients:
- 1 pound beef stew meat, cubed
- 1 cup canned artichoke hearts, halved
- 1 cup beef stock
- 1 red onion, sliced
- 1 cup tomato sauce
- ½ teaspoon rosemary, dried
- ½ teaspoon coriander, ground
- 1 teaspoon garlic powder
- A drizzle of olive oil
- A pinch of salt and black pepper
- 1 tablespoon chives, chopped

Directions:
1. Grease the Slow Cooker with the oil and mix the beef with the artichokes, stock and the other ingredients inside.
2. Toss, put the lid on and cook on High for 4 hours.
3. Divide the stew into bowls and serve.

Nutrition Info:
- calories 322, fat 5, fiber 4, carbs 12, protein 22

Molasses Baked Beans

Servings: 6 | Cooking Time: 6 1/4 Hours

Ingredients:
- 1 pound dried white beans, rinsed
- 4 cups water
- 2 tablespoons molasses
- 1 tablespoon brown sugar
- 2 tablespoons tomato paste
- 1 cup diced tomatoes
- 1 teaspoon mustard seeds
- Salt and pepper to taste

Directions:
1. Combine all the ingredients in your slow cooker. Season with salt and pepper to taste.
2. Cover with a lid and cook on low settings for 6 hours.
3. Serve the beans warm and fresh.

Veggie Refried Beans

Servings: 6 | Cooking Time: 6 1/4 Hours

Ingredients:
- 2 cans (15 oz. each) black beans, drained
- 1 cup vegetable stock
- 2 tablespoons tomato paste
- 1 chipotle pepper, chopped
- 4 garlic cloves, minced
- 1 tablespoon adobo sauce from chipotle
- Salt and pepper to taste

Directions:
1. Combine all the ingredients in your slow cooker.
2. Add salt and pepper as needed and cook on low settings for 6 hours.
3. Serve the beans warm or chilled.

Red Wine Braised Pork Ribs

Servings: 8 | Cooking Time: 8 1/4 Hours

Ingredients:
- 5 pounds pork short ribs
- 4 tablespoons brown sugar
- 1 tablespoon molasses
- 2 tablespoons olive oil
- 1 teaspoon chili powder
- 1 teaspoon cumin powder
- 1 teaspoon dried thyme
- 1 teaspoon salt
- 1 cup BBQ sauce
- 1 cup red wine

Directions:
1. Mix the brown sugar, molasses, olive oil, chili powder, cumin powder, thyme and salt in a bowl.
2. Spread this mixture over the pork ribs and rub the meat well with the spice. Place in your slow cooker.
3. Add the BBQ sauce and red wine and cook on low settings for 8 hours.
4. Serve the pork ribs warm.

Pork Cannellini Bean Stew

Servings: 6 | Cooking Time: 3 3/4 Hours

Ingredients:
- 1 pound pork tenderloin, cubed
- 2 tablespoons canola oil
- 2 celery stalks, sliced
- 2 carrots, sliced
- 1/2 teaspoon dried basil
- 1/2 teaspoon dried oregano
- 2 red bell peppers, cored and diced
- 1 1/2 cups dried cannellini beans, rinsed
- 3 cups chicken stock
- 1 rosemary sprig
- Salt and pepper to taste

Directions:
1. Heat the oil in a skillet and add the pork. Cook for a few minutes until golden. Transfer the pork in your Slow Cooker.
2. Add the rest of the ingredients and season with salt and pepper as needed.
3. Cook the stew on high settings for 3 1/2 hours.
4. Serve the stew warm and fresh.

Garden Slow Cooker Chili

Servings: 8 | Cooking Time: 8 1/2 Hours

Ingredients:
- 2 shallots, chopped
- 4 garlic cloves, chopped
- 1 can (15 oz.) kidney beans, drained
- 1 cup frozen corn
- 1 head broccoli, cut into florets
- 1/2 head cauliflower, cut into florets
- 2 jalapeno peppers, chopped
- 2 red bell peppers, cored and diced
- 1 large carrot, sliced
- 1 can fire roasted tomatoes
- 1 cup vegetable stock
- 2 potatoes, peeled and cubed
- 1 teaspoon chili powder
- 1/2 teaspoon dried oregano
- Salt and pepper to taste

Directions:
1. Combine the shallots, garlic, kidney beans, corn, broccoli, cauliflower, jalapeno pepper, bell peppers, carrot, tomatoes and stock in your Slow Cooker.
2. Add the potatoes and chili powder, as well as oregano and season with salt and pepper.
3. Cook on low settings for 8 hours.
4. Serve the chili warm and fresh.

Artichoke Black Olive Tagine

Servings: 6 | Cooking Time: 4 1/4 Hours

Ingredients:
- 12 oz. artichoke hearts, chopped
- 1 shallot, chopped
- 1 can (15 oz.) chickpeas, drained
- 2 garlic cloves, chopped
- 1/2 teaspoon smoked paprika
- 1/2 teaspoon cumin powder
- 1 teaspoon turmeric powder
- 1 lime, juiced

- 1/2 cup pitted black olives
- 1/2 teaspoon dried oregano
- 1 cup diced tomatoes
- Salt and pepper to taste

Directions:
1. Combine the artichokes, shallot, chickpeas and the remaining ingredients in your slow cooker.
2. Add salt and pepper to taste and cook on low settings for 4 hours.
3. Serve the tagine warm or chilled.

Cherry Rice

Servings:4 | Cooking Time: 3 Hours

Ingredients:
- 1 cup basmati rice
- 1 cup cherries, raw
- 3 cups of water
- 2 tablespoons of liquid honey
- 1 tablespoon butter, melted

Directions:
1. Put cherries and rice in the Slow Cooker.
2. Add water and cook the meal on high for 3 hours.
3. Meanwhile, mix liquid honey and butter.
4. When the rice is cooked, add liquid honey mixture and carefully stir.

Nutrition Info:
- Per Serving: 249 calories, 3.9g protein, 51.1g carbohydrates, 3.3g fat, 1.4g fiber, 8mg cholesterol, 29mg sodium, 136mg potassium.

Curried Tofu Lentils

Servings: 6 | Cooking Time: 6 1/4 Hours

Ingredients:
- 8 oz. firm tofu, cubed
- 2 tablespoons canola oil
- 2 tablespoons red curry paste
- 1 cup red lentils
- 2 cups vegetable stock
- 2 cups cauliflower florets
- 2 tablespoons tomato paste
- 1 bay leaf
- 1/2 lemongrass stalk, crushed
- 1/2 teaspoon grated ginger
- Salt and pepper to taste

Directions:
1. Heat the oil in a skillet and add the tofu. Cook on all sides until golden brown and crusty then transfer in your Slow Cooker.
2. Add the remaining ingredients and season with salt and pepper.
3. Cook on low settings for 6 hours.
4. Serve the dish warm and fresh.

Roasted Bell Pepper Stew

Servings: 6 | Cooking Time: 2 1/2 Hours

Ingredients:
- 2 tablespoons olive oil
- 1 large onion, chopped
- 3 garlic cloves, minced
- 1 carrot, grated
- 1 parsnip, grated
- 1 large jar roasted red bell pepper, chopped

- 2 tablespoons tomato paste
- 1 cup tomato sauce
- 1/2 cup vegetable stock
- 1/4 teaspoon cumin powder
- 1/4 teaspoon dried oregano
- 1 bay leaf
- 1 thyme sprig
- Salt and pepper to taste

Directions:
1. Heat the oil in a skillet and add the onion, garlic and carrot. Cook for 5 minutes until softened.
2. Transfer in your Slow Cooker and add the remaining ingredients.
3. Season with salt and pepper and cook on high settings for 2 hours.
4. Serve the stew warm and fresh.

Pineapple Cranberry Pork Ham

Servings: 6 | Cooking Time: 7 1/4 Hours

Ingredients:
- 2-3 pounds piece of smoked ham
- 1 cup cranberry sauce
- 1 cup pineapple juice
- 1/2 teaspoon chili powder
- 1/2 teaspoon cumin powder
- 1 cinnamon stick
- 1 star anise
- 1 bay leaf
- Salt and pepper to taste

Directions:
1. Mix the cranberry sauce, pineapple juice, chili powder, cumin powder, cinnamon, star anise and bay leaf in your slow cooker.
2. Place the ham in the pot and season with salt and pepper if needed.
3. Cook on low settings for 7 hours.
4. Serve the ham and sauce warm with your favorite side dish.

Carrot Spinach White Bean Stew

Servings: 6 | Cooking Time: 2 1/4 Hours

Ingredients:
- 2 large carrots, sliced
- 1 can (15 oz.) white beans, drained
- 4 cups fresh spinach, shredded
- 1/4 teaspoon cumin seeds
- 1/4 teaspoon chili powder
- 1 pound potatoes, peeled and cubed
- 1 ripe heirloom tomato, peeled and diced
- 1/2 cup vegetable stock
- Salt and pepper to taste

Directions:
1. Combine all the ingredients in your Slow Cooker, adding salt and pepper to fit your taste.
2. Cover the pot with a lid and cook on high settings for 2 hours.
3. Serve the stew warm or chilled.

Pulled Chicken

Servings: 8 | Cooking Time: 8 1/4 Hours

Ingredients:
- 4 chicken breasts
- 2 large sweet onions, sliced
- 1 teaspoon grated ginger
- 1 cup apple cider
- 1 cup BBQ sauce
- Salt and pepper to taste

Directions:
1. Combine all the ingredients in your slow cooker, adjusting the taste with salt and pepper as needed.
2. Cook on low settings for 8 hours.
3. When done, shred the chicken into fine threads using two forks.
4. Serve the chicken warm.

Fennel Infused Pork Ham

Servings: 8 | Cooking Time: 6 1/4 Hours

Ingredients:
- 4-5 pounds piece of pork ham
- 2 fennel bulbs, sliced
- 1 orange, zested and juiced
- 1/2 cup white wine
- 1 cup chicken stock
- 2 bay leaves
- 1 thyme sprig
- Salt and pepper to taste

Directions:
1. Combine the fennel, orange zest, orange juice, white wine, chicken stock, bay leaves and thyme in your slow cooker.
2. Add salt and pepper and place the ham on top.
3. Cook on low settings for 6 hours.
4. Slice and serve the ham warm.

Paprika Chicken Wings

Servings: 4 | Cooking Time: 3 1/4 Hours

Ingredients:
- 2 pounds chicken wings
- 1 1/2 teaspoons smoked paprika
- 1/2 teaspoon sweet paprika
- 1 tablespoon honey
- Salt and pepper to taste
- 1/2 cup chicken stock

Directions:
1. Combine the chicken wings, paprika, honey, salt and pepper in your slow cooker.
2. Add the stock then cover and cook on high settings for 3 hours.
3. Serve the chicken warm and fresh with your favorite side dish.

Sweet Potato And Clam Chowder

Servings: 2 | Cooking Time: 3 Hours And 30 Minutes

Ingredients:
- 1 small yellow onion, chopped
- 1 carrot, chopped
- 1 red bell pepper, cubed
- 6 ounces canned clams, chopped
- 1 sweet potato, chopped
- 2 cups chicken stock
- ½ cup coconut milk
- 1 teaspoon Worcestershire sauce

Directions:
1. In your Slow Cooker, mix the onion with the carrot, clams and the other ingredients, toss, put the lid on and cook on High for 3 hours.
2. Divide the chowder into bowls and serve for lunch.

Nutrition Info:
- calories 288, fat 15.3, fiber 5.9, carbs 36.4, protein 5

Stuffed Butternut Squash

Servings: 6 | Cooking Time: 6 1/2 Hours

Ingredients:
- 1 large butternut squash, halved
- 2 cups cooked lentils
- 1 shallot, chopped
- 2 garlic cloves, minced
- 1/2 teaspoon cumin powder
- 1/4 teaspoon chili powder
- Salt and pepper to taste
- 1/2 cup vegetable stock

Directions:
1. Place the butternut squash in your slow cooker.
2. Mix the lentils, shallot, garlic, cumin powder and chili powder in a bowl. Add salt and pepper to taste then spoon the mixture into the butternut squash halves.
3. Add the stock in the slow cooker as well and cook on low settings for 6 hours.
4. Serve the butternut squash warm and fresh.

Beef Broccoli Sauté

Servings: 4 | Cooking Time: 2 1/4 Hours

Ingredients:
- 2 flank steaks, cut into thin strips
- 1 tablespoon peanut oil
- 1 pound broccoli florets
- 1/4 cup peanuts, chopped
- 1 tablespoon tomato paste
- 2 tablespoons soy sauce
- 1/4 cup beef stock
- 1 teaspoon hot sauce
- 1/2 teaspoon sesame oil
- 1 tablespoon sesame seeds
- Salt and pepper to taste

Directions:
1. Combine all the ingredients in your slow cooker.
2. Add salt and pepper to taste and cook on high settings for 2 hours.
3. Serve the sauté warm.

Ground Beef Bbq

Servings: 8 | Cooking Time: 7 1/4 Hours

Ingredients:
- 3 pounds ground beef
- 1 large onion, chopped
- 4 garlic cloves, chopped
- 2 celery stalks, chopped
- 1 tablespoon apple cider vinegar
- 1 teaspoon Dijon mustard
- 1 tablespoon brown sugar
- 1 1/2 cups BBQ sauce
- 1/2 cup beef sauce
- Salt and pepper to taste

Directions:
1. Combine all the ingredients in your slow cooker.
2. Season with salt and pepper and cook on low settings for 7 hours.
3. Serve the BBQ beef warm.

Butternut Squash Curry

Servings: 6 | Cooking Time: 6 1/2 Hours

Ingredients:
- 2 shallots, chopped
- 4 garlic cloves, chopped
- 4 cups butternut squash
- 1 can (15 oz.) chickpeas, drained
- 1 cup diced tomatoes
- 1 cup coconut milk
- 1 cup vegetable stock
- 2 tablespoons red curry paste
- Salt and pepper to taste
- 2 cups fresh spinach
- 2 tablespoons chopped parsley

Directions:
1. Combine the shallots, garlic, butternut squash, chickpeas, tomatoes, coconut milk and stock in your Slow Cooker.
2. Add the rest of the ingredients and season with salt and pepper.
3. Cook on low settings for 6 hours.
4. Serve the squash warm and fresh.

Thai Chicken Vegetable Medley

Servings: 6 | Cooking Time: 4 1/4 Hours

Ingredients:
- 2 chicken breasts, cut into strips
- 2 zucchinis, sliced
- 2 red bell peppers, cored and sliced
- 2 heirloom tomatoes, peeled and diced
- 2 cups button mushrooms
- 4 garlic cloves, minced
- 1 leek, sliced
- 1 tablespoon red Thai curry paste
- 1 cup coconut milk
- 1/2 cup vegetable stock
- Salt and pepper to taste

Directions:
1. Combine all the ingredients in your slow cooker.
2. Add salt and pepper to taste and cover with a lid.
3. Cook on low settings for 4 hours.
4. Serve the dish warm or chilled.

Fruity Pork Tenderloin

Servings: 8 | Cooking Time: 8 1/4 Hours

Ingredients:
- 3 pounds pork tenderloin
- 1/2 pound plums, pitted and sliced
- 1/2 cup chopped dried apricots
- 1/2 cup frozen cranberries
- 1/2 cup golden raisins
- 1 cup apple juice
- 1 onion, chopped
- 1/2 teaspoon garlic powder
- 1 cinnamon stick
- 1 star anise
- Salt and pepper to taste

Directions:
1. Combine the fruits, onion, garlic powder, spices, salt and pepper in your slow cooker.
2. Place the pork tenderloin on top and cover with a lid.
3. Cook on low settings for 8 hours.
4. Serve the pork roast tenderloin warm, topped with the fruits found in the pot.

Fall Slow Cooker Roast

Servings: 6 | Cooking Time: 6 Hours

Ingredients:
- 2 sweet potatoes, cubed
- 2 carrots, chopped
- 2 pounds beef chuck roast, cubed
- ¼ cup celery, chopped
- 1 tablespoon canola oil
- 2 garlic cloves, minced
- 1 yellow onion, chopped
- 1 tablespoon flour
- 1 tablespoon brown sugar
- 1 tablespoon sugar
- 1 teaspoon cumin, ground
- Salt and black pepper to the taste
- ¾ teaspoon coriander, ground
- ½ teaspoon oregano, dried
- 1 teaspoon chili powder
- 1/8 teaspoon cinnamon powder
- ¾ teaspoon orange peel grated
- 15 ounces tomato sauce

Directions:
1. In your Slow Cooker, mix potatoes with carrots, beef cubes, celery, oil, garlic, onion, flour, brown sugar, sugar, cumin, salt pepper, coriander, oregano, chili powder, cinnamon, orange peel and tomato sauce, stir, cover and cook on Low for 6 hours.
2. Divide into bowls and serve for lunch.

Nutrition Info:
- calories 278, fat 12, fiber 2, carbs 16, protein 25

Red Cabbage Pork Stew

Servings: 6 | Cooking Time: 4 1/4 Hours

Ingredients:
- 1 head red cabbage, shredded
- 1 1/2 pounds pork roast, cubed
- 2 tablespoons canola oil
- 1 large onion, chopped
- 4 garlic cloves, minced
- 1 tablespoon maple syrup
- 1 teaspoon chili powder
- 1/4 cup apple cider vinegar
- Salt and pepper to taste

Directions:
1. Combine all the ingredients in your slow cooker.
2. Add salt and pepper to taste and cook the dish on low settings for 4 hours.
3. Serve the stew warm and fresh.

Shrimp Stew

Servings: 2 | Cooking Time: 3 Hours

Ingredients:
- 1 garlic clove, minced
- 1 red onion, chopped
- 1 cup canned tomatoes, crushed
- 1 cup veggie stock
- ½ teaspoon turmeric powder
- 1 pound shrimp, peeled and deveined
- ½ teaspoon coriander, ground
- ½ teaspoon thyme, dried
- ½ teaspoon basil, dried
- A pinch of salt and black pepper
- A pinch of red pepper flakes

Directions:
1. In your Slow Cooker, mix the onion with the garlic, shrimp and the other ingredients, toss, put the lid on and cook on High for 3 hours.
2. Divide the stew into bowls and serve.

Nutrition Info:
- calories 313, fat 4.2, fiber 2.5, carbs 13.2, protein 53.3

Honey Apple Pork Chops

Servings: 4 | Cooking Time: 5 1/4 Hours

Ingredients:
- 4 pork chops
- 2 red, tart apples, peeled, cored and cubed
- 1 shallot, chopped
- 2 garlic cloves, chopped
- 1 tablespoon olive oil
- 1 red chili, chopped
- 1 heirloom tomato, peeled and diced
- 1 cup apple cider
- 2 tablespoons honey
- Salt and pepper to taste

Directions:
1. Mix all the ingredients in your slow cooker.
2. Add salt and pepper to taste and cook on low settings for 5 hours.
3. Serve the chops warm and fresh.

Pork And Chorizo Lunch Mix

Servings: 8 | Cooking Time: 4 Hours

Ingredients:
- 1 pound chorizo, ground
- 1 pound pork, ground
- 3 tablespoons olive oil
- 1 tomato, chopped
- 1 avocado, pitted, peeled and chopped
- Salt and black pepper to the taste
- 1 small red onion, chopped
- 2 tablespoons enchilada sauce

Directions:
1. Heat up a pan with the oil over medium-high heat, add pork, stir, brown for a couple of minutes, transfer to your Slow Cooker, add salt, pepper, chorizo, onion and enchilada sauce, stir, cover and cook on Low for 4 hours.
2. Divide between plates and serve with chopped tomato and avocado on top.

Nutrition Info:
- calories 300, fat 12, fiber 3, carbs 15, protein 17

Turkey And Mushrooms

Servings: 2 | Cooking Time: 7 Hours And 10 Minutes

Ingredients:
- 1 red onion, sliced
- 2 garlic cloves, minced
- 1 pound turkey breast, skinless, boneless and cubed
- 1 tablespoon olive oil
- 1 teaspoon oregano, dried
- 1 teaspoon basil, dried
- A pinch of red pepper flakes
- 1 cup mushrooms, sliced
- ¼ cup chicken stock
- ½ cup canned tomatoes, chopped
- A pinch of salt and black pepper

Directions:
1. Heat up a pan with the oil over medium-high heat, add the onion , garlic and the meat, brown for 10 minutes and transfer to the Slow Cooker.
2. Add the oregano, basil and the other ingredients, toss, put the lid on and cook on Low for 7 hours.
3. Divide into bowls and serve for lunch.

Nutrition Info:
- calories 240, fat 4, fiber 6, carbs 18, protein 10

No Fuss Vegetarian Chili

Servings: 8 | Cooking Time: 8 1/4 Hours

Ingredients:
- 10 oz. firm tofu, cubed
- 1 can fire roasted tomatoes
- 2 red bell peppers, cored and diced
- 1 yellow bell pepper, cored and diced
- 4 garlic cloves, chopped
- 2 sweet onions, chopped
- 2 cups dried kidney beans
- 4 cups water
- 1/2 teaspoon chili powder
- 1/2 teaspoon cumin powder
- 1/4 teaspoon chili flakes
- Salt and pepper to taste

- Chopped cilantro for serving

Directions:

1. Combine the tofu, tomatoes, bell peppers, garlic, onions, kidney beans, water, chili powder, cumin powder and chili flakes in your slow cooker.
2. Add salt and pepper to taste and cook on low settings for 8 hours.
3. Serve the chili warm and fresh, topped with chopped cilantro.

Thai Style Chicken

Servings: 4 | Cooking Time: 2 1/4 Hours

Ingredients:

- 2 chicken breasts, cut into thin strips
- 2 tablespoons soy sauce
- 1 tablespoon hot sauce
- 1/4 cup smooth peanut butter
- 1 tablespoon lime juice
- 1 teaspoon honey

Directions:

1. Combine all the ingredients in your slow cooker.
2. Cook the chicken on high settings for 2 hours.
3. Serve the chicken warm and fresh.

Bok Choy Shiitake Slow Cooker Fry Up

Servings: 6 | Cooking Time: 2 1/4 Hours

Ingredients:

- 2 garlic cloves, minced
- 1 teaspoon grated ginger
- 1 sweet onion, sliced
- 2 tablespoons canola oil
- 1 cup chopped shiitake mushrooms
- 2 cups sliced button mushrooms
- 2 tablespoons bok choy
- 2 green onions, chopped
- 1 teaspoon sesame oil
- 1/4 teaspoon chili powder

Directions:

1. Heat the oil in a skillet and stir in the garlic, ginger and onion. Cook for 1 minute until fragrant then transfer in your slow cooker.
2. Add the remaining ingredients and cook on high settings for 2 hours.
3. Serve the fry up warm.

Beef Sloppy Joes

Servings: 8 | Cooking Time: 7 1/4 Hours

Ingredients:

- 2 pounds ground beef
- 2 large onions, finely chopped
- 1 tablespoon Worcestershire sauce
- 1/4 cup hot ketchup
- 1/2 cup tomato juice
- 1/2 cup beef stock
- Salt and pepper to taste
- Bread buns for serving

Directions:

1. Combine all the ingredients in your Slow Cooker.
2. Add salt and pepper to taste and cook on low settings for 7 hours.
3. When done, serve the dish in bread buns.

Chicken Shrimp Jambalaya

Servings: 8 | Cooking Time: 8 1/4 Hours

Ingredients:

- 2 tablespoons olive oil
- 1 1/2 pounds skinless chicken breasts, cubed
- 2 large onions, chopped
- 2 red bell peppers, cored and diced
- 1 celery stalk, sliced
- 2 garlic cloves, chopped
- 1/2 teaspoon dried oregano
- 1 cup diced tomato
- 1 1/2 cups chicken stock
- Salt and pepper to taste
- 1 pound fresh shrimps, peeled and cleaned
- Cooked white rice for serving

Directions:

1. Heat the oil in a skillet and add the chicken. Cook for 5 minutes until golden then transfer in your slow cooker.
2. Add the onions, bell peppers, celery, garlic, oregano, tomato and stock.
3. Add salt and pepper to taste and cook on low settings for 6 hours.
4. At this point, add the shrimps and cook for 2 more hours.
5. Serve the jambalaya warm and fresh.

Root Vegetable Beef Stew

Servings: 8 | Cooking Time: 8 1/2 Hours

Ingredients:

- 3 pounds beef sirloin roast, cubed
- 4 carrots, sliced
- 2 parsnips, sliced
- 1 celery root, peeled and cubed
- 4 garlic cloves, chopped
- 4 large potatoes, peeled and cubed
- 1 turnip, peeled and cubed
- 1 bay leaf
- 1 lemon, juiced
- 1 teaspoon Worcestershire sauce
- 1 cup beef stock
- Salt and pepper to taste

Directions:

1. Combine the beef, carrots, parsnips, celery root, garlic, potatoes, turnip, bay leaf, lemon juice, Worcestershire sauce and stock in your slow cooker.
2. Add salt and pepper to taste and cover with its lid.
3. Cook on low settings for 8 hours.
4. Serve the roast and vegetables warm.

Jamaican Jerk Chicken

Servings: 4 | Cooking Time: 7 1/2 Hours

Ingredients:

- 4 chicken breasts
- 2 tablespoons jerk seasoning
- 2 tablespoons olive oil
- 1/2 cup chicken stock
- 1/4 cup brewed coffee
- 1 jalapeno pepper, chopped
- Salt and pepper to taste

Directions:

1. Season the chicken with salt, pepper and jerk seasoning.

2. Combine the seasoned chicken, stock and coffee, as well as jalapeno pepper in your Slow Cooker.
3. Cover with a lid and cook on low settings for 7 hours.
4. Serve the chicken warm and fresh.

Puttanesca Pizza

Servings: 6 | Cooking Time: 2 1/2 Hours

Ingredients:
- Dough:
- 2 cups all-purpose flour
- 1 teaspoon active dry yeast
- 1 cup warm water
- 1/4 teaspoon salt
- 2 tablespoons olive oil
- Topping:
- 1/2 cup crushed fire roasted tomatoes
- 1/4 cup Kalamata olives, pitted and sliced
- 1/4 cup green olives, sliced
- 1 tablespoon capers, chopped
- 1/2 teaspoon dried basil
- 1/2 teaspoon dried oregano

Directions:
1. To make the dough, combine all the ingredients in a bowl and knead for a few minutes in a bowl.
2. Roll the dough into a round that fits in your Slow Cooker.
3. Top with tomatoes, olives, capers and dried herbs.
4. Cook on high settings for 1 1/2 hours.
5. Serve the pizza warm.

Shrimp Stew

Servings: 8 | Cooking Time: 4 Hours And 30 Minutes

Ingredients:
- 29 ounces canned tomatoes, chopped
- 2 yellow onions, chopped
- 2 celery ribs, chopped
- ½ cup fish stock
- 4 garlic cloves, minced
- 1 tablespoon red vinegar
- 2 tablespoons olive oil
- 3 pounds shrimp, peeled and deveined
- 6 ounces canned clams
- 2 tablespoons cilantro, chopped

Directions:
1. In your Slow Cooker, mix tomatoes with onion, celery, stock, vinegar and oil, stir, cover and cook on Low for 4 hours.
2. Add shrimp, clams and cilantro, stir, cover, cook on Low for 30 minutes more, divide into bowls and serve for lunch.

Nutrition Info:
- calories 255, fat 4, fiber 3, carbs 14, protein 26

Green Pea Chicken With Biscuit Topping

Servings: 6 | Cooking Time: 6 1/2 Hours

Ingredients:
- 1 shallot, chopped
- 1 leek, sliced
- 2 garlic cloves, chopped
- 2 chicken breasts, cubed
- 1 1/2 cups green peas
- 1/2 pound baby carrots
- 1 tablespoon cornstarch

- 1 cup vegetables tock
- 1/4 cup white wine
- 1 cup all-purpose flour
- 1/2 cup butter, chilled and cubed
- 1/2 cup buttermilk, chilled
- Salt and pepper to taste

Directions:
1. Combine the shallot, leek, garlic, chicken, green peas, baby carrots, cornstarch, stock and wine in your slow cooker.
2. Season with salt and pepper.
3. For the topping, mix the flour, butter, buttermilk, salt and pepper in your food processor.
4. Pulse just until mixed then spoon the mixture over the vegetables in the slow cooker.
5. Cover and cook on low settings for 6 hours.
6. Serve the dish warm.

Summer Lasagna

Servings: 8 | Cooking Time: 6 1/2 Hours

Ingredients:
- 1 large zucchini
- 1 large eggplant
- 1 can diced tomatoes
- 1 cup white rice
- 1 celery stalk, diced
- 1/2 teaspoon dried oregano
- 2 tablespoons chopped parsley
- 2 cups vegetable stock
- Salt and pepper to taste
- 1 1/2 cups shredded mozzarella

Directions:
1. Cut the zucchini and eggplant into thin ribbons using a vegetable peeler.
2. Mix the tomatoes, white rice, celery, oregano, parsley, salt and pepper.
3. Layer the zucchini, eggplant and rice mixture in your Slow Cooker.
4. Add the stock and top with cheese.
5. Cook on low settings for 6 hours.
6. Serve the lasagna warm.

Spicy Hot Chicken Thighs

Servings: 8 | Cooking Time: 8 1/4 Hours

Ingredients:
- 8 chicken thighs
- 1/4 cup hot sauce
- 2 tablespoons butter
- 1/2 teaspoon garlic powder
- 1/2 cup tomato sauce
- 1/2 cup vegetable stock
- 1/2 teaspoon cumin powder
- Salt and pepper to taste

Directions:
1. Combine the chicken thighs with the rest of the ingredients, including salt and pepper in your slow cooker.
2. Cover with a lid and cook on low settings for 8 hours.
3. Serve the chicken thighs warm and fresh.

Chapter 12 Dessert Recipes

Chapter 12 Dessert Recipes

Double Chocolate Cake

Servings: 8 | Cooking Time: 4 1/4 Hours

Ingredients:
- 1 1/2 cups all-purpose flour
- 1 1/2 teaspoons baking powder
- 1/4 teaspoon salt
- 1/4 cup cocoa powder
- 1/2 cup vegetable oil
- 1 cup water
- 1 cup sour cream
- 4 eggs
- 1 teaspoon vanilla extract
- 1 cup dark chocolate chips

Directions:
1. Mix the flour, baking powder, salt, cocoa powder in a bowl.
2. Stir in the water, oil, sour cream, eggs, vanilla extract and give it a quick mix.
3. Pour the batter in your Slow Cooker and top with chocolate chips.
4. Cover and cook on low settings for 4 hours.
5. Allow the cake to cool before serving.

No Crust Lemon Cheesecake

Servings: 8 | Cooking Time: 6 1/4 Hours

Ingredients:
- 24 oz. cream cheese
- 1 lemon, zested and juiced
- 2 tablespoons cornstarch
- 1/2 cup white sugar
- 4 eggs
- 1 teaspoon vanilla extract
- 1/4 cup butter, melted

Directions:
1. Mix all the ingredients in a bowl.
2. Pour the cheesecake mix in a greased Slow Cooker and cook on low settings for 6 hours.
3. Allow the cheesecake to cool in the pot before slicing and serving.

Vanilla Cookies

Servings: 12 | Cooking Time: 2 Hours And 30 Minutes

Ingredients:
- 2 eggs
- ¼ cup vegetable oil
- 1 cup sugar
- ½ teaspoon vanilla extract
- 1 teaspoon baking powder
- 1 and ½ cups almond meal
- ½ cup almonds, chopped

Directions:
1. In a bowl, mix oil with sugar, vanilla extract and eggs and whisk.
2. Add baking powder, almond meal and almonds and stir well.
3. Line your Slow Cooker with parchment paper, spread cookie

mix on the bottom of the Slow Cooker, cover and cook on Low for 2 hours and 30 minutes.
4. Leave cookie sheet to cool down, cut into medium pieces and serve.

Nutrition Info:
- calories 220, fat 2, fiber 1, carbs 3, protein 6

Cherry Jam

Servings:4 | Cooking Time: 3 Hours

Ingredients:
- 2 cups cherries, pitted
- ½ cup of sugar
- 1 tablespoon agar
- 3 tablespoons water

Directions:
1. Mix sugar with cherries and put in the Slow Cooker.
2. Then mix water and agar and pour the liquid in the Slow Cooker too.
3. Stir well and close the lid.
4. Cook the jam on high for 3 hours.
5. Then transfer the jam in the glass cans and store it in the fridge for up to 2 months.

Nutrition Info:
- Per Serving: 139 calories, 0.5g protein, 36.1g carbohydrates, 0g fat, 1.5g fiber, 0mg cholesterol, 0mg sodium, 3mg potassium.

Cardamom Apple Jam

Servings:4 | Cooking Time: 2.5 Hours

Ingredients:
- 1 cup apples, chopped
- 1 teaspoon ground cardamom
- 2 tablespoons brown sugar
- 1 teaspoon agar

Directions:
1. Mix apples with brown sugar and transfer in the Slow Cooker.
2. Leave the apples until they get the juice.
3. Then add ground cardamom and agar. Mix the mixture.
4. Close the lid and cook the jam on High for 2.5 hours.
5. Then blend the mixture until smooth and cool to room temperature.

Nutrition Info:
- Per Serving: 48 calories, 0.2g protein, 12.5g carbohydrates, 0.1g fat, 1.5g fiber, 0mg cholesterol, 2mg sodium, 72mg potassium.

Peanut Butter Cake

Servings: 8 | Cooking Time: 2 Hours And 30 Minutes

Ingredients:
- 1 cup sugar
- 1 cup flour
- 3 tablespoons cocoa powder+ ½ cup
- 1 and ½ teaspoons baking powder
- ½ cup milk
- 2 tablespoons vegetable oil
- 2 cups hot water

- 1 teaspoon vanilla extract
- ½ cup peanut butter
- Cooking spray

Directions:
1. In a bowl, mix half of the sugar with 3 tablespoons cocoa, flour, baking powder, oil, vanilla and milk, stir well and pour into your Slow Cooker greased with cooking spray.
2. In another bowl, mix the rest of the sugar with the rest of the cocoa, peanut butter and hot water, stir well and pour over the batter in the Slow Cooker.
3. Cover Slow Cooker, cook on High for 2 hours and 30 minutes, slice cake and serve.

Nutrition Info:
- calories 242, fat 4, fiber 7, carbs 8, protein 4

Coconut And Lemon Pie

Servings:6 | Cooking Time: 4.5 Hours

Ingredients:
- 1 teaspoon baking powder
- 1 lemon, sliced
- 1 cup coconut flour
- 1 cup all-purpose flour
- 1 teaspoon vanilla extract
- 4 tablespoons sugar
- 1 cup skim milk
- 2 tablespoons coconut shred
- Cooking spray

Directions:
1. Spray the Slow Cooker with cooking spray from inside.
2. Then mix skim milk with sugar, vanilla extract, all types of flour, and baking powder.
3. When you get a homogenous mixture, pour it in the Slow Cooker.
4. Then sprinkle the dough with sliced lemon and shredded coconut.
5. Close the lid and cook the pie on High for 4.5 hours.

Nutrition Info:
- Per Serving: 223 calories, 6.3g protein, 41.3g carbohydrates, 3.9g fat, 9.2g fiber, 1mg cholesterol, 24mg sodium, 184mg potassium.

Cardamom Coconut Rice Pudding

Servings: 6 | Cooking Time: 6 1/4 Hours

Ingredients:
- 1 1/4 cups Arborio rice
- 2 cups coconut milk
- 1 cup coconut water
- 1/2 cup coconut sugar
- 4 cardamom pods, crushed
- Sliced peaches for serving

Directions:
1. Combine all the ingredients in your slow cooker.
2. Cover the pot and cook on low settings for 6 hours.
3. The pudding is best served warm, although it tastes good chilled as well. For more flavor, top the pudding with sliced peaches just before serving.

Sweet Zucchini Pie

Servings:6 | Cooking Time: 4 Hours

Ingredients:
- 2 cups zucchini, chopped
- ½ cup of sugar
- 2 cups all-purpose flour
- 1 teaspoon baking powder
- 4 eggs, beaten
- 1 tablespoon butter, melted
- 1 cup milk
- 1 teaspoon vanilla extract

Directions:
1. Mix sugar with flour, baking powder, eggs, butter, milk, and vanilla extract.
2. Stir the mixture until smooth.
3. Then line the Slow Cooker with baking paper and pour the smooth dough inside.
4. Top the dough with zucchini and close the lid.
5. Cook the pie on High for 4 hours.

Nutrition Info:
- Per Serving: 302 calories, 9.8g protein, 52.4g carbohydrates, 6.2g fat, 1.6g fiber, 118mg cholesterol, 79mg sodium, 291mg potassium.

Raspberry Biscuits

Servings:8 | Cooking Time: 6.5 Hours

Ingredients:
- 4 eggs, beaten
- 1 cup of sugar
- 1 cup flour
- 1 teaspoon ground cinnamon
- 1 tablespoon coconut flakes
- 1 cup raspberries
- Cooking spray

Directions:
1. Blend the eggs with sugar until you get a smooth and fluffy mixture.
2. Add flour, ground cinnamon, and coconut flakes. Mix the mixture until smooth.
3. Spray the Slow Cooker with cooking spray and pour the dough inside.
4. Then sprinkle the dough with raspberries and close the lid.
5. Cook the meal on Low for 6.5 hours.
6. After this, remove the cooked dessert from the Slow Cooker and cut into servings.

Nutrition Info:
- Per Serving: 193 calories, 4.6g protein, 39.3g carbohydrates, 2.7g fat, 1.6g fiber, 82mg cholesterol, 31mg sodium, 73mg potassium.

Coconut Vanilla Pudding

Servings: 4 | Cooking Time: 1 Hr.

Ingredients:
- 1 and 2/3 cups of coconut milk
- 1 tbsp gelatin
- 6 tbsp sugar
- 3 egg yolks
- ½ tsp vanilla extract

Directions:
1. Whisk gelatin with 1 tbsp coconut milk in a bowl.
2. Transfer this gelatin mixture to the insert of Slow Cooker.
3. Stir in milk, egg yolks, sugar, and vanilla.
4. Put the cooker's lid on and set the cooking time to 1 hour on High settings.
5. Serve chilled.

Nutrition Info:
- Per Serving: Calories: 170, Total Fat: 2g, Fiber: 0g, Total Carbs: 6g, Protein: 2g

Tapioca Pearls Pudding

Servings: 6 | Cooking Time: 1 Hr.

Ingredients:
- 1 and ¼ cups of milk
- 1/3 cup tapioca pearls, rinsed
- ½ cup of water
- ½ cup of sugar
- Zest of ½ lemon

Directions:
1. Whisk tapioca with milk, sugar, lemon zest, and water in the insert of Slow Cooker.
2. Put the cooker's lid on and set the cooking time to 1 hour on Low settings.
3. Serve.

Nutrition Info:
- Per Serving: Calories: 200, Total Fat: 4g, Fiber: 2g, Total Carbs: 37g, Protein: 3g

Amaretto Pear Butter

Servings: 6 | Cooking Time: 6 1/2 Hours

Ingredients:
- 4 pounds ripe pears, peeled, cored and sliced
- 1 1/2 cups white sugar
- 1/4 cup dark brown sugar
- 1/4 cup Amaretto liqueur
- 1/2 teaspoon cinnamon powder

Directions:
1. Combine all the ingredients in your Slow Cooker.
2. Cover the pot and cook on low settings for 6 hours.
3. When done, pour the batter in your glass jars and seal with a lid while still hot.
4. Allow to cool before serving.

Apricot And Peaches Cream

Servings: 2 | Cooking Time: 2 Hours

Ingredients:
- 1 cup apricots, pitted and chopped
- 1 cup peaches, pitted and chopped
- 1 cup heavy cream
- 3 tablespoons brown sugar
- 1 teaspoon vanilla extract

Directions:
1. In a blender, mix the apricots with the peaches and the other ingredients, and pulse well.
2. Put the cream in the Slow Cooker, put the lid on, cook on High for 2 hours, divide into bowls and serve.

Nutrition Info:
- calories 200, fat 4, fiber 5, carbs 10, protein 4

Berry Marmalade

Servings: 12 | Cooking Time: 3 Hours

Ingredients:
- 1 pound cranberries
- 1 pound strawberries
- ½ pound blueberries
- 3.5 ounces black currant
- 2 pounds sugar
- Zest of 1 lemon
- 2 tablespoon water

Directions:
1. In your Slow Cooker, mix strawberries with cranberries, blueberries, currants, lemon zest, sugar and water, cover, cook on High for 3 hours, divide into jars and serve cold.

Nutrition Info:
- calories 100, fat 4, fiber 3, carbs 12, protein 3

Pumpkin Pie

Servings: 10 | Cooking Time: 2 Hours And 20 Minutes

Ingredients:
- 1 and ½ teaspoons baking powder
- Cooking spray
- 1 cup pumpkin puree
- 2 cups flour
- ½ teaspoon baking soda
- 1 and ½ teaspoons cinnamon powder
- ¼ teaspoon ginger, grated
- 1 tablespoon vegetable oil
- 2 eggs
- 1 tablespoon vanilla extract
- 1/3 cup maple syrup
- 1 teaspoon lemon juice

Directions:
1. In a bowl, flour with baking powder, baking soda, cinnamon, ginger, eggs, oil, vanilla, pumpkin puree, maple syrup and lemon juice, stir and pour in your Slow Cooker greased with cooking spray and lined.
2. Cover Slow Cooker and cook on Low for 2 hours and 20 minutes.
3. Leave the cake to cool down, slice and serve.

Nutrition Info:
- calories 182, fat 3, fiber 2, carbs 10, protein 3

Mascarpone With Strawberry Jelly

Servings:6 | Cooking Time: 1 Hour

Ingredients:
- 2 cups strawberries, chopped
- 1 tablespoon gelatin
- 3 tablespoons sugar
- ¼ cup of water
- 1 cup mascarpone

Directions:
1. Mix strawberries with sugar and blend the mixture until smooth.
2. Transfer it in the Slow Cooker and cook on High for 1 hour.
3. Meanwhile, mix water with gelatin.
4. Whisk the mascarpone well.
5. When the strawberry mixture is cooked, cool it little and add gelatin. Carefully mix it.
6. Pour the strawberry mixture in the ramekins and refrigerate for 2 hours.
7. Then top the jelly with whisked mascarpone.

Nutrition Info:
- Per Serving: 125 calories, 9g protein, 11g carbohydrates, 5.5g fat, 1g fiber, 21mg cholesterol, 45mg sodium, 118mg potassium.

Coconut Clouds

Servings:4 | Cooking Time: 2.5 Hours

Ingredients:
- 2 egg whites
- 1 cup coconut shred
- 2 tablespoons of sugar powder

Directions:
1. Whisk the egg whites until you get firm peaks.
2. Add sugar powder and coconut shred and carefully mix the mixture.
3. Then line the Slow Cooker with baking paper.
4. With the help of the spoon put the small amount of coconut mixture in the Slow Cooker to get the cookies in the shape of clouds.
5. Cook them on High for 2.5 hours.

Nutrition Info:
- Per Serving: 246 calories, 3g protein, 12g carbohydrates, 22g fat, 4g fiber, 80mg cholesterol, 40mg sodium, 0mg potassium.

Pears Jam

Servings: 12 | Cooking Time: 3 Hours

Ingredients:
- 8 pears, cored and cut into quarters
- 2 apples, peeled, cored and cut into quarters
- ½ cup apple juice
- 1 teaspoon cinnamon, ground

Directions:
1. In your Slow Cooker, mix pears with apples, cinnamon and apple juice, stir, cover and cook on High for 3 hours.
2. Blend using an immersion blender, divide jam into jars and keep in a cold place until you serve it.

Nutrition Info:
- calories 100, fat 1, fiber 2, carbs 20, protein 3

Cocoa Cake

Servings:8 | Cooking Time: 2 Hours

Ingredients:
- 1 cup milk
- 1 cup of sugar
- ½ cup of cocoa powder
- 1 teaspoon baking soda
- 1 tablespoon lemon juice
- 1 teaspoon vanilla extract
- 2 cups flour
- 3 tablespoons sunflower oil

Directions:
1. Line the bottom of the Slow Cooker with baking paper.
2. In the food processor mix all ingredients and blend until smooth.
3. Pour the liquid dough in the Slow Cooker, flatten the surface of the dough well with the help of the spatula and close the lid.
4. Cook the cake on High for 2 hours.
5. Then cool the pie well ad cut it into servings.

Nutrition Info:
- Per Serving: 283 calories, 5.2g protein, 53.4g carbohydrates, 6.9g fat, 2.5g fiber, 3mg cholesterol, 175mg sodium, 189mg potassium.

Chocolate Whipped Cream

Servings:4 | Cooking Time: 2 Hours

Ingredients:
- ½ cup of chocolate chips
- 1 cup heavy cream
- 1 tablespoon sugar
- 1 teaspoon vanilla extract
- ½ teaspoon lime zest, sliced

Directions:
1. Mix chocolate chips with vanilla extract and put it in the Slow Cooker.
2. Close the lid and cook them on Low for 2 hours.
3. Meanwhile, whip the heavy cream and mix it with sugar.
4. Transfer the whipped cream in the serving ramekins.
5. Then sprinkle it with melted chocolate chips.
6. Top every serving with lime zest.

Nutrition Info:
- Per Serving: 230 calories, 2.2g protein, 16.5g carbohydrates, 17.3g fat, 6.4g fiber, 46mg cholesterol, 28mg sodium, 103mg potassium.

Bananas And Sweet Sauce

Servings: 4 | Cooking Time: 2 Hours

Ingredients:
- Juice of ½ lemon
- 3 tablespoons agave nectar
- 1 tablespoon vegetable oil
- 4 bananas, peeled and sliced
- ½ teaspoon cardamom seeds

Directions:
1. Put the bananas in your Slow Cooker, add agave nectar, lemon juice, oil and cardamom, cover, cook on Low for 2 hours, divide bananas between plates, drizzle agave sauce all over and serve.

Nutrition Info:
- calories 120, fat 1, fiber 2, carbs 8, protein 3

Cardamom Rice Porridge

Servings:2 | Cooking Time: 4 Hours

Ingredients:
- ¼ cup basmati rice
- 1 cup milk
- ½ cup of water
- 1 teaspoon butter
- 1 teaspoon ground cardamom

Directions:
1. Put all ingredients in the Slow Cooker.
2. Close the lid and cook the dessert on high for 4 hours.
3. Cool the cooked meal and add sugar if desired.

Nutrition Info:
- Per Serving: 165 calories, 5.8g protein, 25.2g carbohydrates, 4.6g fat, 0.6g fiber, 15mg cholesterol, 74mg sodium, 109mg potassium.

Peach Cobbler

Servings: 8 | Cooking Time: 6 1/2 Hours

Ingredients:
- 2 pounds ripe peaches, pitted and sliced
- 1 tablespoon cornstarch
- 2 tablespoons brown sugar
- 1 1/2 cups all-purpose flour
- 1/2 teaspoon baking powder
- 1/4 teaspoon salt
- 1/4 cup sugar
- 1/2 cup butter, chilled and cubed
- 2/3 cup buttermilk, chilled

Directions:
1. Mix the peaches, cornstarch and brown sugar in your Slow Cooker.
2. Combine the flour, baking powder, salt, sugar and butter in a bowl and rub the mixture well until sandy.
3. Stir in the buttermilk and give it a quick mix then spoon the batter over the peaches.
4. Cover and cook on low settings for 6 hours.
5. The cobbler is best served slightly warm or chilled.

Pecan Muffins

Servings:5 | Cooking Time: 3 Hours

Ingredients:
- 4 pecans, chopped
- ½ cup plain yogurt
- 1 egg, beaten
- 1 teaspoon ground clove
- 1 cup flour
- 2 tablespoons olive oil
- 2 tablespoons brown sugar

Directions:
1. Mix all ingredients except pecans in the mixing bowl.
2. When you get a smooth batter, add chopped pecans and carefully mix them with the help of the spoon.
3. Pour the muffin batter in the muffin molds (fill ½ part of every muffin mold) and transfer them in the Slow Cooker.
4. Cook the dessert on High for 3 hours.

Nutrition Info:
- Per Serving: 262 calories, 6.3g protein, 26.3g carbohydrates, 15.1g fat, 2g fiber, 221mg cholesterol, 32mg sodium, 152mg potassium.

Mexican Chocolate Cake

Servings: 8 | Cooking Time: 6 1/4 Hours

Ingredients:
- 1 cup all-purpose flour
- 1/2 cup cocoa powder
- 1 teaspoon baking soda
- 1/4 teaspoon salt
- 1/4 teaspoon chili powder
- 1 cup buttermilk
- 2 eggs
- 1/2 cup corn oil
- 1 teaspoon vanilla extract
- 1 cup dulce de leche to frost the cake

Directions:
1. Mix the dry ingredients in your Slow Cooker.
2. Add the wet ingredients and give it a quick mix just until combined.
3. Pour the batter in a grease Slow Cooker and bake for 6 hours on low settings.
4. Allow the cake to cool completely then frost it with dulce de leche.
5. Slice and serve fresh.

Dulce De Leche

Servings: 4 | Cooking Time: 8 Hours

Ingredients:
- 1 can (14 oz.) sweetened condensed milk
- Water as needed

Directions:
1. Make 2-3 holes in the condensed milk can, preferably on the top side.
2. Place the can in your Slow Cooker and add enough water to cover it 3/4.
3. Cover the slow cooker with its lid and cook on low settings for 8 hours.
4. Serve the dulce de leche chilled.

Plums Stew

Servings: 2 | Cooking Time: 1 Hour

Ingredients:
- 1 pound plums, pitted and halved
- ½ teaspoon nutmeg, ground
- 1 cup water
- 1 and ½ tablespoons sugar
- 1 tablespoon vanilla extract

Directions:
1. In your Slow Cooker, mix the plums with the water and the other ingredients, toss gently, put the lid on and cook on High for 1 hour.
2. Divide the mix into bowls and serve.

Nutrition Info:
- calories 200, fat 2, fiber 1, carbs 5, protein 4

Dried Fruit Rice Pudding

Servings: 8 | Cooking Time: 6 1/4 Hours

Ingredients:
- 2 cups white rice
- 1/2 cup golden raisins
- 1/2 cup dried apricots, chopped
- 1/4 cup dried cranberries
- 1/2 cup white sugar
- 3 cups whole milk
- 1 1/4 cups heavy cream
- 1 cinnamon stick

Directions:
1. Mix the rice, raisins, apricots, cranberries, sugar, milk, cream and cinnamon in your slow cooker.
2. Cover the pot and cook for 6 hours on low settings.
3. The rice pudding is best served chilled.

Cinnamon And Chocolate Peaches

Servings: 2 | Cooking Time: 2 Hours

Ingredients:
- 4 peaches, stoned and halved
- 1 tablespoon cinnamon powder
- 1 tablespoon cocoa powder
- 2 tablespoons coconut oil, melted
- 2 tablespoons sugar
- 1 cup heavy cream

Directions:
1. In your Slow Cooker, mix the peaches with the cinnamon, cocoa and the other ingredients, toss, put the lid on and cook on Low for 2 hours.
2. Divide the mix into bowls and serve cold.

Nutrition Info:
- calories 40, fat 1, fiber 1, carbs 5, protein 0

Choco Liquor Crème

Servings: 4 | Cooking Time: 2 Hrs.

Ingredients:
- 3.5 oz. crème Fraiche
- 3.5 oz. dark chocolate, cut into chunks
- 1 tsp liquor
- 1 tsp sugar

Directions:
1. Whisk crème Fraiche with sugar, liquor, and chocolate in the insert of Slow Cooker.
2. Put the cooker's lid on and set the cooking time to 2 hours on High settings.
3. Serve chilled.

Nutrition Info:
- Per Serving: Calories: 200, Total Fat: 12g, Fiber: 4g, Total Carbs: 6g, Protein: 3g

Peppermint Chocolate Clusters

Servings: 20 | Cooking Time: 4 1/4 Hours

Ingredients:
- 2 cups pretzels, chopped
- 1 1/2 cups dark chocolate chips
- 1/2 cup milk chocolate chips
- 1 teaspoon peppermint extract
- 1 cup pecans, chopped

Directions:
1. Combine all the ingredients in your Slow Cooker.
2. Cover the pot and cook on low settings for 4 hours.
3. When done, drop small clusters of mixture on a baking tray lined with baking paper.
4. Allow to cool and set before serving.

Espresso Ricotta Cream

Servings: 10 | Cooking Time: 1 Hr.

Ingredients:
- ½ cup hot coffee
- 2 cups ricotta cheese
- 2 and ½ tsp gelatin
- 1 tsp vanilla extract
- 1 tsp espresso powder
- 1 tsp sugar
- 1 cup whipping cream

Directions:
1. Whisk coffee with gelatin in a bowl and leave it for 10 minutes.
2. Add espresso, ricotta, vanilla extract, sugar, cream, and coffee mixture to the insert of Slow Cooker.
3. Put the cooker's lid on and set the cooking time to 1 hour on Low settings.
4. Refrigerate this cream mixture for 2 hours.
5. Serve.

Nutrition Info:
- Per Serving: Calories: 200, Total Fat: 13g, Fiber: 0g, Total Carbs: 5g, Protein: 7g

Milk Fondue

Servings:3 | Cooking Time: 4 Hours

Ingredients:
- 5 oz milk chocolate, chopped
- 1 tablespoon butter
- 1 teaspoon vanilla extract
- ¼ cup milk

Directions:
1. Put the chocolate in the Slow Cooker in one layer.
2. Then top it with butter, vanilla extract, and milk.
3. Close the lid and cook the dessert on Low for 4 hours.
4. Gently stir the cooked fondue and transfer in the ramekins.

Nutrition Info:
- Per Serving: 301 calories, 4.3g protein, 29.3g carbohydrates, 18.3g fat, 1.6g fiber, 23mg cholesterol, 74mg sodium, 191mg potassium.

Amaranth Bars

Servings:7 | Cooking Time: 1 Hour

Ingredients:
- ½ cup amaranth
- 4 oz peanuts, chopped
- ¼ cup of coconut oil
- 3 oz milk chocolate, chopped

Directions:
1. Put all ingredients in the Slow Cooker and cook on High for 1 hour.
2. Then transfer the melted amaranth mixture in the silicone mold, flatten it, and refrigerate until solid.
3. Cut the dessert into bars.

Nutrition Info:
- Per Serving: 276 calories, 7.1g protein, 19.1g carbohydrates, 20.3g fat, 3.1g fiber, 3mg cholesterol, 15mg sodium, 210mg potassium.

Saucy Peach And Apple Dessert

Servings: 4 | Cooking Time: 4 1/4 Hours

Ingredients:
- 2 Granny Smith apples, peeled, cored and sliced
- 2 ripe peaches, pitted and sliced
- 1 cinnamon stick
- 1 cup fresh orange juice
- 1 teaspoon orange zest
- 3 tablespoons honey
- 1 teaspoon cornstarch
- Ice cream or whipped cream for serving

Directions:
1. Combine all the ingredients in your Slow Cooker.
2. Cover the pot and cook for 4 hours on low settings.
3. Allow the dessert to cool in the pot before serving.
4. Ice cream or whipped cream can be a great match for this dessert.

Lemon Jam

Servings: 2 | Cooking Time: 3 Hours

Ingredients:
- ½ cup lemon juice
- 1 orange, peeled and cut into segments
- 1 lemon, peeled and cut into segments
- ½ cup water
- 2 tablespoons lemon zest, grated
- ¼ cup sugar
- A pinch of cinnamon powder
- ½ tablespoon cornstarch

Directions:
1. In your Slow Cooker, mix the lemon juice with the sugar, water and the other ingredients, whisk, put the lid on and cook on Low for 3 hours.
2. Divide into small jars and serve cold.

Nutrition Info:
- calories 70, fat 1, fiber 3, carbs 13, protein 1

Vanilla Peach Cream

Servings: 2 | Cooking Time: 3 Hours

Ingredients:
- ¼ teaspoon cinnamon powder
- 1 cup peaches, pitted and chopped
- ¼ cup heavy cream
- Cooking spray
- 1 tablespoon maple syrup
- ½ teaspoons vanilla extract
- 2 tablespoons sugar

Directions:
1. In a blender, mix the peaches with the cinnamon and the other ingredients except the cooking spray and pulse well.
2. Grease the Slow Cooker with the cooking spray, pour the cream mix inside, put the lid on and cook on Low for 3 hours.
3. Divide the cream into bowls and serve cold.

Nutrition Info:
- calories 200, fat 3, fiber 4, carbs 10, protein 9

Almonds, Walnuts And Mango Bowls

Servings: 2 | Cooking Time: 2 Hours

Ingredients:
- 1 cup walnuts, chopped
- 2 tablespoons almonds, chopped
- 1 cup mango, peeled and roughly cubed
- 1 cup heavy cream
- ½ teaspoon vanilla extract
- 1 teaspoon almond extract
- 1 tablespoon brown sugar

Directions:
1. In your Slow Cooker, mix the nuts with the mango, cream and the other ingredients, toss, put the lid on and cook on High for 2 hours.
2. Divide the mix into bowls and serve.

Nutrition Info:
- calories 220, fat 4, fiber 2, carbs 4, protein 6

Sweet Baked Milk

Servings:5 | Cooking Time: 10 Hours

Ingredients:
- 4 cups of milk
- 3 tablespoons sugar
- ½ teaspoon vanilla extract

Directions:
1. Mix milk with sugar and vanilla extract and stir until sugar is dissolved.
2. Then pour the liquid in the Slow Cooker and close the lid.
3. Cook the milk on Low for 10 hours.

Nutrition Info:
- Per Serving: 126 calories, 6.4g protein, 16.9g carbohydrates, 4g fat, 3g fiber, 16mg cholesterol, 92mg sodium, 113mg potassium.

Sour Cream Cheesecake

Servings: 8 | Cooking Time: 4 1/4 Hours

Ingredients:
- Crust:
- 1 1/2 cups crushed graham crackers
- 1/2 cup butter, melted
- Filling:
- 12 oz. cream cheese
- 12 oz. sour cream
- 4 eggs
- 1/2 cup white sugar
- 1 tablespoon cornstarch
- 1 tablespoon vanilla extract
- 1/2 teaspoon almond extract

Directions:
1. For the crust, mix the graham crackers with the butter in a bowl then transfer this mixture in a Slow Cooker and press it well in the pot.
2. For the filling, combine the cream cheese, sour cream, eggs, sugar, cornstarch, vanilla and almond extract in a bowl. Pour the mixture over the crust.
3. Cook for 4 hours on low settings.
4. Allow the cheesecake to cool in the pot before slicing and serving.

Pure Berry Crumble

Servings: 8 | Cooking Time: 5 1/4 Hours

Ingredients:
- 1 pound fresh mixed berries
- 1 tablespoon cornstarch
- 1/4 cup white sugar
- 1 teaspoon lemon zest
- 1 cup all-purpose flour
- 1/4 cup cornstarch
- 1 pinch salt
- 1/2 teaspoon baking powder
- 1/2 cup butter, chilled and cubed
- 2 tablespoons sugar

Directions:
1. Mix the berries, cornstarch, 1/4 cup sugar and lemon zest in your slow cooker.
2. For the topping, combine the flour, cornstarch, salt and baking powder in a bowl. Add the butter and mix well until the mixture is grainy.
3. Spread the mixture over the berries and cook on low settings for 5 hours.
4. Serve the crumble chilled.

Avocado Cake

Servings: 2 | Cooking Time: 2 Hours

Ingredients:
- ½ cup brown sugar
- 2 tablespoons coconut oil, melted
- 1 cup avocado, peeled and mashed
- ½ teaspoon vanilla extract
- 1 egg
- ½ teaspoon baking powder
- 1 cup almond flour
- ¼ cup almond milk
- Cooking spray

Directions:
1. In a bowl, mix the sugar with the oil, avocado and the other ingredients except the cooking spray and whisk well.
2. Grease your Slow Cooker with cooking spray, add the cake batter, spread, put the lid on and cook on High for 2 hours.
3. Leave the cake to cool down, slice and serve.

Nutrition Info:
- calories 300, fat 4, fiber 4, carbs 27, protein 4

Milky Custard

Servings:6 | Cooking Time: 7 Hours

Ingredients:
- 3 cups of milk
- 3 tablespoons corn starch
- 1 teaspoon ground cardamom
- 1 cup of sugar

Directions:
1. Mix sugar with ground cardamom and corn starch.
2. Add milk and whisk the mixture until smooth.
3. After this, pour the liquid in the Slow Cooker and cook it on Low for 7 hours. Stir the mixture every 1 hour.
4. Then cool the cooked custard well and transfer in the ramekins.

Nutrition Info:
- Per Serving: 205 calories, 4g protein, 44.1g carbohydrates, 2.5g fat, 0.1g fiber, 10mg cholesterol, 58mg sodium, 74mg potassium.

Ricotta Lemon Cake

Servings: 8 | Cooking Time: 5 1/4 Hours

Ingredients:
- 1 1/2 cups ricotta cheese
- 1/4 cup butter, melted
- 1/2 cup white sugar
- 1 teaspoon vanilla extract
- 1 tablespoon lemon zest
- 4 eggs, separated
- 1 1/2 cups all-purpose flour
- 1 1/2 teaspoons baking powder
- 1/4 teaspoon salt

Directions:
1. Grease your Slow Cooker with butter.
2. Mix the ricotta, butter, sugar, egg yolks, vanilla and lemon zest in a bowl. Fold in the flour, baking powder and salt.
3. Whip the egg whites until stiff then fold them into the batter.
4. Pour the batter in your slow cooker and cook on low settings for 5 hours.
5. Allow the cake to cool in the pot before slicing and serving.

Vanilla Cheesecake

Servings: 8 | Cooking Time: 3 Hrs.

Ingredients:
- 2 cups cream cheese
- ½ cup sour cream
- 5 eggs
- 8 oz graham cookies
- ½ cup butter, melted
- 1 cup of sugar
- 1 tsp vanilla extract
- 1 tsp lemon zest

Directions:

1. Whisk cream cheese, sour cream, sugar, lemon zest, and vanilla extract in a mixing bowl.
2. Add eggs to the mixture while beating it with a hand mixer.
3. Mix melted butter and crushed graham cookies in a blender.
4. Spread this mixture in a pan lined with a parchment sheet.
5. Fill this crust with the cream cheese mixture.
6. Add 1 cup water into the insert of Slow Cooker and place steel rack inside.
7. Place the baking pan with the prepared cheesecake batter in the Slow Cooker.
8. Put the cooker's lid on and set the cooking time to 3 hours on Low settings.
9. Slice and serve when chilled.

Nutrition Info:
• Per Serving: Calories: 551, Total Fat: 39.2g, Fiber: 1g, Total Carbs: 38.36g, Protein: 12g

Cinnamon Apple Butter
Servings: 6 | Cooking Time: 6 Hrs.

Ingredients:
• 1 lb. sweet apples, peeled and chopped
• 6 oz white sugar
• 2 oz cinnamon stick
• ¼ tsp salt
• ¼ tsp ground ginger

Directions:
1. Add apples, white sugar, cinnamon stick, salt, and ground ginger to the insert of Slow Cooker.
2. Put the cooker's lid on and set the cooking time to 3.5 hours on High settings.
3. Discard the cinnamon stick and blend the remaining apple mixture.
4. Put the cooker's lid on and set the cooking time to 3 hours on Low settings.
5. Serve when chilled.

Nutrition Info:
• Per Serving: Calories: 222, Total Fat: 14.1g, Fiber: 9g, Total Carbs: 27.15g, Protein: 3g

Cornmeal Apricot Pudding
Servings: 6 | Cooking Time: 7 Hrs.

Ingredients:
• 4 oz. cornmeal
• 10 oz. milk
• ¼ tsp salt
• 2 oz. butter
• 1 egg
• 2 oz. molasses
• 1 tsp vanilla extract
• 1/3 tsp ground ginger
• 3 tbsp dried apricots, chopped

Directions:
1. Grease the insert of your Slow Cooker with butter.
2. Put the cooker's lid on and set the cooking time to 10 minutes on High settings.
3. Mix milk with cornmeal in a separate bowl.
4. Stir in vanilla extract, salt, ground ginger, molasses, and whisked egg then mix until smooth.
5. Spread this cornmeal batter in the greased insert of Slow Cooker.
6. Add dried apricots on top of this batter.

7. Put the cooker's lid on and set the cooking time to 7 hours on Low settings.
8. Serve when chilled.

Nutrition Info:
• Per Serving: Calories: 234, Total Fat: 11.2g, Fiber: 1g, Total Carbs: 28.97g, Protein: 5g

Cinnamon Rolls
Servings: 8 | Cooking Time: 6 Hours

Ingredients:
• 4 cups all-purpose flour
• 1/2 teaspoon salt
• 1 1/4 teaspoons active dry yeast
• 2 eggs
• 1 3/4 cups milk
• 1/4 cup sour cream
• 1/4 cup white sugar
• 1 cup light brown sugar
• 1 teaspoon cinnamon powder
• 1/2 cup butter, softened

Directions:
1. Mix the flour, salt and yeast in a bowl.
2. Add the eggs, milk, sour cream and white sugar and mix well with a spoon then knead for 10 minutes until elastic and smooth.
3. Allow the dough to rise for 40 minutes.
4. Transfer the dough on a floured working surface and roll it into a thin rectangle.
5. Spread the softened butter over the dough and top with brown sugar and cinnamon.
6. Roll the dough as tight as possible then cut the roll into thick slices and arrange them all in your Slow Cooker.
7. Allow to rise for 20 additional minutes then bake for 4 1/2 hours on low settings.
8. Serve warm or chilled.

Mint Summer Drink
Servings:6 | Cooking Time: 3 Hours

Ingredients:
• 1 cup fresh mint, chopped
• 7 cups of water
• 1 orange, sliced
• 1 lemon, sliced
• 1 cup agave syrup
• 1 cup strawberries

Directions:
1. Put all ingredients in the Slow Cooker.
2. Close the lid and cook the drink on High for 3 hours.
3. Then refrigerate the drink until cool.

Nutrition Info:
• Per Serving: 200 calories, 1.1g protein, 51.8g carbohydrates, 0.3g fat, 2.5g fiber, 0mg cholesterol, 51mg sodium, 211mg potassium.

Printed in Great Britain
by Amazon

13464173R00079